The Best of Everything for Your Baby

Les Krantz

Sharon Ludman-Exley

PRENTICE HALL PRESS

Library of Congress Cataloging-in-Publication Data

Ludman-Exley, Sharon
The best of everything for your baby / Sharon Ludman-Exley with Les Krantz.
p. cm.
Includes bibliographical references and index.
ISBN 0-7352-0032-7 (pbk.)
1. Infants (Newborn)—Care. 2. Infants—Care. 3. Infants—Development. 4. Consumer education. I. Krantz, Les. II. Title.
RJ61.L953 1999
649'.122—dc21 99-34098
CIP

This book contains and reflects the opinions and ideas of the authors, collected from different sources. All information and suggestions are to be used at the reader's sole discretion. The publication of the book does not reflect any endorsement by the publisher, and the publisher does not assume any responsibility for, the information and advice contained in the book or the products and services it describes. The product descriptions and prices within this book are accurate as of the time it was written. Due to periodic price and style changes, as well as any product safety recalls that may occur, readers should check with the appropriate manufacturer for current models and safety information.

Printed in the United States of America

10 9 8 7 6 5 4 3 2 1

ISBN 0-7352-0032-7

PRENTICE HALL PRESS
Paramus, NJ 07652

On the World Wide Web at http://www.phdirect.com

Dedicated to:

My "baby," Emma, and my husband, Peter, with love and thanks;

and to my parents, Sally and Nathan, for letting me always be their "baby."

Sharon Ludman-Exley

Contents

Baby's Body — Looking after baby's body from diapers to powders, ointments to medicine spoons.

Bath Time—What's best for bathing baby?

Parental Peace — How to get it when you need it. The best products to keep you sane, from tranquillity tapes to family activities.

Organizing The Nursery and Your Life—Top products to help you organize baby, yourself and your growing family, from calendars to closet organizers and more.

Toys—The best learning toys, the best new toys, the classics.

Going Places With Baby 267

Going places: Essential Equipment and tips to help you get around while you and baby are on the go — from little errands to international air travel.

INTRODUCTION

All parents-to-be want the best for their baby—but "the best" can be an elusive and subjective definition. This book will make some of the seemingly endless decision-making a little more straightforward with its objective descriptions, reviews and recommendations on the best of everything for your baby. Your first child will undoubtedly be the biggest single change in your life to date.

Speaking from experience, we think first dates, final exams, marriage and all of those other milestones can't hold a candle to the birth of your child. It's a magical event and the beginning of a marvelous journey for your family. We hope this book will make some of those changes a little less distracting. It will provide informative recommendations about "Gearing Up" for your baby and how to give your best in those stressful, yet wonderful, first two years. Even if this isn't your first child, you'll find this book really useful. Products, technology and equipment are constantly changing and we think you'll find many new and updated items suggested that you'll wish had been around the last time. We found a lot of things in this category!

As with most things in life, you can always expect the unexpected. When we brought our baby home from the hospital, she came with no instructions. We called our parents a lot, and read from Dr. Spock and several other books, so we thought we "knew what to expect . . . " Many books, our pediatrician (and sometimes the blurred memories of our parents) encouraged and helped us with many things relating to baby's behavior, the development of newborns and our many concerns about medical issues.

These sources helped tell us why our baby wasn't sleeping, what to do about that diaper rash and when (and what) to feed her.

Frustration begins to set in when new parents are faced with making many purchases for all sorts of uses—baby equipment, baby food, baby's safety and more. Some of your purchases will be essential; you couldn't do without them. Some will be selected for comfort, some for aesthetics, and others for security. Some will be luxury items. Some products will surprise and delight you with their usefulness and ingenuity. We have discovered some of the best for inclusion in this book. Remember to confer with other parents, too. All of you are going through similar learning experiences and sharing similar parental challenges. Find a family with an infant slightly older than yours and tap into their resources and experiences. Reciprocate the favor by being a mentor to someone whose baby is due to arrive. Our daughter made lots of friends in the park while her parents discussed with other new moms and dads the best diaper and the merits of the latest play-gym. We've even found some great support groups on the world wide web via the internet, too.

As parents, we spent endless hours in the big baby-supply superstore, and in the intimate (and expensive) baby clothing store (the one where parents have shopped for five generations and where a personal shopper is on hand to assist you). In researching this book, those experiences were recalled, and these stores (plus catalogs and the internet) have been revisited with hindsight and new perspective.

Not being sure what was essential made us very confused new parents. We'd wonder what might propel our baby ahead educationally or stimulate her in appropriate ways. Often, it seemed that in making a purchase the decision was complicated by price, function and design. We agonized over stroller choices, craving certain colors, and expecting (even wishing for) certain functions. In the end we had to buy two strollers (never actually getting the color we wanted). There just wasn't one multipurpose stroller that satisfied all of our needs and requirements (weatherproof for walks downtown in the chilly northeast winters and lightweight for easy use on airplanes and public transportation). Every parent's needs will be different and will be affected by lifestyle, resources, and even personal recollections.

Supplemented with reviews, recommendations and analysis, *The Best of Everything For Your Baby* will help you make informed decisions about the kinds of products your baby really needs. We've listed those that will hopefully make your baby's life—and your own—easier, more comfortable, more pleasurable, and more efficient. We found some truly fabulous things for your baby which are described within these pages. Some are singled out as "Cool Classics," timeless quality products that are tried and true; tested and used by generations of babies and their families. We offer some criteria and make recommendations based on pragmatic issues, such as safety and budget. We also point out developmental issues—what kinds of things encourage your baby, stimulate her, or educate her—in her first months and in the years to come. We have indicated "Best Baby Buys" for some items that represent outstanding value, while our "Designer's Choice" award celebrates products that we consider to be well designed in terms of function and aesthetic appeal. *The Best of Everything For Your Baby* also takes into account the more intangible criteria of design and style, and balances those with concerns of budget. First and foremost, we recognize products that perform well and offer good value for the expense—and applaud those that go the extra mile to look and feel good, too. Beyond merely describing products, we have also included creative ideas and helpful hints on the use of these products from multiple perspectives—yours and your baby's. Throughout *The Best Of Everything For Your Baby,* safety is always our prime consideration. The text addresses safety recommendations and guidelines used by manufacturers, and also includes an important section about recalls on baby products and equipment. Look for our "Safety Savvy" sections within each chapter, too. Armed with this information, look out for some of the highly recommended products that are highlighted—we've ranked the best products and made special mention of those that excel.

In his timeless bestseller, Dr. Benjamin Spock answered questions about baby's well-being (and before you go much further, if you don't already own his book, it's time to get it). We strive to answer some of the questions you will invariably have about baby's possessions, such as which items to choose and where to find them. Equipping a baby can sometimes feel overwhelming. This book is sure to make some of the necessary preparations and purchases a little more straightforward and informed.

Having a baby is also a special time. During the first two years as you and your child get to know each other, we hope you'll reach for this book and find some of the best of everything for your baby.

Good luck, congratulations, and have fun.

Gearing Up

In the midst of pregnancy, to prepare for baby's arrival is an irresistible and natural urge, not just for parents, but for grandparents, too. Every parent has an image of what baby's room will be like. No longer is it as simple as the old-fashioned stereotypes—pink for girls and blue for boys. It's wise to be ahead of the game with some of the nursery preparations; if your child-to-be is lucky enough to have his or her own room, make sure that it's decorated well ahead of schedule. Paint fumes aren't appropriate to welcome baby home, and in the final hectic and uncomfortable weeks of pregnancy, neither parent (especially Mom) needs the inconvenience of decorating or the scramble to buy a crib at the last minute. Be warned, many furniture items are made to order, or are not typically kept in stock. Optimistically, some stores will claim to have stock, but that might only be one or two of an item. Shops may even consider their floor sample part of stock (and you may not want a gently used item, at least not without a significant discount).

Throughout the furniture industry, it is not unheard of to have to wait 13 weeks (an entire quarter of a year) for an item to be delivered. This will be especially true for more luxurious cribs, or ones that offer some customization, or different color finishes and schemes. A manufacturer will probably be producing this from scratch for you. We ordered our crib 12 weeks in advance of our due date, exactly as prescribed by the salesperson in the baby store. We made calls to inquire of its arrival within the last month but only received delivery about two days before contractions started. It wasn't the end of the world, but life was getting a little topsy-turvy by that stage, and worrying about a crib was something we didn't need to be doing. We are sure we would have survived the crisis, but what if baby had arrived early?

The moral of this tale is, if at all possible, try not to wait until the last minute, especially if you want the widest range of choices for your selection. If you are shopping at the last minute, don't agonize. Your selections will be more limited, but there are still a lot of things out there; the big baby stores and many catalogs have good inventory. If you elect to purchase any floor models, check very carefully that everything is properly assembled and complete, and of course in good working order.

It seems obvious to point out, but one thing that all new parents should be prepared for is that life will never be the same again. The tidy living room or minimal furniture arrangement will forever be cluttered with toys; the elegant bathroom littered with baby powders and paraphernalia. Organized individuals should note that even they will not be immune to the spontaneity of parenthood with all of its unexpected quirks. Part of the pre-arrival organization should involve determining what items are essential and need to be bought in advance of the big day. Take into consideration what reflects best the budget and design sensibilities of your family. There are lots of affordable, good-value products out there; the JCPenney Company is an excellent source for one-stop shopping on a budget. There are also many higher-priced items that might find their way onto your wish-list. We really recommend coming up with a realistic budget and then seeing how your wish-list reconciles against it.

If your baby's grandparents and other relatives ask if there is anything they can help with, be specific with your requests and help them understand your criteria in selecting the right products for your baby. The following guide reviews nursery items essential for gearing up for baby's arrival. Don't forget that there are other indispensable items to be found in other parts of this book that have to be pre-purchased, too. (See "Going Places" for car seats—you'll need one of these to get baby home if she is born in a hospital.)

The Modern Nursery

The modern day nursery is a marvel of equipment and products that, in your pre-parent life, you never would have imagined existed. Every baby comes with an awful lot of equipment. Where do you put it all? How do you organize it? How do you decorate the nursery? What are essential items and how do you choose? Read on, we are about to cover a lot of ground.

First and foremost, there is the nursery itself to be considered. It doesn't have to be a separate room, if your limited space (and budget) won't allow it. Family sleeping schedules, access from your bedroom, play areas and storage spaces may also affect your decision. For us, the "nursery" was a section of our bedroom as the extra available space (still limited) we had was better suited for play. Perhaps there's an area you can convert, or maybe you have a room you want to transform. If you didn't paint or wallpaper while you were pregnant you may find some of our favorite products and suggestions helpful in making your nursery comfortable, safe and attractive for baby and for you.

We do recommend, if you have both the budget and space, hiring an architect or qualified interior designer to lay out your nursery and to make recommendations regarding lighting, materials, color and finishes. Find an architect who has designed playrooms and nurseries and you'll likely find a master of space-saving ideas. You'll help that architect or designer greatly if you have a good sense of exactly what your budget is (don't forget that their fee will be included in this), as well as having a list of likes and don't likes. If you have the time, and are working far enough in advance, collect magazine clippings, articles and pictures of things you like. Pick up some paint samples, or fabric memos, if you have access to them. A good designer will welcome your input and understanding. If you're hooked on doing it yourself, check out our space-saver products.

Planning and Designing the Nursery

Even if you have an architect on board, try to make a scale drawing of the space you will use for a nursery. Identify where permanent fixtures and openings are—windows, doors, electrical outlets, heaters, etc. Make a few copies of the basic space and then try out some possible furniture arrangements. Remember to allow clearance for doors and dresser drawers, and don't forget to keep access to electrical outlets. Leave space for play and quiet activities as well as for storage. If you can get creative, your child will enjoy a secret, safe space, too.

Nurseries seem to reflect our own feelings about childhood. They are special places intended, and hopefully, designed for the special needs of early childhood. For a while, nurseries and playrooms were quite in vogue; 100 years ago, architects like Frank Lloyd Wright and Charles Renee Macintosh proudly designed them for their clients. Later, parents couldn't afford the space for baby's nurse (where the name "nursery" is derived from); and nurseries became rooms of the wealthy, eventually losing their popularity.

Today new parents, designers and artists have rediscovered the importance of creating a special place for your child—a place of discovery, exploration and security. Craftsmen and artists are conceiving, painting and creating objects of usefulness and beauty for the nursery.

Architects who understand the psychology of a child's environment will often use scale to give your child a sense of independence and control. Your child will understand and realize that "this is my space" and the nursery will become an empowering place. It should also have within it a comfortable area for the parents to bond with their baby—as mom and dad will also spend a great deal of time here. New technologies and materials help to increase the design options—such as convertible furniture (furniture that grows with your child) and easy-care fabrics and surface materials.

Ultimately, your nursery should reflect your child's growing awareness of her growing world.

Selecting a Design Style for Your Nursery

Today we can match style with physical and emotional comfort as manufacturers and designers have tuned into the early childhood market. Parents are persuasive consumers, and more money is being spent on nurseries, their design and their furniture than ever before. You can select a crib in Victorian, Shaker, Arts and Crafts or just plain "fantasy" styles. You can design a nursery that's buttons and bows, frills and lace or minimalist in black, white and gray.

Stylistic decisions should be based on:

- Aesthetics—What looks good to you?
- Function—What will work best for you?
- Budget—What can you afford?
- Reflection—What are you comfortable with? What is reminiscent of your childhood?

Ask yourself what you like. What do you picture in your mind? Does the style reflect your home's style? If you have a Queen Anne home, you may wish the nursery to maintain its design integrity. Or maybe you have a 50s split-level you're renovating with echoes of the same era. Traditional looks might suggest to you the nature of continuity and family values. Or do you just want something cute and simple, with Mickey Mouse or Winnie the Pooh to inform the design? Whether your design theme is historical, traditional, contemporary or styled from fantasy, today's nursery should integrate your baby's needs, sensibilities and aesthetics along with your sense of style, budget and personality.

Personalizing the Nursery

Personalizing the nursery will help define your baby's identity (whether you're designing it yourself or giving direction to your architect or designer). Today, you can hire muralists or buy ready-to-use decorative borders. You can select a custom, personalized crib or repaint an heirloom. Take a child's scribble and turn it into a stamp to pattern the walls. Your favorite and fondly remembered characters are now available on everything from bedding to lamps. Putting your personal touch on the nursery can be based on:

- family tradition
- personal favorites—color, characters, stories and themes
- gender
- stimulation and education

In terms of planning, however, remember a nursery isn't a nursery for very long. Six months after baby is born, great changes come about. Baby will become more mobile, exploring her space and claiming it for herself. The nursery can either become divided by use into a bedroom and a playroom or unified into a multi-purpose room for sleep, play and learning (not to mention diapering, washing and dressing). Creating a space that does all of this and more can be terribly exciting and challenging. And because children love to use their body in their space, don't forget to incorporate areas for secret hiding places, nooks, crannies and quiet spaces for reading and reflection. Remember bedtime spaces benefit from predictability; built-in furniture or accessories are often useful. The play areas benefit from flexibility—the ability to transform or create one's own world—and what could be better than that?

If you want professional design help with your nursery, contact either the AIA (American Institute of Architects), or the ASID (American Society of Interior Designers). Refer to your yellow pages; both national organizations list their local offices in the yellow pages. The local chapters of these organizations carry lists of architects and designers experienced in specific project types, and with expertise in working on projects with particular budgets (in the big picture of things, a nursery is a very small project, but one that many architects and designers with residential architectural experience will be quite interested in).

Look at AIA on-line (www.e-architect.com) and also search for designers who have worked for "clients" under the age of two. If you're going it on your own, you might want to pick up a few helpful books.

Nursery Comfort–Yours and Your Baby's

Location We like to suggest putting the nursery near your own bedroom (late-night feedings get tiring) and also near a bathroom (diaper pails are best out of the nursery—remember about those odors, and deodorizers). Adjacent, convenient accessibility to mom, dad, and water sources is very practical if at all possible.

Convenience It's the middle of the night and you have to feed your baby. You plop down in the glider or comfortable arm chair conveniently placed near the crib. Remember, you don't have to get the expensive rocker that matches that custom crib; just pick a chair that will be comfortable and roomy enough for two. Look for one with armrests for support during breast or bottle feeding. We will mention that a rocker or glider might be an investment worth making. Don't just take our word for it; most parents you speak to who owned a rocker will probably swear by it. As always, ask your friends for opinions and recommendations, too. Adding a footstool or hassock is also a good idea, to give you a place to prop your feet up. Open shelving allows you to reach for supplies and toys one-handed, especially convenient in the middle of the night. Also, be sure there's an outlet available for a tape player or CD player as well as a night-light. Music can soothe baby's soul (or maybe just your frayed nerves). Either way, you'll want access to it.

Rocking Chairs and Gliders

When we went crib shopping, we were told we must have the matching and very costly rocker. "Every new mother needs one," we were informed. Well, rockers and gliders are certainly comfortable for soothing your baby, but not a necessity if you have budget and space limitations. Babies were being born long before the invention of sophisticated furniture! A rocker is a wonderful thing, however, so if you have the room and the budget as well as the inclination, then check out those mentioned. It will likely be a comfort and joy long after you and baby have stopped sharing it.

Traditional Glider Fare Dutailier® is the name in gliders, and most of their models are traditional in style. If you have more modern furniture this may not be a great aesthetic choice, although a comfortable one. What Dutailier® does better than most, is provide a smooth glider that is strong and nicely finished. These are special order selections, so you can choose the finish—from royal cherry to harvest oak. We like #11370 for its more simple frame; some of the other models are quite large in scale. They come with a one year warranty. JCPenney has included a mini-Dutailier® selection at a more affordable price. Cosco makes a glider you can pick up (inexpensively) at your local Toys "R" Us. In comparing gliders versus rockers, the glider has a safer mechanism in that it reduces the risk of little fingers getting trapped or squished. Usually, they are more complex, take up more floor space and for some parents, they are not stylish or contemporary enough. You decide.

Dutailier®—the name in gliders

Dutailier® Contemporary Style Rocker

Prices: $239.99 rocker #R343-8314C; $109.99 ottoman #R 343-8330C
Available through: JCPenney Catalog
(800) 222-6161

This is a white, more relaxed style glider than the traditional ones Dutailier® is known for. It comes with a relaxed blue and white gingham check in 100% cotton. An extra we really like is the built-in organizer located on one armrest so you can keep things handy. There's a matching ottoman—if you go with the glider you'll want the ottoman, too.

Dutailier® Traditional Style Rocker

Prices: $199.99 #R343-8298C rocker; $109.99 #R 343-8306C ottoman
Available through: JCPenney Catalog
(800) 222-6161

This is a much more traditional choice, and you can select a wood finish. Pick either cherry with blue velour upholstery or oak with a multi-dot upholstery. Petite armpads at the elbow add to your comfort.

Little Miss Liberty Glider and Ottoman

Prices: $274 glider; $88 ottoman
Manufacturer: Little Miss Liberty Round Crib Company™
Contact: (800) RND-CRIB

Here's a glider with ottoman from an unusual source, the Little Miss Liberty Round Crib Company™. This glider and ottoman combination comes in a choice of wood finishes (natural, cherry, glossy white and unfinished) and you can order it upholstered in any of the Little Miss Liberty fabrics. If you have one of their round cribs you can match it, but even on its own with your own nursery collection, it's a good solid purchase.

Rocking Chairs

Designer's Choice

Emily

Price: $699.00
Available through: Pottery Barn
(800) 922-5507

Emily is a good-looking rocking chair that also provides the comfort and ease of a cushy club chair. Its foam-wrapped hardwood frame and foam cushions are upholstered in a cotton-linen blend. Its design is sophisticated and casual. Pick this season's colors—natural or cranberry.

Designer's Choice:

Riley

Price: $549.95
Available through: Room & Board
(800) 486-6554

Riley's rocker is comfortable and classic. Its full size makes it very inviting for new parents, whether to lounge in alone or to cuddle up with baby. If you want to start off keeping it pristine, you may choose to buy one of the slip covers sold separately. Room & Board gives you an option of fabrics from appealing plaids to "Daryl" solids. That's a nice option that allows you to match the Riley to your nursery decor.

Nursery Safety Savvy

The most important consideration in selecting or designing anything for your baby is safety. Keep drapery cords, electrical outlets, and appliance cords out of your baby's reach. Cords, even from some balloon decorations, have caused strangulation deaths. Roll up any dangling strings and fasten them securely out of reach. The U.S. Consumer Product Safety Commission (CPSC) and the American Window Covering Manufacturers Association recommend clipping the cord to itself or to the window covering with a clothespin or cord clip. The method we prefer is to wrap it around a cleat mounted high up on the window frame. Use outlet covers for unused electrical sockets. Shield radiators or heating ducts, without blocking air flow. Don't place plants or any other object where your baby can pull them down on herself. If in doubt remove things altogether, or seek the advice of a safety consultant. Contact the Window Covering Safety Council (WCSC) at 800-506-4653 for information for parents on the need to check and childproof their window cords for safety.

Really think about what the room will be like for the 3 A.M. feeding and position furniture so you won't be bumping into things late at night. Have a qualified electrician install a UL (Underwriters Laboratories) listed dimmer switch for the overhead light. Most switches and dimmers will be too high for baby and toddler to reach, but make sure of this so that your baby isn't tempted to play with it. It's also very important to secure your nursery windows, and to keep furniture away from any upper-story windows. Also check your window screens to see they are fastened securely. The best bet on window safety is to secure the window to open just far enough for air to circulate—it's the best way to keep baby safe.

Night-Light Your Way Safely

A few words regarding the fire hazard presented by night-lights: To reduce the chance of fire, locate night-lights away from cribs and beds, and place them away from where the bulb might touch flammable materials. Purchase night-lights tested by Underwriters Laboratories and marked "UL approved." (Read our section on safety considerations.) Also, consider night-lights that use cooler, mini-neon bulbs instead of four- or seven-watt bulbs. Another suggestion is to use a lamp for a night-light. Pick one with a flame-resistant shade and a 15-watt bulb and place it on the dresser, or simply use a dimmer switch on the overhead light.

We keep finding innovative products which use amazing technology. Why not for night-lights as well?

Night-lights and More

Dusk to Dawn Night-light

Price: $12.95
Available through: One Step Ahead® Catalog
(800) 274-8440

Available only from our friends at the One Step Ahead Catalog, this is a great value night-light. Featuring a built-in light sensor, the night-light will go on at dusk and turn off at morning's first light. The neon tube never heats up, so it is safe as well. Little fingers won't get burned. It also outlasts ordinary bulbs and since they figured we'd want one for the nursery and one for the hallway, it comes paired up.

Kid Switch

Price: $8
Manufacturer: Perfectly Safe

When your toddler needs to get out of bed to go potty, he'll be unable to reach that light switch. To solve this problem, pick up this plate extender, which brings the light switch down to your toddler's level. You and your child can have access to the same switch and no wiring is required. It's easy to install; just replace the current wall switch plate with the Kid Switch.

Moon and Stars Night Light Set

Price: $12.95 set
Available through: One Step Ahead Catalog
(800) 274-8440

Mount the moon and the stars on a wall or stand them on a dresser. Just a touch will turn these on and off. Baby will not be disturbed by a bright light; just the glow of the moon and stars to keep her feeling reassured.

Soothing Sounds Crib Light (Model #1563)

Price: $19
Manufacturer: Fisher-Price

This is a crib-side night-light and when baby activates it with her voice, it produces soothing sounds. We think this is a wonderful concept. Sometimes it will take a few moments for you to get to baby's side, and this device can provide some familiar reassurance that baby will appreciate. A friend's newborn really responded to this crib light.

Light, Texture and Color (and Some Basic Color Theory)

Nothing conveys mood and attitude like color, texture and light. We often feel the nursery palette should be made up of soothing colors, such as peach, pale pinks, blues and ivory. Washes of warm color should enrich the space with gentle lighting, suggestive yet without eerie shadows. Now, however, darker colors are also in baby's palette, and they can add a rich, suggestive, almost magical touch to a nursery. Black and white, not previously considered appropriate for children, is now not only appropriate but suggested. The patterned black and white products developed to stimulate baby's senses have infiltrated early childhood product lines. In part, this is because babies react most to high-contrast illustrations in their first few weeks of life and are not able to distinguish subtler shades. You can purchase bedding, mobiles and even wallpaper borders. The mix of the bold geometric patterns is especially stylish, yet whimsical.

Which color should you make baby's room? If you have no idea, no favorite shade, then perhaps you'd like to refer to basic color theory to see how children typically react to color. Many color theorists and psychologists think color can be used very effectively for children, so let's take a peek at some of their basic theories:

- Red can make a room lively, invigorated and even happy. In tests, when children saw red, it released epinephrine, a hormone that causes the heart to beat faster and the body temperature to rise. Kids will feel energetic and excited.
- Pink can help create a calm and soothing environment. Kids seem to quiet down when in the pink.
- Blue helps infuse a serene and calm scene. When "blue" (in a blue room), blood pressure lowers, allowing children to relax, and maybe even think more clearly and reason more logically.
- Being in the "green" gives one a feeling of well-being. The brain releases dopamine, a neurotransmitter that gives off a feel-good effect. Green is also thought to be a nurturing color; it calms and lowers stress.
- Yellow boosts creativity (use sparingly!). The hypothalamus (the motivational center of the brain) is stimulated by yellow but too much of it can make kids irritable and edgy.

Today's kids grow up design-conscious, so don't just stick to primary colors. If you are inclined to do something more sophisticated, go ahead and check out the forecast for the color palette 2000 (colors expected to appear in consumer markets shortly): "Wild Berry," "Innocent Blush," "Biscotti," "Wasabi," "Royal Plum," "Aluminum Foil" and even, "Colorado Mist." Check the paint chips at your local Home Depot and know that whatever color or colors you select, children's rooms are perfect for painted decorations. It's easy, quick, (mostly) affordable, changeable (when baby decides she can't tolerate pastel pink a minute longer) and effective. Stencils and murals can be applied by a professional, or you can do it yourself. To make a paint job last a bit longer, paint the main portion of the room a solid color and utilize some of the decorative wallpaper borders which are readily available.

Babies spend a lot of their time looking up, lying on their backs. Ceilings can become a wonderful focus for the nursery or bedroom. You can use paint or paper to create skies, galaxies or rainbows. Decorative trims, borders and mobiles will all keep your baby interested and even entertained. Remember to put some of your decorations, such as those over the crib and changing table, at your baby's eye level. Some friends recently framed art prints and hung them at baby eye level off the floor—the little art lover looks at them while playing and crawling around the nursery. Apparently, the mother of famous architect Frank Lloyd Wright hung prints of the great European cathedrals around the young Frank's crib. Legend has it that she hoped to direct his career aspirations toward architecture. Perhaps even the most subtle design considerations in baby's room could have life-influencing consequences.

Contrasts of light and dark are often fascinating for babies. Your baby will love products like prism stickers and night lights which emit streams of colorful light into the nursery. Natural lighting is also stimulating. Place the crib near a window to offer a view, but avoid direct sunlight.

Painting, Decorating and Hardware

Paint remains the least expensive way to make great changes in a nursery, playroom or even a closet. That's why we love it. Now with the amazing techniques and finishes we can handle like pros, there's no reason not to run out for a few gallons. Here are a few of our favorite products to help make painting and decorating easy.

Crayola Interior Latex Paint

Available through: Benjamin Moore Dealers
(800) 972-4685

What we like more than the tremendous color choices are the super idea pages you can pick up along with a few gallons. If you can't think of what to do with chalkboard or glow-in-the-dark paint, Crayola can. They show you how to make galaxies appear, and even more. If you're unfamiliar with sponge techniques or don't know what ragging, glazing and smooshing are, then these "Neat Idea" hints are for you. Special effect paints are fun and exciting. Crayola paints will help you create a whole universe for your baby, so go ahead and reach for the stars.

Dutch Boy Kid's Room™ Paint

Available through: Sears and wherever Dutch Boy paints are sold
(800) 828-5669

Available at your local Sears, Dutch Boy Kid's Room™ Paint is designed specifically for kids. It's Dutch Boy's most stain resistant and washable satin enamel and it comes in some favorite kid-friendly shades. We really appreciate the low odor formulation which makes painting and moving in more enjoyable. Pick up the "Easy-Does-It-Painting Children's Rooms" booklets which contain simple to follow steps. The planning section is especially helpful if you haven't done a painting project on your own before. This is durable, hard-working paint, only now you can get it in "Twinkle," "Big Shoes Blue," "Ballerina Slippers" or "Home Run Red."

Martha Stewart Everyday Colors

Available at: Kmart and Sears Stores

Martha always does it right; her paint collection has 256 inspiring colors to choose from. They're color coordinated and definitely in fashion. Pick a paint chip or two and do the nursery up like Martha. It's a piece of cake!

Ralph Lauren Paints

Available at: Home Depot

You might think this is a paint line designed for the ultra-sophisticated and not for your baby. But we really enjoy the beauty and ease of the Ralph Lauren techniques and applications. A gallon of gorgeous color and a how-to-do video (The Ralph Lauren Techniques Video) will set you in motion. The specialty brushes and finishes are not inexpensive, but the finished product can be close to professional. The "Denim" and the "Chambray" techniques are lovely translations of fabric into paint. Check out "Canyon Blossom," "Stonewashed Blues," and "Hampton Pink." They'll certainly add new dimensions to baby's nursery. Home Depot offers free how-to clinics on a fairly regular basis. It's over $20 a gallon but you'll get a lot of "look" for that cost!

Transfer Mations™

Available through: Camp Kazoo. Ltd.
(888) 60MURAL

Transfer Mations™ is an easy, imaginative and fun way to paint decoratively in your child's room. You can even take on a full-sized mural. Iron-on patterns transfer directly to bedroom or playroom walls, furniture and fabric accessories. Then just like you used to do in craft kits, paint by the numbers (you paint inside the outlines with designated colors). There are whimsical cowboys and cowgirls, storybook castles, borders, doo-dads, window and ceiling designs, too. This is a really clever aid for painting. A complete instruction guide helps take you through the painting process step-by-step, and there are coloring sheets also included. That way, with markers and pencils you can try out different combinations. If you can't hire that muralist, give Transfer Mations™ a try!

"Transfer mate" your baby's nursery into something special.

Hardware Imagine taking that old bureau you bought at a yard sale. Give it a Martha Stewart coat of paint or two and then to finish it off, pick some extraordinary drawer pulls or knobs. Hardware is not what it used to be. There are so many beautiful, fun, appealing and charming varieties of pulls, knobs and more, you may not even know where to begin. So we decided to share one or two spectacular ones we've found:

Angel Wings

Call for retail sources and prices: Billy-Joe
(803) 973-3540

Isn't every baby an angel? Of course! And to prove it, add some adorable pewter angel wings to a bureau, chest or wardrobe. Billy-Joe's Angel Wings are sophisticated yet child-like.

Designer's Choice

Babyface

Price: $28.00
Available through: Soko
(888) 828-7656

Babyface—oh that babyface! Soko has designed the cutest little babyface knob you'll ever see. Made of solid bronze using the lost wax method of bronze casting, these products are high-quality and high-design. All Soko's products are available in five patinas (finishes): Dove, Black, Antique, Celadon and Natural Bronze. Can you imagine the effect of babyfaces on that little bureau? We can, and it's a beautiful sight.

Buba

Call for retail sources and prices: Billy-Joe
(803) 973-3540

Buba is cute as can be with his little tummy and child's body. Cute aside, it's also a fine pewter handle. If you want something softer, you can order it in pink, blue or lemon frosted resins. Not as expensive as some other knobs we've found, Buba is a good value—functional and adorable.

Flutterbyes

Price: $36.00
Available through: Soko
(888) 828-7656

Flutterbyes are little butterfly knobs available in assorted sizes and made of solid bronze. All Soko's products are available in five patinas (finishes): Dove, Black, Antique, Celadon and Natural Bronze. Let your imagination fly away on the wings of Flutterbyes!!

Flutterbyes will charm an old bureau, baby and you.

Manhandles™

Price: $130.00–150.00
Available through: Soko
(888) 828-7656

Manhandles™ are a collection of sculptural, distinctive hardware designed by American designer Cari Jaye Sokoloff. Art, craft and function combined, these pulls and knobs are not for everyone. Soko's Manhandles™ are very costly yet very effective. They dance, move and arabesque around your furnishings (you may want these for yourself).

Arabesquing Manhandles will decorate any furnishing.

Crib Toys, Mobiles and More

We already mentioned that mobiles can be a welcome distraction as well as a fabulous decorative addition to the nursery. Crib toys can also keep baby entertained and challenged. Stuffed toys (plush friends) are endearing and help baby feel secure. Just remember that when your baby is a newborn, keep soft stuffed toys and pillows out of the crib—it is a suffocation hazard. Here are just a few of the toys, teddies, mobiles and more.

Mobiles

Another aesthetic personal decision is, which crib mobile is best for baby? Is it balloons and teddies or black and white patterns and shapes designed for stimulation? Look through your catalogs; often there's one to match your nursery decor. Perhaps it coordinates with baby's bedding or the nursery theme or maybe you'll want to have something more artistic. Take a look at mobiles and think about what baby will actually see. Look at it from underneath. You'll notice that the more dimensional the mobile is, the more you can see. Perhaps you'll also want a second mobile to hang above the changing table; baby might be pleasantly distracted by it. Here are some of our mobile favorites:

Best Baby Buy

Enchanted Garden Musical Mobile

Price: $40.00

Manufacturer: Manhattan Baby

A whimsical blend of music and motion, this Enchanted Garden Musical Mobile will lull baby to sleep. Friendly little characters rotate, smiling at baby, while the sounds of "Brahms' Lullaby" wafts through the air. When baby reaches five months of age, you can cut off the characters and use them as little plush toys. We're enchanted.

Enchanting! A garden mobile with lullaby music and motion.

Designer's Choice and Cool Classic

Infant Stim-Mobile®

Price: $26.00

Manufacturer: Wimmer-Ferguson (800) 747-2454

Here it is—the famous black and white baby mobile which grows and changes with baby's changing visual preferences. We have given the Stim-Mobile® as a baby gift many, many times and each time we hear how popular it is with the child. Our own child liked it so very much we moved it out of reach (when she learned to sit up) and put it over her changing table instead. This award-winning mobile encourages visual activities like learning how to focus, track and scan with its reversible black and white patterns, as well as encouraging baby to reach out. Order the additional set of Color-Cards to add to the Infant Stim-Mobile® as the child grows. The colors will add some visual variety when baby gets a bit older. It's a modern day classic.

Stim-ulate baby! Here's the Infant Stim-Mobile®, a true classic.

The Little Polar Bear Mobile

Price: $9.95
Contact: North-South Books
(212) 463-9736

Brighten up the nursery with the lovely images of Lars, the Little Polar Bear, a real favorite among children everywhere. Lars and friends sway in the breeze and will delight your little polar bear fan. It's made of sturdy board and is printed in full color. Keep out of reach of young children, as with all mobiles.

Rainbow Fish Mobile

Price: $14.95
Contact: North-South Books
(212) 463-9736

If you're a fan (one of many) of the Rainbow Fish, you'll be enamored with this beautiful mobile. Hanging from the arms of an orange starfish, the Rainbow Fish and company can swim together above your baby's crib or changing table. The glitter and shimmer will catch baby's eye and when older, the mobile will remind your child about sharing. As with all mobiles, don't put it in reach of toddlers. It's printed on durable board and is easy to assemble.

Winnie the Pooh Voice Activated Musical Mobile

Price: $28.95
Manufacturer: Dolly, Inc.

When baby cries, this Winnie the Pooh mobile will start rotating and playing music to help soothe baby. It attaches easily to the crib rail, is battery operated and will play 10 minutes before shutting off.

Recalled: The CPSC announced a repair program for about 49,000 Fisher-Price Magic Motion Crib Mobiles. The rotating ring and mirror may unscrew as they turn. It's Model #71153 which is affected. If you're given that mobile, call Fisher-Price at (888) 407-6479 for a free replacement part to repair Magic Motion. This is a very popular mobile and a very good one, so we're hoping Fisher-Price will have this problem worked out in its newer versions.

Crib Toys

Mommy Bear

Price: $17.95

Manufacturer: Dex Baby Products

Age: Newborn +

Mommy Bear is a soft friend for baby. Soft rhythmic sounds (from real recorded sounds of the womb) will help baby to relax and sleep. Mommy Bear is hypo-allergenic, and runs on a battery that plays for 40 minutes and then shuts itself off. The adjustable loop allows you to hook Mommy Bear to the crib or even on the diaper bag (we know baby will want her near).

Cool Classic

Nursery Novel™

Price: $12.00

Manufacturer: Wimmer-Ferguson

Age: Birth–18 months

The Nursery Novel™ is an adorable, stimulating first book which can be tied to baby's crib or changing table. Every child will love discovering those famous black and white graphics and contrasting colors. The fun mirror is an

A novel toy, book and visual delight—the Nursery Novel™!

added bit of enjoyment for baby. She'll adore this and won't even know the Nursery Novel™ helps her engage her visual skills.

Baby will be on Cloud 9 with her Cloud Pull Musical Mobile.

Designer's Choice

Cloud Pull Musical Mobile

Price: $20.00
Manufacturer: Manhattan Baby
(800) 541-1345

Baby will learn all about cause and effect and sunshine and clouds with her Cloud Pull Musical Mobile. The music box plays "You Are My Sunshine" when pulled, and the friendly, smiling faces will reassure baby. Just remember not to leave crib toys with the baby when baby is unattended. Play with the Cloud Pull with baby. It's so cute you'll both be on Cloud 9.

Best Baby Buy

Soft Stories

Price: $20.00 approx.
Manufacturer: Wimmer-Ferguson
(800) 747-2454

Your baby's crib will soon have a great view and a story to tell. Soft Stories attaches with Velcro so you can even take it along on trips. Each foam-filled

Every picture tells a story, and your baby will be captivated by Soft Stories.

design can be placed to create a storyboard, in the country, city or thrown into the back pocket. Baby will enjoy finding the two squeakers and the mirror. Soft Stories is literary fun but also encourages visual activity, eye/hand coordination and helps baby recognize herself as well.

Sweet Slumber Bear

Price: $29.95
Available through: One Step Ahead Catalog
(800) 274-8440

This is a cuddly, baby-safe, battery-operated teddy who plays soothing womb sounds. Hugging the bear, listening to the sounds or cuddling up together in the crib can calm fussy babies. The little bear comes in his own p.j.'s—pick pink, mint or blue velour—and looks ready for bed.

Surfaces and Finishes

You'll want the nursery surfaces and finishes to be hard-wearing; they'll take a fair amount of abuse. With all of the great products available, they don't need to be boring and dull.

Flooring, for example, is costly to replace or refinish. We don't suggest pile carpeting—think of the stains. A low pile wall-to-wall, or even a wood floor would be better. Area carpets, like a bright rag rug, can add color and pattern (remember a non-slip mat underneath). If you have the space and have a defined area (or even room) for play space, try a soft, yet durable flooring. Good choices include cushioned vinyl or low pile carpeting.

Rugs

Bunny Rug

Prices: $750–$1700 (depending on size)
Available through: Rue de France Catalog
(800) 777-0998

Our favorite bunnies keep company on the six inches of tapestry bounding this beautiful tapestry bound wool (60%) and sisal (40%) rug. The illustrations are inspired by Beatrix Potter and will be a thoughtful, sweet addition to any nursery—where budget isn't much of an issue. The sisal gives the rug softness and durability and the latex backing helps protect it. It's available in three sizes; 4' x 6', 6' x 9', and 8' x 10'.

A Bunny Rug inspired by Beatrix Potter

Flower Rug

Prices: $69.00 3'; $199.00 5'; $399.00 7'
Available through: Pottery Barn Stores and Catalog
(800) 922-5507

Flowering rugs—perfect blooms for the nursery floor—are crafted of wool in this season's bold, strong colors; blue and sun yellow. They're canvas backed and look great in pairs or threes spread out around the room.

Susan Sargent Circus Area Rugs

Prices: Vary depending on size
Contact: Susan Sargent Designs Inc.
(800) 245-4767

Susan Sargent is an artist who spent years training with master European artisans and became involved in every aspect of textile creation. She returned to the U.S., and spent the next 20 years developing her skill. Eventually, she incorporated her energetic, lively designs into woven and hand-made rugs and accessories. Her Circus Collection leaps and soars, with bareback riders and lions jumping through hoops. Children will adore the designs, the colors and the spectacle. Susan Sargent Designs continues to add to her collections and the

Circus rugs that leap and soar

now available Classic, Spotted Ponies, Vermont Seasons, Western and Architecture themes will certainly provide something for everyone. Each collection is available in everything from area rugs and pillows to throws and bedding (look for her adorable ABC collection in our bedding section).

Beds, Cribs and More

The bed is a key element in a child's room. It becomes an important "place." Not only is it a comforting place, but your child will even foster a sense of ownership in this safe domain. Although she may kick up a fuss now and then about going to bed, your baby will quickly understand that her "bed" can also be a source of stability, warmth and comfort.

Your child's first "bed" provokes a great deal of thought and research. Moses Baskets, returning to favor, are lightweight and portable for the first few months, and for those on limited budgets, provide a great solution. A bassinet-carriage is also a versatile choice—set it on a stand or clip it to a wheeled frame. Cradles and cribs are even more first options. Shortly, you'll read more about these first "beds." Think about how you want them to function, consider where baby will first sleep and, perhaps, you may even recall some of your own childhood memories of your bed; perhaps that will be a factor in making your decision here.

The first "bed," something you will doubtless agonize over, won't last very long. Baby will outgrow it quickly; of course, it is still an important decision to determine the safest, most appropriate, affordable and attractive place for baby to sleep. You may choose to invest in a well-designed crib that is large enough to keep baby safe when she first becomes mobile. There is now an amazing selection—everything from metal to wood; plain to simple, traditional to contemporary and whimsical or ornate. Cribs in all colors or natural finishes are now available.

Then the first landmark of childhood comes—your baby's first "real" bed. The transition from crib to bed may be difficult for you and your baby. We don't really recommend junior beds; there may be an argument for being able to make an earlier transition, but soon this intermediate transition will lead to a bigger bed. We think that it's best to encourage your baby so she becomes comfortable and proud of the change—and a real grown-up bed is a wonderful incentive at a young age when issues of self-esteem begin to emerge. Just as your toddler will be proud of going potty, so will she brag about her big bed. Pick a single bed with a firm mattress that will see baby through the beginning of school (at least, if not more).

Save bunk beds or platform style beds for when your child is older or for when other siblings arrive on the scene. Many bunk bed systems can be purchased in parts—allowing you to add the upper bunk later. If you anticipate a two-story sleeping solution at some point, then perhaps planning to expand upward incrementally will help your pocketbook. Just make sure that the upper bunk isn't discontinued before you buy it; check back with your supplier once in a while. You might be able to buy the upper deck during a sale when junior is a little older. If junior's sibling doesn't come right along, that extra bunk is really great for sleep-overs, too!

Cribs and Crib Mattresses Your baby will be sleeping more than 12 hours a day. Sleep is extremely important to development. Naturally, you

Hey There Sleepyhead!

are concerned about creating an environment conducive to these essential sleep periods (and it won't have escaped you that sometimes when baby sleeps, you can too!). This leads to questions about purchasing the right crib and mattress for your baby.

The minute you know you are pregnant is probably not too soon to order a crib. Cribs and crib mattresses are fundamentals in the nursery. They deserve some extra thought and consideration, as well as some extra budgeting.

There is an incredible selection to choose from which makes it all the more difficult to determine how much you need to spend, what is the best size, and whether you really need a premium mattress. What about a cradle or a bassinet—do you need one? What's a bedside cradle?

Here are a few of our favorite things to keep in mind:

Cribs and mattresses are furniture purchases. That means order early and use care and common sense in your selection. Also, remember that unlike your other furniture purchases, nursery items outlive their usefulness rather quickly. If any of your friends have used products advertised to grow with baby, ask them if it was worth the extra cost. We were prodded into buying a changing table that could become a student desk. Did it? By the time a desk was needed, the nursery was a school-ager's bedroom. The original piece was an awkward size and color for a pre-teen's room. What was nice about this costly grow-with-baby item was that it was sturdy and safe, not its proposed future use. It was a great changing table with lots of storage, but as a desk, it was rather poorly designed with awkward ergonomics for a child. Sometimes you will hear sales rhetoric about versatile furniture. In many cases, we are prone to consider this only a minor consideration in influencing selection. Select furniture for its primary function, not some perceived future "flexibility." There are some new convertible cribs out there that we do like; they turn into very suitable and affordable first beds. Keep in mind that you should assess these items carefully before you buy.

When do you really need to firm up the selection of your baby's crib and place that order? We think as early as possible. Although some baby specialty stores say four to six weeks is all it takes to order many brands, our experience was more like four to six months. Shop early and make it a priority decision. See if you can pay a deposit, with the balance due just prior to delivery. Such an arrangement helps your cash flow and provides incentives for the store to keep on top of your order.

Most of our favorite baby stores are small and don't stock cribs and mattresses. Our projected lead time until delivery was four to six months, but this afforded us the additional choice of trim colors. We traded lead time for a more custom crib at a slightly less than custom price. What do you do if baby comes early? It could (and does) happen—ask at your favorite shop if they have any floor samples, in case of this scenario. Using a bassinet or cradle for a bit will also bide you some time until you get that crib. If you're pregnant now, spend some time shopping and looking about. Order in your fifth or sixth month for imported, sixth or seventh for domestic cribs. Order sooner rather than later!

Where will you find your crib? Your choices are baby stores (usually exclusive and generally more costly), department/discount stores (generally with large variety, perhaps with limited delivery), mail-order and on-line catalogs (selection and variety are fairly good, but check shipping costs and remember you're on your own with set-up and assembly), and superstores with their good selection and lower prices. What are the pros and cons of where you will shop? Specialty baby stores seem to have very knowledgeable staff. They will know a lot about the lines they carry but that knowledge often costs. These stores tend to carry gorgeous, costly pieces, often imported. Since your baby's crib is the most important item in the nursery, you may want to spend your baby bucks here; but staff may also pressure you to have the matching changing table, rocker and bureau. If you can withstand the sales push, the crib might be well worth it. Superstores, on the other hand, don't have baby specialists in their employ but you'll get variety, availability and price. Look in your catalogs, visit that chic small store, search the mega store on-line, and don't forget your local department store (they will probably be somewhere in the middle in terms of knowledge, service and stock). Think about the features you really want and those you really need. Don't skimp on this item but don't break into the piggy bank either. Remember it is a temporary piece of furniture.

Crib Safety Savvy

Is a crib just a crib? In terms of functionality, we would have to answer yes. Safety-wise, we think not (do not compromise your baby's safety). Feature wise, again, we say no. Aesthetically we shriek no. We can easily see when looking at cribs that some are very unstable and not at all what we want to have our little one sleeping in. The crib is the most important piece of furniture you will buy for the nursery. All new American cribs are built to the same safety guidelines, so you shouldn't need to pull out a measuring tape and determine the space between the slats (the maximum distance between crib slats should be 2 3/8 inches). Basic cribs are 55 inches long and about 30 inches wide. Say no to cribs with corner posts higher than 1/16 of an inch above the end panel. Posts offer an opportunity for clothing to get caught—very dangerous. Should you borrow or buy a crib with posts too high, unscrew them or saw them off and sand down the remaining end panel. If you go European, just as with pillows, the crib might be an unusual size—order a mattress to go with it to avoid the problem of locating an odd-sized one.

Pay attention that the crib you select meets the ASTM F1169, the Standard Consumer Safety Specification for cribs. Basic vigilance, understanding consumer safety guidelines and careful assembly should offer some peace of mind. If you elect to borrow or purchase a used crib, please make sure that you follow these safety guidelines in assessing crib safety before using it for your baby. Many older cribs do not conform to current standards and guidelines and for this reason, we recommend purchasing a new crib that does meet these parameters of safety.

Sudden Infant Death Syndrome

SIDS (Sudden Infant Death Syndrome) is not a diagnosis or a disease. It is the sudden and unexpected death of an apparently healthy infant. The death remains unexplained even after autopsy and examination of the circumstances. It is the number one cause of death in Canada for infants between one week and one year of age. In the U.S. many more children die of SIDS in a year than all who die of cancer, heart disease, pneumonia, child abuse, AIDS, cystic fibrosis and muscular dystrophy combined. For answers to your frequently asked questions regarding SIDS, call your doctor. The following sources can also provide research data and links to other related sites:

American SIDS Institute
www.sids.org
(404) 843-1030

Back to Sleep
(800) 505-2742

The Canadian Foundation for the Study of Infant Deaths
(800) ENDSIDS and (416) 488-3260

The SIDS Alliance
www.sidsalliance.org
(410) 653-8226

One of the most important things you can do to help reduce the risk of SIDS is put your baby to sleep on her back, for a nap or for the night. Discuss this with your baby's doctor as some babies may have a health condition which requires that they sleep on their stomach. If baby doesn't seem to like this, remember she'll soon adapt and this, if your doctor agrees, is most likely the best sleeping position she can take.

Also be sure that baby sleeps on a firm mattress and don't use fluffy blankets or comforters. Don't let your baby sleep on a waterbed, sheepskin or a pillow. And when your baby is just newborn, keep soft stuffed toys and pillows out of the crib—they are a suffocation hazard.

Check with your doctor on all of these recommendations as well as the other standards in risk reduction of SIDS that the U.S. Public Health Service, the American Academy of Pediatrics, SIDS Alliance and Association of SIDS and Infant Mortality Programs usually state:

- keeping temperature not too warm, just comfortable
- creating a smoke-free zone around baby
- see baby gets proper medical care and attention and all vaccinations
- consider breast-feeding

Remember, sadly, there is still no definitive cause or causes of SIDS. Speak with your doctors and also check out those web sites and organizations listed above.

Will you want a baby "propper," one of the new products to help position babies on their side or back? Manufacturers tout these to lessen the incidence of SIDS, but proppers can also be a hazard. They are usually firm bolsters, but like pillows, they can still be dangerous. Baby's airway could become blocked should her neck become trapped over the edge of the propper. Ask your pediatrician for advice and information on SIDS, and ask whether he or she recommends purchasing a baby propper for your infant.

Prop-a-Baby

Price: $8.99–14.99
Manufacturer: Dex

Two soft wedges of flannel cushions can be positioned on each side of your baby, creating support. They stay in place with Velcro.

Safe and Sound Sleep System with Bonus Tape

Price: $18.95
Available through: One Step Ahead Catalog
(800) 274-8440

One Step Ahead has put together a nice sleep package for your baby—flannel-covered wedges, head support, and special sheet protector—all designed to keep your baby from rolling over onto her tummy. It includes "Sounds of the Womb," a 30-minute tape to help baby relax. The nest is machine washable, and fastened with Velcro so it's adjustable for added comfort.

Crib Features

Side Railing Release Mechanism and Ease of Release We really liked the drop side feature on our crib. It was foot operated; look for this feature, or for one that is easily operated with one hand. Your other hand is very often busy with baby. Most models now have a similar foot kick bar which releases the drop side. You will use this feature a lot so be sure to test and retest it in the store. Is it easy enough for you to do while you have a baby in one arm? Can you manage the operation of it? If the locking mechanism for the rail has exposed hardware (not necessarily a safety issue), annoying and unwanted noise might be an issue (that ugly screech may wake a baby you have just spent an hour coaxing to sleep!).

Mattress Height Adjustment An additional feature we prefer in crib selection is the option of adjustable mattress height. Initially, your newborn gets the highest setting—the higher baby is, the easier it is for you to reach in and pick her up. Once she can pull herself up, you will want to set the mattress to a lower level. Picking her up is less of an issue, as she's able to stand along the rail. If possible, the mattress should lower to many positions. So you have an idea, some of the more expensive cribs offer at least four positions while some Canadian ones have two. Both are better than just one, in our opinion. Remember, the lower the mattress can sit in the crib, the longer junior will be safely tucked in, and not as easily able to get out and about. There are two systems of accomplishing this task: using bolts and screws, or with a hooked bracket. Watch out for uncoated bolts which may strip the holes on the post over time, weakening the frame. We personally like hooked brackets where the mattress lays on top of the springs and is anchored to the crib frame. Child Craft, Simmons and other manufacturers use this system of hooked brackets and we feel it really provides more support and safety—a little catch prevents a sibling from getting underneath and pushing the mattress up.

Mattress Support What should be holding up your baby's mattress? Look underneath and see whether the crib has vinyl straps, cardboard deck, metal bars or springs. The best choice (if you can afford it) is a crib with a set of springs, providing mattress support and a springy surface for your toddler to stand and jump on later. This is largely an issue of comfort, rather than safety.

Crib Wheels or No Wheels? Whether to have wheels is a personal choice. Wheels make changing the bedding a bit easier but not much else. Moving the crib around, remember, is really going to happen only within the one room—a crib is wider than most single doorways, so it will stay, wheels or no wheels, where it is set up when delivered. Metal wheels or plastic? We think metal and wide rather than thin, if possible. If you buy a crib that doesn't have such great casters and you desire better mobility, pick up some better ones at your local hardware store—most are standard dimensions and will be interchangeable.

What is a teething rail? This is a rather practical feature of some cribs. When a baby starts to teethe, the top rail on the crib is often a good place to gnash. Although the paint used on cribs is nontoxic, a teething rail will keep the crib looking fresh and keep baby from getting things in his mouth that you'd rather not have there. If you do choose a crib without a teething rail, don't worry. There are some manufacturers thinking about this type of problem—check the listing that follows our crib list; we've added a teething crib rail that easily mounts on almost any crib.

Cost You decided and you have placed your order. So what will your crib with teething rail, four mattress height and side drop with foot control cost you? Cribs begin at about $100 and go up from there. We'll be repeating this, but you do get more or less what you pay for. If you're hoping for more than one child, you may get a better deal by buying a better quality, more expensive crib the first time around that will hold up to the wear and tear of several children.

Assembly and Delivery We think it's worth the extra $25 to $50 to have your baby's crib delivered and set-up. Cribs are often missing a few screws or have a part slightly defective and it is easier to rectify if someone else is handling it.

If you do purchase a crib from a discount store or mail-order and need to assemble it yourself, most are assembled without a great deal of difficulty and usually with ordinary tools. You may want to preview some assembly instructions—stores usually have copies nearby. Frankly, we insist that you follow instructions—save your do-it-yourself creativity for other projects that don't compromise the safety of a family member. If in doubt, call the manufacturer; they will be happy to help—it is in everyone's best interests.

Cribs We Like

Some of the best cribs we found were made by Bellini, Child Craft, Morigeau-Lépine, Inc., Stork Craft, and Ragazzi. Those are the names we often think of when we consider cribs and first beds. There are also some trusted names in furniture who have expanded their "adult" furniture lines and are now manufacturing some fine cribs. Look at the aesthetic beauty of cribs by Stickley or Room & Board. Here's why we especially like these manufacturers:

Bellini

(516) 234-7716

Bellini makes some wonderful, contemporary cribs. The "Avanti" line is stylish and has many coordinating pieces such as the "Milano" crib plus an armoire, a glider and a chest. Design unfortunately costs.

Child Craft

(812) 883-3111

Child Craft offers cribs in contemporary to traditional styles at reasonable prices and has been doing so for over 85 years. You can call for a current catalog and a listing of dealers or skim your JCPenney catalog. We also like the Child Craft safety features: the release mechanism via a foot bar is easy to use as is the mattress height adjustment system. There's also a very complete range of baby beds, from cribs to convertible beds and chests to multi-use changing tables. Here are a few of their cribs we think are value wrapped up in good looks:

Child Craft Crib 'n Bed

Price: $579.99 (#R 343C3042C)
Available through: JCPenney Catalog
(800) 222-6161

We like this "grow with your child" crib and bed. It's got simple styling, lots of added features and comes in natural or honey oak finishes. As a crib, you get a built-in changing table and even several drawers. Its a multi-purpose multi-age hit! It converts easily to a youth bed, low for toddlers and complete with an-underbed storage drawer. We like it without the headboard but it's your choice—a nice option. If all that built-in space still isn't enough for baby's clutter, order the matching four-drawer chest.

Child Craft Encore Crib, Daybed and Double Bed

Style: #33301
Contact: Child Craft for dealer nearest you
(812) 883-3111

We've seen how well Child Craft creates the "grow with your child" crib and bed, but the Encore's got all the features it needs, plus it's extremely versatile. Crib, daybed or double bed, the Encore is a winner. Order it in natural maple and see if the 5-drawer chest or computer desk fit into your toddler's room—she'll be needing them. The natural maple finish is one that compliments most decors; it ages beautifully and isn't too grainy.

Child Craft Shaker Style

Price: $299.99 (#R 343C6797A)
Available through: JCPenney Catalog
(800) 222-6161

This Child Craft crib is stylish, with Shaker simplicity in natural-finish wood trim. Complete with all the Child Craft features we like (single drop-side and plastic teething rail), this crib is a good, fairly economical choice. You can order a three-drawer chest/changer and also a four-drawer chest to match. What we like about ordering from JCPenney is an added value—order a crib and a mattress and your savings increase. *Design Detail: Replacing the knobs on the chest and drawers with something fanciful will spice up the ensemble.*

Designer's Choice

Morigeau-Lépine, Inc.

(800) 326-2121
Available in Canada and the U.S.

For over 50 years, this juvenile furniture company in Quebec, Canada has made some very stylish cribs. You'll find the Morigeau line well-made and attractive, yet a bit pricey in comparison to some of the other cribs that we've reviewed. There's a wide range of accessories and while we don't believe you need a matching set of nursery furniture, Morigeau pieces are quite elegant and sophisticated. From some wonderful finishes and color choices, we selected a light gray finish with yellow trim for our baby. You really feel you are tailoring a custom order to match your own decor and sensibilities. Design-wise we really adore the unusual headboard styles—like the moon and swan—which are now available. If budget is an issue, choose from the smaller collection of the sister line, Lepine. Fewer options mean slightly lower prices, and Lepine can still offer many similar designs.

Our Morigeau crib seemed very pricey at first. Then when we really looked at other cribs we loved the size, stability and safety it provided. Although we didn't have another child, our crib has kept two other children (and probably more to follow) comforted and sleeping soundly. It's true that a less expensive crib will suffice, but if you intend to have more than one child you just might want to consider a crib that will easily outlast two or more active toddlers. Morigeau's full-size crib allows you to put off one decision (the first bed) for a little while longer. Some less expensive cribs that are less well made may struggle to last through more than a couple of babies without extra care or some refinishing.

Ragazzi

(514) 324-7886

Available in Canada and the U.S.

If money is no object and you're designing a sophisticated nursery, go ahead and look into cribs by Ragazzi, know as the fashion leader in children's furniture. The two-tone wood finishes are very elegant in grown-up colors like forest green or deep burgundy and Ragazzi caters to a very specific high-end market. But we think you can get style and safety and get it for less somewhere else. Take a look and decide for yourself. We do like the three-child warranty. If you like their cribs, take a look at their very sophisticated youth furniture lines.

Ragazzi 500 Series Crib

Looking for a sleigh-style crib? Here it is, the 500 series by Ragazzi is probably what you had in mind. The details like cute drawer pulls on the series help make it fashionable (however, you can do that yourself to almost any chest or set of drawers).

Designer's Choice

Room & Board® Kids Collection

(800) 486-6554

Room & Board® has developed a kids collection of fine furniture, classic and with fine lines. There's even a line of great-looking linens and accessories to go along with your purchase. What we really like is that any piece you select you can match up to any of Room & Board's sensible storage pieces. They have two really good-looking cribs that we adore—the Bainbridge and the Savoy—that are clearly influenced by Scandinavian design (with very clean, classic modern lines).

Room & Board® Bainbridge Crib

Solid maple, this Scandinavian-styled crib features a single drop side, a height adjustable mattress support and two locking casters. Good looking and made well—what more could anyone want? Room and Board also support their products with excellent customer service, although you may find some of their shipping costs quite high compared to other retailers, if you are shopping via their catalog.

Room & Board® Dearborn Crib

The Dearborn is available in natural maple or white painted maple. It also features a single drop side, a height adjustable mattress support and two locking casters. Pick up a changing table to complete the nursery. Both the Room and Board showrooms, and the catalog are set up to show a complete line of furniture, complete with decor and props. It's actually a good place not only to see the furniture itself, but how it might look in the nursery.

Stork Craft

(604) 274-5121

Available in Canada and the U.S.

Another good source for solid, reasonably priced cribs, Stork Craft is available throughout the U.S. and Canada. Stork Craft is manufactured in Canada but has the features we like. Some of their cribs have two different releases and others have a two-handed drop-side release. Stork Craft has contemporary styling and reasonable costs.

Unusual Cribs

Do you want the unusual in nursery decor and are you willing to pay for it? If you are, we've found a few elegant and unusual cribs we couldn't resist mentioning. They aren't for all of us, but they are truly special:

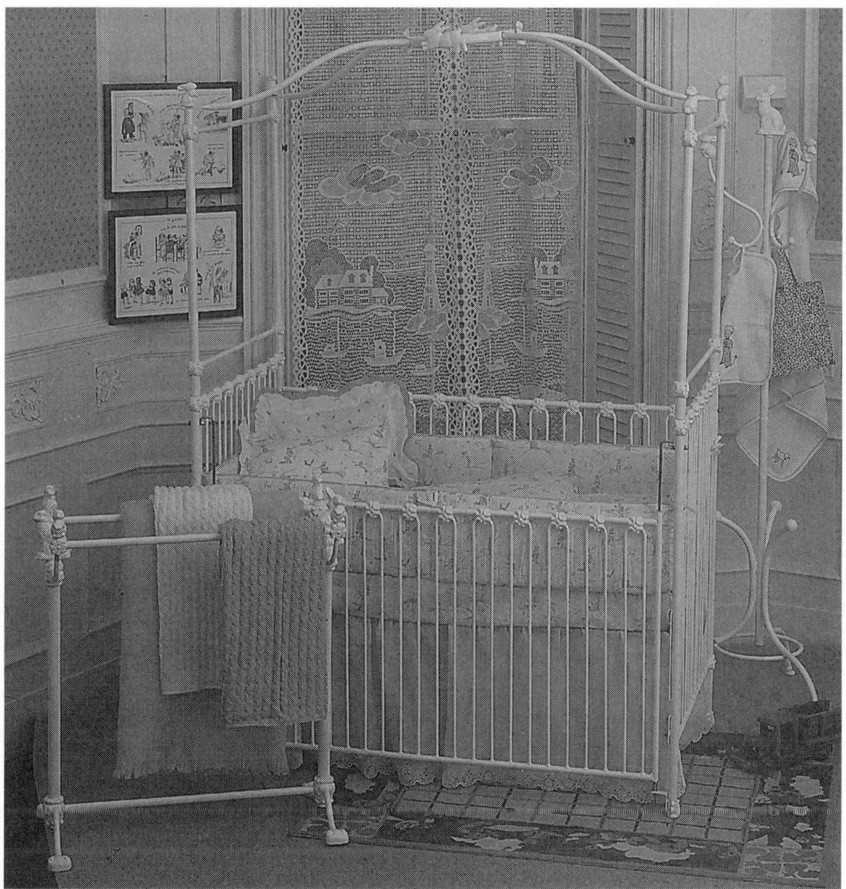

A canopy for baby to dream under, the Lapin Crib—courtesy of Rue de France

Designer's Choice

Lapin Canopy Crib and Rack Set

Price: $1600

Rue de France

(800) 777-0998

Here it is—the money is no object crib! This is a beautiful, old-fashioned ironwork crib, lovely and sweet. It has the standard crib issue—white enamel coating that's rust-protected and safe, side rails lock in place and lower for access, and adjustable height spring frame. It's a canopy crib, very unusual in today's market. You can even push that budget further (another $800 or so) and order the matching quilt rack and coat rack. If the sky is the limit, then this is the nursery addition you may be searching for.

Little Miss Liberty Round Crib (Wood with 5" mattress)

Prices: $ 738–858
Little Miss Liberty Round Crib Company™
(800) RND-CRIB

Know what your favorite celebrities are wearing these days? Sure you do, courtesy of every fashion magazine. But do you know what kind of crib your favorite celebrity parents are buying? They are, of course, buying unusual round cribs from the Little Miss Liberty Round Crib Company™.

Round cribs have been around historically but seemed to disappear until three years or so ago, when the Little Miss Liberty Round Crib Company introduce its round crib designs. Now just select a finish for your hardwood crib: everything from Lacquer (even in black), Standard Wood, Iron Forged, Shaker Wedgwood or Bunny McKenzie (handpainted). Pick a crib type: standard round, canopy round, round dome, fluted dome and more. The rounded edges, according to Little Miss Liberty, reduce many safety hazards associated with corners of typical cribs. Round cribs do offer more visibility, easy access and use less floor space than typical cribs. When you buy your round crib, it comes with double laminated high density foam mattress; bedding is extra. And that's a big extra!

Little Miss Liberty's round cribs are for the stars—they're unusual, enticing and expensive. If you can afford it, you'll probably go for the works: the elaborate bedding (even in silk), the matching window dressings, and even the matching diaper stacker. What can we say, most babies don't need half of what we purchase. If you're inclined and can afford it, why not start your baby off in a round crib?

Dura-Crib (and 3-inch mattress)

Prices: $418–450
Manufacturer: Little Miss Liberty Round Crib Company™
Contact: (800) RND-CRIB

For those of us pinching pennies, Little Miss Liberty has come out with Dura-Crib™, fabricated from Polyplastic components. It offers the same increased child visibility, has no corners to endanger children and uses less floor space than typical rectangular cribs. There's a sweet-as-ice-cream bedding collection to drool over—"a-lot-of-Gelato"—with canopies and diaper stackers to match. Bedding is bought as a set so once you've splurged you get the coverlet, bumper guard, dust ruffle, drapes and canopy cover (and a bit more).

Double Delight™ Twin Crib

NeNe Quality Baby Products
(213) 890-4449

We also looked at a Double Delight™ Twin Crib because the idea of twins sleeping close to each other seemed so intriguing. This is basically two cribs that turn a corner; there are double drop gates and a plexi-divider so the twins can look at each other. The cost, a whopping $1199, does include double bedding in "Hippo Pink or Blue" or "Pink or Blue Plaid" and if you've one of each, you can mix and match it. If you are crunched for space (and we bet that the surprise of twins will tax many for square footage), the Twin Crib is more efficient than two cribs. But from a price perspective, we weren't convinced about the necessity of a dual crib; wouldn't two well-made, medium priced cribs in view of each other still keep twins close? Maybe moms and dads of twins could let us know!

Teething Rails

Remember we mentioned teething rails—if your crib doesn't have one, order two of these, one for each side of the crib. For some reason, this is one product that you usually need two of, but never seems to be packed in pairs:

Teething Crib Rail

Price: $14.95 #01130012
Available through: The Right Start Catalog
(800) 548-8531

This crib rail helps protect your baby's tender gums. It's a clear plastic cover made of soft, safe rubber teething material. It attaches easily with pressure-sensitive tape and will bond to wood, metal or plastic without harming the finish. You can even trim it to fit your crib. Just don't forget you need enough for both sides.

Crib Mattresses

A more utilitarian quest is the selection of a crib mattress. Base this choice on function; you can momentarily put aside aesthetics. The big question will be: Should you choose foam or innerspring? How do you select the right one for your baby? Remember, if you need to cut costs, do it on the crib and not on the mattress. Your pediatrician might even voice an opinion on this matter. Our top mattress pick is firm, firm, firm. Firm is better; blocked breathing can occur when baby is sleeping on her stomach and sinks into the mattress. Sudden Infant Death Syndrome (SIDS) has increased risk when a baby is sleeping on her stomach. It is recommended by the American Academy of Pediatrics that you try to prevent baby from sleeping in such a position. We've mentioned some aids that might also help prop baby up. Once in a while, a baby can get his hands and feet caught between a poorly fitting mattress edge and the crib. A firm mattress will lessen that gap and that danger.

So what exactly is the difference between foam and innerspring? Which is better? There are pluses and minuses for each. Foam mattresses cost less and weigh less. We give good grades to high density foam mattresses for retaining their shape well. Best of all, the lighter weight makes it easier to turn or lift the mattress when changing sheets; you will be doing this often. This is a large benefit. If going with foam, make sure the mattress has square corners (no gaps for trapping baby), a waterproof covering and ventilation holes.

Innersprings, on the other hand, typically cost more than foam but keep their shape better. They generally have a metal spring unit with layers of padding and insulators keeping the padding separate from the springs. These layers are usually covered in wet-resistant ticking material.

Foam or innerspring, low-priced mattresses have ticking that is only one layer of vinyl. It's best to have mattresses with quilted or multiple vinyl layers laminated together and reinforced. What that means for your baby is that the mattress will be more waterproof and more resistant to tears or holes. Look also for fabric binding as opposed to vinyl. The fabric will breathe, allowing air to escape as your baby moves around and pushes against the mattress. That pressure might otherwise cause vinyl binding to eventually split.

Vent holes are holes you do want. They help alleviate air pressure against the seams and also allow odors to escape. Go for as many vents as you can find or afford as they really also keep the mattress fresher longer.

Is coil count important? Are 150 coils less comfortable than 600 coils? Don't just look at the count. Look at each manufacturer's mattress carefully for all of the previous features and for firmness.

So, what does a high quality mattress having all of the above cost? Prices will begin at about $100.00 and are well worth the expense. When your mattress arrives, immediately dispose of the plastic it was shipped in; all plastic bags pose a suffocation danger to your baby.

We want to mention one thing we felt was essential. A very kind grandmother bought us a fitted crib pad. The vinyl inside helped keep our mattress somewhat dryer and definitely in better shape than if we hadn't gotten one (actually we liked it so much we bought an extra one).

Baby Posturepedic Crib Mattress

Price: $100.00
Manufacturer: Sealy®

One of the best, the Sealy Posturepedic mattress is popular for good reason. This model has a "sense and respond" coil system; a Staph-Gard hypo-allergenic, laminated cover which resists bacteria; hypo-allergenic Perma-Foam for softness; a heavy-gauge border for edge support; and perhaps best of all, a warranty that far exceeds baby's use of it (a lifetime warranty).

Bumpa Bed™ Crib Mattress

Prices: $115.00 ($139.00 for one that folds in half for portability)
Manufacturer: The Bumpa Bed Co.
(800) 241-1848

Like so many children's products we love, the Bumpa Bed mattress was invented by some parents-to-be. They were so concerned over mattress safety, they conceived of the idea of the Bumpa Bed system. It fits snugly into any standard-size crib. The bottom and sides are sculpted from a single piece of firm foam. Because of this special design, gaps, loose bumper pad strings and sagging materials are nonexistent problems, which means less worry for you and lots of comfort for your baby. You can also use the Bumpa Bed on the floor or on its custom platform (additional cost but maybe worth it) as baby's first bed. That "safe nest" which protected baby so well will also keep your growing toddler from rolling out of bed at night; the familiarity will be so comforting. An added bonus—the Bumpa Bed mattress packs up in a convenient carrying case. Baby can sleep well when on the go.

Deluxe Crib Mattress

Price: $80.00
Manufacturer: Carter's

Another sound mattress, Carter's has therapeutic soft zones on the top to provide extra comfort for your baby, hypo-allergenic Perma-Foam wrap, and a tough cushion which supports the bottom side for toddlers. The innerspring construction has added strength on the outer edges.

Infant Advantage Crib Mattress and Sound and Motion Unit®

For retail sources and prices call: Infant Advantage®
(800) INFANT-A

The Infant Advantage crib mattress will fit into any ordinary (standard size) crib; however, it is most "un-ordinary." The mattress itself can have the Sound and Motion Unit installed into it, which, for those of us who didn't know, is a sleeping system that replicates both the womb conditions and the security of being held closely. Surrounded by soothing and familiar sounds and motion, your baby will supposedly sleep more easily and longer. You program the sound and motion to decrease over 17 weeks which gradually weans baby from this created "womb-like" environment. Not for those on a restricted budget, the Infant Advantage is really part of a big picture and total system—you can start with the bassinet and then remove the unit for its installation into their manufactured crib mattress. If you think this is for you the Advantage Sound and Motion Unit can be rented for $249.00; the bassinet retails for $129.00; and the crib mattress retails for $199.00.

Other Sources We mention just a few mattresses because many stores where you're making your crib purchase will also have mattresses and that one-stop-shopping is very convenient. Room & Board, for example, carries a line of fine mattresses so you can order crib and essentials at the same time. Always ask at the store; often there's even a price break that comes with that one-stop-shopping.

Cradles, Bedside Cradles and Bassinets

Some baby terminology is quite confusing (we hope this book is helping). One of the things that really stumped us was the bassinet. You're about to learn the proper definitions of *cradle* and *bassinet,* as well as answers to those nagging questions—Do you need one, or both, or none?

Technically, a bassinet is a basket with approximate dimensions of two and a half feet long, a foot deep and a foot and a half wide. It has firm sides, a hard bottom and a thin mattress. Some have handles or wheels for added convenience. Bassinets are viable sleeping solutions for only the first three months of a baby's life. Trekking to the nursery in the middle of the night every single time baby wakes for feeding and changing is a pretty good reason to spend that extra $40 for this early sleeping arrangement. Convenience is always a valid reason, particularly for overworked new parents, and that sweet little bassinet can be right by your bed. Unlike cribs, bassinets are good items to borrow, but your safety check for a new or borrowed bassinet should include a snug-fitting mattress, a sturdy base or stand, and secure wheels, if applicable. A bassinet mattress isn't very expensive so that's an easy item to replace if a used one seems worn or soiled. If you are purchasing one, you might want to choose one with a removable "Moses basket" that separates from the base. Yes, it is indeed named after the one in which Moses floated down the Nile—though you'll find most models are manufactured out of something a little more hi-tech than woven reeds. These newer models are easy to carry with you around the house or even out to dinner. However, baby should always be transported in a car seat when in a vehicle, so the added work between the car seat and bassinet might be too inconvenient for a short stay at a restaurant. We bet that baby will be just as happy in her portable car seat. Be sure to follow manufacturer's weight guidelines. Some say baby really feels secure in the little confines of a bassinet. We just liked having baby close to us for those first nights. We could have managed very well without one, too, so if your budget is tight, don't feel that baby is going without by not having a bassinet. On the opposite side of the coin, our friends at Eco Baby (who make a wonderful Moses Basket) reminded us that for some people, a crib is a luxury. For them, a Moses Basket would fill all of the early sleeping needs of an infant until baby could sleep with Mom and Dad (avoiding a crib altogether). This is a good, viable solution for those who are on a tight budget.

Okay, bassinets sound pretty good, so what then is a cradle? Slightly larger than a bassinet, cradles are suspended on a frame and the larger dimensions mean you can use it for about four months or a month longer than a bassinet. Cradles can rock baby to sleep or help calm him down. Some new parents don't want to rock their babies to sleep believing it might become a bedtime habit they'd rather not start. That's another personal choice. What we do know is cradles could be a family heirloom or a new purchase, available in wood, metal or even brass. They can even match your nursery decor or highlight it. A cost imperative is that a cradle, like a crib, needs to have bumpers and sheets. Remember, most bassinets are lined so they don't need a bumper.

Cradle and Bassinet Safety Savvy

Although they are alternatives to putting your little newborn in her large crib, unfortunately bassinets, carrycots and cradles are not covered by the federal safety standards that cover cribs and portable cribs. What you need to remember if you opt for a cradle or bassinet is:

- Cradles must comply with all crib standards: slats, like slats on cribs, should have no spaces more than 2 3/8 inches wide.
- The cradle mattress must be a snug fit, allowing no areas for your baby to become wedged into, particularly between the mattress and the side of the cradle.
- Follow manufacturer's weight guidelines carefully.
- Choose one with a sturdy bottom and a wide base. (They are often unstable, be careful).
- Stop using when your baby can pull herself up.

Cradles, Bedside Cradles and Bassinets to Choose From

The bedside cradle is a relatively new invention, at least to us. It offers the advantage of having baby close and yet not sleeping in your bed. What some call the "Family Bed" or even "attachment parenting" is a philosophy of cosleeping, so that when baby wakes up next to Mom and Dad she feels secure, helping her go back to sleep. The downside of cosleeping, for those who worry a lot, was the possibility of Mom or Dad turning over onto baby. The bedside cradle eliminates such worries because the baby is actually in her own cradle. Here are some we like and we'd like to mention that should you wish to replace the foam mattress that comes with your bedside cradle, Eco Baby (888-ECO BABY) makes an all-natural one:

Bedside Cradles

Bedside Co-Sleeper

Price: $189.95

Available through: Baby Catalog of America
(800) 752-9736

Babies sleeping next to parents do seem to fall asleep with ease and sleep well. This Bedside Co-Sleeper allows you to accomplish this without sleeping in the same bed. This little portable crib links to your bed, so your newborn can sleep within your reach. This is especially helpful if you can't lift (due to a cesarean section). The system will convert later to a play yard. As a play yard it also allows wheelchair users or people of short stature to have easy access to baby. To top it off, the entire system folds up into its own carrying bag and will easily fit into an airplane's overhead compartment. This is a multi-use, multi-purpose product and one we especially like for its universal accessibility.

Cuddle Me Close Bedside Cradle

Price: $149.95
Available through: One Step Ahead Catalog
(800) 274-8440

Cuddle up with your baby at night while sleeping in your own bed. Just place this bedside cradle next to your own bed and it will seem like baby is in the bed with you. When baby grows out of the cradle, at about six months, convert it to a little (traditionally styled) toddler bench. Many of our friends have been telling us that baby often sleeps with them. This cradle is a good compromise because everyone is in his or her own bed, side-by-side. Baby will sense how close you are and you can relax and have her within arm's reach. Go ahead and cuddle up close.

Cradles, Bassinets and Moses Baskets

Infant Advantage Bassinet®

For retail sources and prices call: Infant Advantage®
(800) INFANT-A

Here's an oversized bassinet for babies up to four months which has a sturdy and foldable stand. The surfaces wipe clean and the bassinet can be easily moved from room to room. The makers say this bassinet would be a great choice even if it didn't have the Sound and Motion System and we agree (it can be used without it). The Sound and Motion, as mentioned earlier, is a sleeping system that replicates both the womb conditions and the security of being held closely. Surrounded by soothing and familiar sounds and motion, your baby will supposedly sleep better. You program the sound and motion to decrease over 17 weeks which gradually weans baby from this created "womb-like" environment. Not for those on a restricted budget, the Infant Advantage is really part of a total system —the bassinet Sound and Motion Unit removes to then be installed into their manufactured crib mattress. The crib mattress fits into any standard sized crib and at the end of the four months of the program it can be used as a premium crib mattress. Some parents swear by it; however, keep in mind its higher cost. (The Infant Advantage Sound and Motion Unit can be rented for $249.00; the bassinet retails for $129.00; and the crib mattress retails for $199.00).

Other Sources: Here are three additional catalog sources that offer good value, quality cradles, bassinets and Moses baskets:

The Baby Catalog of America

(800) 752-9736

The Baby Catalog of America carries a nice selection: a bedside bassinet and a Moses basket and the bedding each will need. These are pretty traditional in styling yet one bassinet does have Classic Pooh bedding.

The One Step Ahead Catalog

(800) 274-8440

Call The One Step Ahead Catalog for its new Sit N'Soothe Portable Bassinet. At sleepytime it reclines fully while a gentle vibrating action helps send baby off to dreamland. When baby wakes, the Sit N'Soothe converts to an upright seat. It even comes with a head cushion, a three-point harness (a great safety feature for a bassinet), and mesh sides for air circulation. The canopy is retractable and the entire bassinet fits easily into its own carrying case. A really good mix of uses make the Sit N'Soothe a more versatile purchase than most bassinets.

The Right Start Catalog

(800) 548-8531

The Right Start Catalog has a beautiful Moses Basket made of willow. The set includes the basket and all of the bedding in a soft, lovely ivory check.

Toddler Beds

We learned a lot when we began searching for the perfect crib for our baby and then we learned even more when picking that first all-important bed. This is a landmark, as we mentioned earlier, a transition point. The first bed can be an empowering experience. Your baby will be so proud of her achievement and she'll want to sleep in her new bed. You'll want that, too, and you'll also want a bed that will last and is safe and strong. When is baby ready for a big kid bed? They'll probably let you know (maybe by climbing out of the crib) but often if your child has reached 35 inches or the crib railing is at mid-chest level, she might be ready for more room. All of your toddler's favorite security objects (blankies and cuddly toys) should make the move with her.

Let's face it, beds are not inexpensive items so you'll want one with lasting power—durability, and timeless or adaptable design. If you like an Arts and Crafts style bed, the simplicity of its fine design will also work with everything from Winnie the Pooh to tie-dyed bedding. An iron work classic beauty will look wonderful in ribbons and bows, Barbie pink or more sophisticated Laura Ashley patterns. Wood finishes can offer masculine or feminine touches if desired. A spindle maple bed would work in NFL hero sheets and also classic patchwork.

Toddler Bed Safety Savvy

As with cribs, pick a good, firm mattress, the best you can afford. Don't forget that during toilet training, you'll want to have waterproof mattress pads and covers to help protect that new mattress and keep it like new. Keeping in mind that the least expensive item to change is the bedding might lead you to a more classic or contemporary bed choice.

Toddler beds shouldn't be more than two feet off the floor. Remove the box spring if it's higher. Room & Board make their children's beds so they don't need a box spring avoiding this problem. Remember that bunk and four-posters are really for older children—it's a long fall from a top bunk and clothes could get caught on the four-poster. If you're in love with a four poster (and who wouldn't be) or a bunk, you can always go ahead and place your order. Then, until your toddler is a bit older (maybe two and a half or three), you can place the mattress on the floor and let your child get ready for that big kid bed. We've shown some wonderful beds of these types. Just wait a bit until you use them, then they'll be wise purchases.

Here are those first kid beds we favor for their strong good looks and their ability to adapt with changing decor:

Designer's Choice

Arts and Crafts Bed, Trundle

Price: $579.00 Twin—$399.00 Trundle
Available through: The Land of Nod Catalog
(800) 933-9904

Arts and Crafts style will never be out of fashion, and this selection is made of solid maple with clean, classic lines. We've found a trundle bed to be an efficient spacesaver—and even if you think your toddler won't be doing sleepovers for a while, you may enjoy the convenience on those nights when you're needed in his room. The Arts and Crafts bed and trundle are handcrafted in the U.S., something we forget to mention enough. This is a good looking, nicely constructed version at a good price.

Betsy Cameron's Storybook Collection

Lexington Furniture

Do you have a little princess at home? This premier collection, designed by famed romantic photographer Betsy Cameron, is timeless, innocent and whimsical. Crafted from select hardwood in a snowy white finish, the Victorian and French designs make any toddler's room into a storybook. If you like the traditional look of antiques and heirlooms, this is the modern version. Cameron believes that children's furniture is very special, embodying the love and memories lasting a lifetime. Working with Lexington Furniture and their designers, Cameron created the Storybook Collection which drew from her story of Princess Sleepyhead's search for the perfect bed. Here it is. Not for everyone of course, just some special little princess.

Belle

Price: $599.95 Twin

Available at: Room & Board® Stores

(800) 486-6554

Little girls will adore the Belle bed. It's handcrafted in white-painted steel with a clear lacquer finish. This is really a bed for your child to grow into—you may even want to put off the purchase until she's a little bit older. You can always pick it out, order it and get it ready for her third birthday. When she is ready, you'll want to drape that canopy with fabric and create a warm, enchanting look for your little beauty.

Curling Iron Bed

Price: $649.00 Twin

Available through: The Land of Nod Catalog

(800) 933-9904

Here's an elegant iron bed, a new heirloom. There's an aged or distressed finish to choose from—green with cream castings or antique white. It's got the classic good looks we admire at a price we think is pretty good. Even the shipping isn't out of line. The Curling Iron Bed is an awfully pretty first bed—it will look lovely all made up (again, you may want to wait a bit).

Darby Loft With Twin Bed or Bunk

Prices: $799.95–1109.95 Twin to Bunk
Available at: Room & Board® Stores
(800) 486-6554

This is one of Room & Board®s great designs, simple and with many options for parents whose needs often differ. We really like the loft configuration if you have room. Your little one can grow into the top bunk, and in the meantime, she'll take the bottom. You can add a Brighton Nightstand which will suit it perfectly, it'll fit under the top bunk, too. It comes with a ladder and two guard fences. Remember that the Darby Bunk can also be converted into two twins, until your child is ready for that top bunk. Darby is a maple classic, especially good for a growing family.

Forestdale Twin, Bunk & Trundle

Prices: $449.95–1099.95 Twin to Bunk
Available at: Room & Board® Stores
(800) 486-6554

Room & Board® provides clean, classic designs and this is one of them. The Forestdale Collection offers many variables—you can choose from bunk beds or twins, add a trundle and also order a two-door storage cabinet and bedside table. It's quite a complete collection and a good looking one as well. The twin bed has an optional single guard rail so it's a terrific first bed. Pick white ash or just sealed with a clear lacquer (ginger or natural finish). Forestdale is a collection your child will grow into, not out of.

Cool Classic

Le Petit Lapin Trundle Bed

Price: $1100.00
Available through: Rue de France Catalog
(800) 777-0998

Here is one of the sweetest (and most expensive) trundles we've seen. It's definitely for a little princess, one who adores bunnies. The sturdy bed's posts are topped with cast-iron *petits lapins* (handpainted); your little one will love it. It's available in Matte White, Gloss White or Antique Cream. It's the ultimate in little girl's beds, and the trundle is a bonus you'll get lots of use out of in nights to come.

Bunnies perched up high on the posts of a classic trundle bed—Courtesy of Rue de France

Kidplay Sleep & Store

Available through: Kids' Studio
(213) 655-4178

What could be better than a twin bed that combines good looks, storage and all the qualities we look for in a toddler's first bed? Kidplay Sleep & Store does all of that and much more. If you spring for the matching Kidplay Show & Store shelf unit, you'll get some needed storage in a child-proportioned piece (with an adjustable configuration of shelves possible). Kidplay is a great first bed and all the little (hidden, sort of) shelves and bins are cute and fun. The semi-circular panels can be used vertically or horizontally as headboard, guardrail, back supports, footboard, shelf and even side table. Just gear the use to your child's age and you'll discover how best to use Kidplay. The collection is made from Finnish plywood and parts of the pieces are tinted green, yellow and red.

Picket Fence Bed

Price: $890.00 Twin
Available through: The Land of Nod Catalog
(800) 933-9904

Tom Sawyer would like the privilege of whitewashing this picket fence bed. It's crafted of maple planks, made in the U.S.A.—and comes in a white lacquer finish, of course. There's even a little nightstand to match. This bed is adorable—you can just imagine it outfitted in lovely garden-like sheets.

Vermont Spindle Bunk, Trundle, Bed

Prices: $1095.00 Bunk; $340.00 Trundle
Available through: The Land of Nod Catalog
(800) 933-9904

Until junior's ready for those great bunks, you can separate these into two perfect twins. The Vermont Spindle Bunk is made of natural ash or painted white maple and is solid and sturdy. The bunk set includes a ladder and two safety rails. You can get both storage drawers and a trundle bed—providing the premium in spacesaving. The Vermont Spindle Bunk is contemporary and clean looking, and (did we mention?) a good value.

Monitors

Having an electronic device to monitor your infant isn't a necessity, but for some parents it can be very reassuring. One of my biggest fears was that I would sleep so soundly I wouldn't hear my baby's cries. Most monitors are audio—one-way walkie-talkies so you can hear your infant. Some of the newest and most technologically advanced monitors provide both visual and audio assurance using a simple video camera. A monitor does allow you to keep tabs on your baby, by letting you listen in, watch, or both when you are in a separate part of your home.

Audio Monitoring

Cellular phones, taxi dispatchers and others often cause interference with these monitors. You may even pick up the monitor next door. The base of a monitor acts as the transmitter and the parent's unit is the receiver. Sometimes switching to another channel (if you have that option) works, or modifying the range, but you might have to switch to another model entirely. Also remember that someone may be able to hear your conversation in the nursery as well. Some cordless phones may also cause problems with your monitor. Hopefully your cordless has additional channels so you can try for clear reception. If that doesn't work the two might just be incompatible. We suggest careful testing of all portable electronic devices in your home for compatibility, as soon as you get them. Keep your receipts, and if things don't work out, exchange your monitor or cordless telephone. They may be small, but you'll find that most babies have a pretty good cry or scream, and it's likely you'll hear it live, too, just as well as that monitor picks it up, especially in a small home.

Now if you still want the convenience of monitoring from slightly afar, purchase a monitor that is best for you. Be sure to choose one that can run on battery and also has an AC adapter. Monitors seem to eat up batteries, but some of the newer models have rechargeable ones, a definite bonus.

Video Monitoring

If we thought a regular monitor wasn't always necessary, the newest video monitors really might be excessive. Unless, of course, you're into state-of-the-art gadgets and want to be the first on your block with one. These units feature a wireless camera for transmitting a black and white picture of your baby, along with sound, to your monitor. You'll pay for the technology.

Monitoring Safety Savvy

Keep monitors out of baby's reach; the cord or adapter could pose a strangulation threat. Most transmitters work best at distances less than 10 feet. Put yours close enough to pick up the sounds of your child yet far enough away that the cord is always out of reach. If baby has an older sibling, have a talk with them about the monitor so that they understand that this is for baby's well being, and is not a walkie-talkie toy for them.

Sounds of silence are not always sounds of a healthy baby. Nothing will monitor your baby better than you doing it in person.

Recalled: Manufactured between 1988 and 1990, the Gerry Deluxe Baby Monitor (model #602) has been recalled. Wiring could overheat and catch fire. If someone offers you one as a hand-me-down, hand-it-over to Gerry for a free replacement. Call (800) 672-6289.

Monitors

Baby Call

Price: $50

Manufacturer: Sony Corporation

Baby Call looks good, especially with that rounded antenna. It is costlier, but the sound is clear and with little static. This is a good standard monitor without a light display but with a good range. If you like Sony, you'll probably like this monitor.

Baby View Portable Monitor and Camera Set

Price: $179.00

Manufacturer: Safety 1st®

This is high technology baby monitoring and we like it (unless your pediatrician recommends it, we still think that it's a luxury item). Even when it's dark, the infrared LEDs light up a wide-angled view of your sleeping beauty. The camera can sit on a bedside table or be wall mounted. The sound is pretty good, too. If you're in the nursery relaxing and want to watch the news, the monitor can also work as a black and white TV. It might remind you of James Bond, but it's a sound purchase for the nursery that must have everything.

Crisp and Clear

Price: $69.95

Manufacturer: First Years

Another great monitor at a good price, with rechargeable batteries, this one uses advanced 900 MHz frequency for better reception (this helps a lot with interference and static). It also has a dual sound/light display. It's fully portable and compact in size. First Years has a monitoring winner here!

Look 'n Listen

Price: $45

Manufacturer: Gerry

A good basic monitor with a light display and workable on either batteries or regular current, the Look 'n Listen does just that. You'll "see" and hear if baby needs you.

Sound & Lights Monitor (#71565)

Price: $50
Manufacturer: Fisher-Price
(800) 828-4000

One of the most popular monitors around, the Sound & Lights has all the essentials—plus a lighted display—at a reasonable price. Really useful features are that you can transmit and receive on battery or electric power (so it's a good monitor for traveling as well) and it comes with a range selector for added privacy. The Direct Link Privacy Monitor #71566 is another Fisher-Price choice and a good one.

Ultra-Sensitive Nursery Monitor

Price: $26.99
Manufacturer: Gerry

We like the handy pocket size for the caregiver's unit which has LED "sound lights" to let you know there's been some sound in the nursery. A belt clip is even included. This is a simple addition, but if you are prone to lose your TV remote control (and who isn't), this simple inclusion will save a lot of frustration, so long as you use it! There's a control for the volume and two separate channels to help avoid interference.

Changing Tables

Just like cribs, changing tables come in all varieties: wheeled, folding, and railed. They can be made of plastic or wood. The factor they have in common is, of course, safety. Also like cribs and high chairs, your baby is placed high for your own convenience and so they, too, present the danger of falls. Usually this happens when your baby, who seems to always lie so still, is suddenly pushing herself around with great strength (enough strength to push right off the table). Or perhaps you turn around for an instant to get some wipes and your baby decides then and there to move!

In actual fact, anything can be a changing table—the floor, your bed or the kitchen table. However, we do recommend purchasing a changing table rather than adapting a low dresser. If you're insistent on that, you can buy an indented foam pad (about three inches thick), covered with vinyl. Don't forget to attach a strap which can snap onto the back of the dresser. Add a changing table pad, like the one manufactured by Rumple Tuff.

Keeping everything you need to change baby right by the changing table is a good start toward safety. Washcloths, fresh clothing, wipes and other necessities should be right at hand. If your changing table doesn't have convenient storage, there are some hanging compartments listed below.

A sturdy changing table is important. Tipping over is also a hazard—so look for a wide stance if the changing table is lightweight. We did what we call the "rattle test," pushing, poking and rattling the tables we looked at to see how sturdy and steady they were. We found wooden changing tables were the most sturdy of those we looked at. What we think you should avoid is the fold-down wooden adapter for the top of a chest. When babies are placed on the outer edge, the weight can cause the chest and adapter to tip over.

Changing Table Safety Savvy

1. Never leave baby alone. Let the phone ring. Don't answer the door.
2. Everything you need should be within reach—washcloths, clean clothes, diapers, ointments, cotton balls, etc.
3. One hand should be holding baby firmly at all times while changing her.
4. Check the weight limitations on your model. Some infants grow rather quickly and as the construction of changing tables varies, some may hold more weight than others.
5. If using a fold-up changing table be sure that at each use, it is opened fully, stable, and secure.

Changing Table Criteria

1. Your changing table should be at a comfortable height for you, waist-high is a good level.
2. You will need a flat, wide surface to give sufficient room to work (extra room also gives you a few extra precious seconds to take action should baby be in danger of falling. The larger surface also affords enough room to change a toddler. That's the age diapering can sometimes become a battle—diapering a squirming child can be a challenge!
3. If you purchase one with drawers underneath (and we did), be sure they have metal glides. That will mean an easy slide and locking mechanisms will keep the drawers from flying out.

Changing tables are a good item to buy used or to have handed-down. Manufacturers seem to keep parts current longer than on other products and you may even be able to get instructions along with those missing screws. Again as with cribs, if you're planning to have more than one child, ordering that slightly more expensive, wooden changing table might become more cost-effective when it sees you through changing your third child.

There are many changing tables available that match your crib. Ours did. The Morigeau changing table we selected was also a great buy. It was made of wood, nicely finished, with a high rail, and a safety belt. The Morigeau was also extremely sturdy even on its casters. It met all of our criteria. Child Craft, Ragazzi, Morigeau-Lépine, Inc. all make good quality changing tables. Many convert to three-drawer dressers which might be useful for a toddler's room. Of course, these come with a higher price tag, around $300 to $500. Again, we want to remind you that if you're planning more than one child, it becomes a more cost-effective purchase. Here are those manufacturers who produce high quality changing tables:

Child Craft
(812) 883-3111

Morigeau-Lépine, Inc.
(800) 326-2121

Ragazzi
(514) 324-7886

For those of you who don't really need or want to match your crib furniture, or want to curb those nursery costs, here are some other models we like:

Badger Changing Table with Rails and Drawers

Price: $129.99
Available through: Baby Catalog of America
(800) 752-9736

Here's a sturdy hardwood table with two roomy shelves and complete with a pad and restraining strap. This is an easily assembled item, available in white or natural finishes.

Carver Changing Table

Price: $799.95–899.95
Available at: Room & Board® Stores
(800) 486-6554

Here's a multi-use changing table which is also the ultimate in storage solutions. The Carver is at an easy-to-reach height so it becomes a comfortable changing station. It's available in all sorts of finishes from cherry, maple, and red oak with changeable details like drawer pulls (pick from the available collection). This is a functional piece with clean, contemporary styling, which will become your toddler's first dresser or storage cabinet. Carver might seem like an investment; and it is. It's a worthwhile one.

Changing Table

Manufacturer: Gerry

Gerry makes a full-size hardwood changing table (model 3610) which has two shelves for storage and safety railings on all sides. It comes with the necessities: a safety belt and changing pad. You can order an optional drawer kit.

Changer-N-Desk

Manufacturer: Kinderkraft

Here's a wood changing table with a high rail on all sides, a shelf and a storage drawer for baby essentials. What's nice is that it can convert into an art board or a desk table. The white surface wipes clean. The Changer-N-Desk comes in many finishes: natural, aspen and cherry.

Changing Table Accessories

These are some accessories which might be helpful to you as you change your baby (over and over again). These are easily available in your favorite baby catalogs and also at Toys "R" Us, Sears, Walmart and other favorite stores.

- Wipe Holder—a compact little shelf that can hold those wipes, a wipe warmer or other baby essentials. Some also have a middle section which holds diapers and allows access from the bottom. The one we liked in the Right Start catalog (800-548-8531) even has removable side compartments.

- Organizers—these often attach and hang off the edge of your changing table and help you store all of those essentials for diapering.
- Terry Covers— cover the plastic changing mat with a layer of materials to prevent the baby from sticking to the mat and to absorb any moisture that results from changing the baby.
- Laundry Bag—pick one which can drape over the side of the changing table and one which is washable. Some tie closed but it might be better to find one which fastens with Velcro.
- Diaper Stacker—this was also something we wondered about. It's an item you certainly don't need but may want. It will keep a stack of diapers convenient and tidy. Diaper Stackers today even match sheets or themes of your nursery, so you'll easily find a Winnie the Pooh one and many more to choose from.
- Chucks and Lap Pads—we have to say we never used these at all. My changing table came with a lovely terry cover which was easily washable but just in case you want to know—chucks are disposable plastic-filled paper liners that go under baby's tush when you're changing her and lap pads work the same way only they're rubber pads covered usually in flannel.

Here is a specific diapering helper we really like:

Diaper Depot

Price: $16.95
Available through: One Step Ahead Catalog
(800) 274-8440

Here's an organizer for your changing table that will help you to be efficient and free of the distractions of searching for something. You'll know where everything is and it will be within reach with the Diaper Depot. It hooks over the side of the changing table and holds up to 16 diapers of any size which you can easily pull out one at a time from the bottom. Wipes sit on the top where you can reach them and the convenient side pockets hold other necessities. If you wrap the wipe warmer accessory ($19.95) around your container, you'll have a totally complete diapering station.

Bedding for Cribs and Toddler Beds

Have you thought of everything for your baby's nursery? In the rush of crib shopping, mattress evaluation and equipment purchases, you may have overlooked the most simple of necessities—baby's bedding. We were very excited with some Mickey Mouse bedding we found because it was mostly black, white and red (the same colors used in the educational toys we were also purchasing) and the patterns were lively and recognizable. The bedding also went really well with our Morigeau crib, a soft gray color. Most importantly, it fit into our budget, our design sensibilities, and was soft, 100% cotton.

When you purchase the all-important first bed, your big kid's first bedding should also get similar consideration. Spend time thinking about how your growing child will react and use this first bed. Do you want the bedding to reflect interests and provide reassuring, friendly images?

Select bedding, for cribs and first beds, with the same priorities in mind which you used to decorate the nursery: aesthetics, function, budget and reflection/attitude. We found bedding with Winnie the Pooh, the Rainbow Fish, Sesame Street and just about all of our favorite characters. We also found designs using the sky, the garden and the simplicity of children's drawings for imagery. Bedding can make quite a visual impact on a nursery as well. The energetic or soft colors, the fanciful or traditional patterns and shapes and imagery all add to a room's signature feeling.

Some bedding is quite expensive these days such as items which are handcrafted, appliquéd or imported. We suggest that if you adore some of these, picking up just a single piece can set the tone in a nursery or bedroom. A bumper guard or cover, for example, are items which are instantly visible and also receive a great deal of use. Add some solid or similar patterned sheets and more that are more in your budget and you've retained the design aesthetic and saved some of the cost. There are some wonderful basics around and they can be found in fleece, flannel and the softest of cottons.

Bedding has become really tied into the fashion industry and coordinates include much more than sheets. There are comforters, pillow shams, dust ruffles and skirts, wallpapers, friezes, diaper stackers and even, canopy covers to choose from. You can also find favorite custom fabrics and have them turned into bedding coordinates. There's even educational-styled bedding—those now famous black and white patterns we're used to seeing in learning toys are appearing nightly on baby's sheets. Mix and match your way through bedding choices, and remember that one day junior may turn to you and say no to those sheets you adore. Children will start influencing these design decisions quicker than you know. For now, however, the choice is yours. Go by what you feel is right for your baby, attractive, well made and affordable.

Bedding Safety Savvy

- Babies should not be placed to sleep on soft surfaces such as pillows, sofa cushions, adult beds or other surfaces not designed specifically for infant sleep.
- Use only a fitted crib sheet, mattress pad and/or a waterproof pad between your baby and the crib mattress.
- Select bumper pads that fit around the entire crib and tie or snap securely in place. Trim off any excess lengths after straps are tied (this also keeps your baby from chewing on or becoming entangled in the bumper straps, ties and ribbons).
- Quilts, comforters and blankets should be placed only on top of your sleeping baby (never under the baby).
- Use bumper pads only until your child can pull up to a standing position. Then remove them. They can become a way for baby to climb over the railing and fall.
- Pillows and plush toys should only be used for decoration. Remove them when your baby is asleep or unattended.

Bedding For Cribs and Bassinets

Baby Alphabet Crib Quilts

Price: $79.95
Available from: Blue Tiffany, a Division of Maple Springs
(215) 234-0812

A lovely handcrafted quilt with the alphabet and all of baby's favorite friends for you to wrap her up in. Pick either pastel or primary colors and have it embroidered with baby's name and date of birth.

Bundle baby up in a handcrafted alphabet quilt. Courtesy of Maple Springs.

Bassinet Bedding

Prices: $12.99–69.99

Available through: JCPenney Stores and Catalog

JCPenney offers a few choices for typical bassinets—pick from lace, star light, and even knit sheets. At these reasonable prices, you won't mind that baby won't be using them for long.

Best Baby Buys

Bedding Sets–5 pc.

Price: $69.99

Available through: JCPenney Stores and Catalog

What a bargain! Crib bedding for a really remarkable price and it's cute, too. Pick from Sesame Street "Elmo," Looney Tunes, Noah's Ark (by Red Calliope), and In the Tree Tops (baby animals settling down to rest in the trees). Sets include a comforter, a bumper, crib ruffle, crib sheet and receiving blanket. What more do you need?

Cotton Nursery Bedding in a Rainbow of Colors

Prices: $12.95–15.95
Available through: One Step Ahead Catalog
(800) 274-8440

Here is one-stop shopping for all of your bedding needs, an incredible and colorful selection of nursery sheets and blankets. All are 100% cotton for baby's comfort and there's crib and bassinet sheets as well as blankets, top sheets and more. Order the matching cotton thermal crib blankets and receiving blankets to carry a coordinated look throughout the nursery. Or have fun and mix and match; with over 15 colors to choose from (3 pinks!) you'll love the entire collection.

Designer's Choice

Galaxy and Garden Crib Bedding Sets

Prices: $365.00–370.00 sets; $25–40 fitted sheets
Available through: The Land of Nod Catalog
(800) 933-9904

From flowering tulips to evening galaxies, here's some crib bedding we really love. It's well-designed, cute, 100% cotton and very soft. These crib sets contain 4 pieces: a generous bumper, a coverlet, fitted sheet and crib skirt. If you don't want to spend so much on bedding, consider choosing just one piece, such as the bumper or the coverlet, and mix and match with some lower priced coordinates. That way junior can still enjoy the stars and planets or snails and ladybugs. You can even purchase some curtain panels in either design which will help add just the right tone to baby's nursery.

Infant Flannel & Fuzzy Friends Crib Ensembles

Prices: $16.00–55.00
Contact: Land's End Catalog
(800) 332-0103

Want a really soft (4.7 oz. cotton) flannel sheet for baby's bed? Land's End makes a great line of crib bedding in solids or Fuzzy Friends (an animal print that reverses to polka dots). You'll love the crib sheets, coverlets, bumper pads and receiving blankets. These are great to mix and match with your other bedding, too.

Pooh's Friends Forever

Price: $39.99
Manufacturer: Little Bedding Co.

Baby will love Winnie the Pooh and her crib set featuring her favorite friends. At a very reasonable price, the set includes a comforter, bumper and fitted sheet and is part of the themed nursery collection, Friends Forever.

Stick Figures Crib Bedding

Price: $299.00 set
Available through: The Land of Nod Catalog
(800) 933-9904

Using children's stick figure style drawings (fish, sun, people) to illustrate this great crib bedding, The Land of Nod offers this collection as a money-saving set of four pieces: a generous bumper, a coverlet, fitted sheet and crib skirt. As these images float on patches of bold color, the set would look great with any colored coordinates in solids or blocks. The drawings are so typical of early artists' works your child will grow to recognize them, naming each and every one.

Susan Sargent Bedding

Prices: $ 25.00–200.00 hand-painted/$40.00–490.00 appliquéd
Contact: Susan Sargent Designs Inc.
(800) 245-4767

We've always loved Susan Sargent's rugs and now we're quite smitten with her coordinates. Her children's bedding collections (we especially like the ABC and Circus ones) are adorable, lively and energetic. The ABC collection is hand-

A circus of a quilt—elegant and fun!

painted and features the alphabet and delightful animals. The Circus collection is appliquéd; choose the lovely crib quilt. Although Sargent's bedding may not fit in everyone's budgets, we certainly value handmade, handpainted items as well as the fine quality of her many collections. Elegant and fun, the Sargent collections are indeed Designer's Choice.

Teddy at Play Crib Quilt and Bumper Pad

Prices: $55.00 bumper pad; $69.00 quilt
Available from: The Company Store Catalog
(800) 285-3696

Teddy bears are nearly irresistible and these are some of the cutest we've seen! Your little bear may fall asleep counting all of the teddies playing on her 100% cotton, handcrafted quilt. Don't forget you can pick up some inexpensive flannels or fleece coordinates to really make this a great buy.

Wick-Away Crib Protector

Price: $15.95 for a 2-pk.
Available through: One Step Ahead Catalog
(800) 274-8440

Here's a crib protector we really like. The special top layer wicks wetness away to be absorbed by the middle layer, and then the waterproof backing keeps the fitted sheet dry and clean. That sounds fairly complicated but using the pad is totally simple. Just tie it to the crib slats to prevent bunching up under your baby and when the time comes, throw it straight into the washer. It even comes in colors now (mine never did) and the array includes light blue, pink, natural, white and mint.

Bedding For Baby's First Bed

Company Kids™

Prices: $12.00–89.99
Available from: The Company Store
(800) 285-3696

Company Kids™ is a great children's collection of bedding and accessories. There's plenty to choose from with these graphic, bold and lively designs. Themes like Transportation, Sports, Animal Family and School Days will perk up a child's first bed with their bright colors and simple, recognizable images.

Haight-Ashbury Tie-Dye Bedding

Prices: $15.00–99.00
Available through: The Land of Nod Catalog
(800) 933-9904

For the hippest of children, here's a T-shirt style bedding collection in 100% cotton jersey knit. Choose from Tangled Up Blue or Green River Tie-Dye to brighten up junior's room with sheets, comforters and even bed skirts. They're naturally cool.

Knit Sheets (for toddlers)

Prices: $24.00–40.00
Contact: Land's End Catalog
(800) 332-0103

This is a great, thoughtful line of bedding for kids in easy-to-care-for jersey knit (no ironing). Kids love the softness and you'll like the deep pockets and shrinkage resistance, not to mention the eight bold and beautiful colors.

Palais Royal Muscaris Bedding

Prices: $76–104.00
Available through: Rue de France Catalog
(800) 777-0998

Fantasy bedding for your little girls. Grape hyacinths scatter blooms across a field of white in what's called the Muscaris pattern. It's gentle, sweet and all girl. Not only that, it's top of the line 100% Egyptian combed cotton, with a 200 thread count. Maybe your little one won't know what that is, but you'll recognize the difference. It doesn't come cheap but it's beautiful and high quality, too.

Sports Bedding

Prices: $14.99–39.99
Available at: JCPenney Stores or Catalog

JCPenney says to let the games begin and your little sport will love choosing bedding with everything from X-games to Major League Soccer, Star Wars to Roadworks. Whatever you choose, you can outfit the entire room; the collections include accent pillows and draperies.

Cool Classic

Susan Sargent Bedding

Prices: $25.00–200.00 hand-painted; $40.00–490.00 appliquéd
Contact: Susan Sargent Designs Inc.
(800) 245-4767

Susan Sargent spins her magic for toddler's bedding collections as well (we especially like the ABC and Circus ones). These are adorable, lively and energetic. The ABC collection is handpainted and we think the pieces to own are the twin duvet and pillow cases, perfect for toddlers learning their alphabet and naming animals. The Circus collection is appliquéd; pick from a twin coverlet, a twin bed skirt, and pillow cases. Although Sargent's bedding may not fit in everyone's budgets, it is elegant and fun. The Sargent collections are truly the Designer's Choice.

Under the big tent or for your child's first bed, a lively Circus Collection!

Tulip Bedding

Prices: $16.00–109.00
Available through: The Land of Nod Catalog
(800) 933-9904

Tulips and spring-like bedding in an endearing combination of appliqué, seersucker, cotton, and T-shirt style jersey knit. The solid lavender jersey sheets are sold in a convenient set. There are appliquéd white sheets with lavender and blue tulips, and small and large checked reversible patterns using the entire color range (lavender, white, green, blue). All of them are 100% cotton and as fresh as springtime. Pick some, pick all, mix and match and enjoy the entire growing collection!

Playpens (and Portable Cribs)

We now think of a portable playpen as a necessity. We used one of the first Graco Pack 'N Play's to appear on the scene. It wasn't pretty, all gray, but it functioned for us as both traveling crib and playpen. At home we used it when we wanted to keep baby safely out of the way—if we were cooking, for example. She loved her Pack 'N Play as we'd pop in different toys for her to play with, offering her varying challenges. Today, portable playpens are incredibly popular and good-looking with even more features and best of all, they are easier to use.

Some of these newer features to look for are canopies, large wheels, and, even, a bassinet. Remember you can use one of these playpens fairly early making it worth the investment. We didn't even take a look, but there are still some very traditional wood playpens available. However, we still prefer the portables made with aluminum tubing, nylon mesh on the sides for ventilation and a vinyl covered mattress. Fold it up in its bag and off you go. When we say a portable playpen is a necessity, we mean you could live without one, but when the prices have gone down and the features up, you may think it's a worthwhile purchase. We do.

Here are our favorites:

Happy Cabana

Price: $100.00 approx.
Manufacturer: Evenflo

From bottles to happy cabanas, Evenflo has created a portable play yard that features a canopy, a bassinet attachment, large wheels and an easy fold-up design. If you're traveling, you'll enjoy wheeling the folded-up Happy Cabana as if it were just another piece of luggage.

Cool Classic

Pack 'N Play With Canopy

Price: $150 approx.
Manufacturer: Graco

The classic portable playpen, Graco's Pack 'N Play couldn't get much better. It now features four snap-action hinges to help you set it up and store it even quicker than before. The padded floorboard doubles as a zippered carrying case. Best of all is the canopy (protecting baby from those UV rays) and side pocket storage and unlike ours, the newest one is a colorful delight!

Baby Best Buy

Pack 'N Play With Bassinet Insert

Price: $150 approx.
Manufacturer: Graco

It's a combination bassinet, crib and play yard with mesh on two sides with a roll-down flap on one side. Like all the Graco playpens, you'll be able to set it up really quickly. The Pack 'N Play attachment works as a bassinet for newborns up to 15 lbs. You can use the Pack 'N Play as a crib and play yard for infants up to 30 pounds. It features Swivel wheels with brakes at one end. You'll love it—just go ahead and pack and play. There's also a Deluxe Bassinet Pack 'N Play in a larger size.

Play Yard

Price: $89.99
Manufacturer: Carter's

Thought they only made clothes? Carter's has entered the portable playpen market with their Play Yard, complete with mesh sides. It also has features you'll look for: it folds easily for storage and it's made of easy to care for nylon.

Repair Alert: The CPSC has announced a repair program for Century Products' Fold 'N Go Care Centers which include a play yard, bassinet and changing table. The fabric may be loose, creating a pocket where baby could suffocate. Call Century at 800-583-4092 for a free repair kit immediately.

Toddler Room Furniture

In our quest for baby's best cribs and beds, we came across a few chairs and beanbags and more that are so irresistible we just had to include them. When your toddler is really mobile and in charge of her environment, it's empowering to provide furniture that is kid-friendly and kid-sized.

Designer's Choice

Eazy Bean™ Lounger, Fruits, Vegetables and Carry-Ons

Manufacturer: Eazy Bean™
(415) 255-8516

Toddlers spend a lot of time on the floor and these Fruits, Vegetables and Balls will look good, be comfortable and keep your little one full of beans, so to speak! Eazy Bean does a take-off on the 60s bean bag chair, updating it and turning it into gardening and sports delights. You'll like cuddling up to read to your child in the Apple, or catching a nap in the 8-Ball or goofing around on the Soccer Ball. Toddlers also really seem to like taking their chair along with them; the Carry-On's are half stools with handles. They'll turn up all over the house, but they're so cute you may not mind! (They come in a multitude of colors from subtle to bold, pastel to primary, durable cotton twill or cozy cotton velveteen).

The Nod Chair

Price: $215.00
Available through: The Land of Nod Catalog
(800) 933-9904

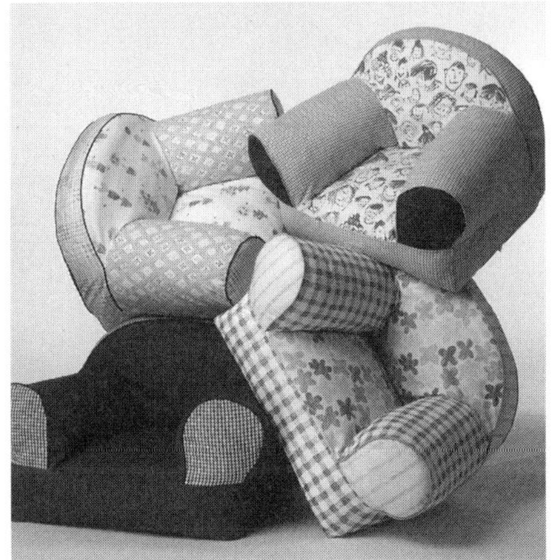

Give this chair a nod for junior's room.

This is the official chair of the Land of Nod and it's no wonder. Perfectly scaled for a child, it's soft and frameless, and made for curling up with a favorite book or just lounging. There are even some large pockets on the back for odds and ends. You'll appreciate that the cotton and denim covers unzip for washing. Especially cute are the faces mixed with jazzy stripes, the bold flowers set against even bolder plaids and the all-star denim chair—it's hard to choose which one your child will nod off in.

Patchwork Chair

Price: $199.95
Available through: Room & Board® Stores
(800) 486-6554

There's nothing like a comfy chair and this is one your toddler will claim as her own. The Patchwork Chair is lightweight enough to move around and the 100% cotton cover can be removed for washing. Best of all, you can choose from plaid or flowers and the bright patterns of either will be perfect for your toddler to snuggle into.

Cool Classic

Polartec Kids Nest

Prices: $38.00 nest pillow plus $70.00 Polartec cover
Contact: Land's End Catalog
(800) 332-0103

Pillow or chair—Land's End calls it a "nest." Whatever it is, it's cushiony and cuddly. Buy the nest pillow and then choose your Polartec cover in an array of ten colors. It's ideal for curling up in, flopping down on and settling in for a nap.

Designer's Choice

Teensy Table & Chairs

Prices: $85.00 per chair; $129.00 table
Available through: Room & Board® Stores
(800) 486-6554

We know it's not inexpensive, but it's quality construction. The Teensy Table and Chairs are made of molded plywood and are formed to fit those little bodies. The lacquer finish allows for easy clean-up and maintenance.

Safety Considerations

Here we want to give you some general safety considerations, discuss certified products and standards, list some favorite childproofing equipment and offer some resources to help with recalls and safety issues. Also, in each chapter we try to cover safety guidelines and offer tips which correspond to those specific areas and products.

Unfortunately, there are a high number of injuries associated with baby products each year. Different government agencies and branches monitor different products: car seats are reviewed by the U.S. National Highway Traffic Safety Administration (NHTSA); baby food is covered by the Department of Agriculture; and skin care products are regulated by the Food and Drug Administration (FDA). Please note that in Canada, for information on issues regarding child safety car seats, contact the Transport Canada's (TC) Road Safety Office or the Canadian Automobile Association (CAA). Cribs and toys are regulated by the U.S. Consumer Product Safety Commission (CPSC) with few requirements. Voluntary standards have been created, usually by manufacturers or advocacy groups, for the consumer's added protection.

You may have seen "JPMA" stamped on some toys. The Juvenile Products Manufacturers Association (JPMA) sponsors a voluntary certification program for certain children's products. Although these guidelines are only as stringent as the Association determines, at least products are now tested on a periodic basis. The JPMA uses an independent laboratory for testing products (Detroit Testing Laboratory) and certify the products if they meet minimum safety performance standards developed by the American Society for Testing and Materials (ASTM). Stickers, stamps and initials are no guarantee of safety. Products without stickers and certification may also still be safe—they may never have been tested. So watch your child playing with and using products. Check them for wear and tear. Watch for recalls and ask friends about any problems they have had. Be cautious. If in doubt, don't use a product.

Who should you call for information, reports and recalls? The worst news item we read this year regarding recalls wasn't about a particular product. It was, in fact, that the news of recalls doesn't often reach the end user or juvenile consumer. Infants and toddlers are in danger. As a new parent, you need to be proactive regarding safety. Check on recalls and check often. When you're in a store like Toys "R" Us, check out the recalls they post (and we thank them and other conscientious stores for doing that). Skim those parenting magazines for recalls and listings of dangerous products and read our chapter on recalls. Newspapers, especially nationally circulated ones, often feature articles that you'll find useful in this regard.

Some useful resources and contacts:

CAA
(613) 247-0117
This is the number for the Canadian Automobile Association (CAA), which works closely with Transport Canada in providing child safety seat information. Call for more details.

CPSC

(800) 638-2772

Call the hotline and listen to updates on product recalls or to report an injury.

FDA

(301) 443-1240

Call the FDA if you would like to complain or hear about recalls about a baby food, formula or skin-care product.

JPMA

(609) 231-8500

Call or write (JPMA, P.O. Box 955, Marlton, NJ 08053) to obtain a listing of certified products.

NHTSA

(800) 424-9393

Call about car safety seats.

TC

(613) 998-1978

For any questions regarding child car safety seats in Canada, contact Transport Canada.

What are the biggest dangers to your baby and how can you best keep her from hazards such as these?

- Strangulation

  We often hear about strangulation danger in recall information. Babies have really soft and vulnerable throats. Pressure applied to the outside of their neck can cut off their air supply. Strings on hooded nightgowns or pacifier cords can get caught on crib posts or baby can slip through the leg holes of strollers or get caught in between the wide-spaced slats of older cribs. They can also strangle when they fall on a low-strung crib mobile which is strung between bars. Such incidents are tragic and scary. What you can do is remove all strings from garments. Crib bumper tie-ons shouldn't be more than nine inches in length, so trim them if they're longer. Check wall decorations or trims for any long or loose strings. Keep baby's crib away from the window and remember to tie up those cords for the blinds. Crib mobiles, remember, need to be removed the instant your baby is sitting up.

- Falls

  Babies will and do fall. They crash into fireplaces and coffee tables with sharp edges. They push themselves out of car seats and strollers. What can you try to do to prevent such accidents? Use seat belts that fasten around the waist and crotch and use them securely. Test the belt each time you use it. Read our chapter on Going Places and all about installing and using car seats safely. Purchase products without sharp edges and buy pads and protectors for furniture.

- Choking

  We often forget that babies are capable of biting off parts of toys and other small objects. Even tips of bottles or foam covering play products can find their way into your baby's mouth. They also often choke on food. We've all heard about hot dog pieces being just the right size to become lodged in baby's throat. Coins, batteries and other household objects can get stuck in your baby's throat, cutting off air supply. Follow all manufacturer's guidelines. When you're washing baby's toys give them an exam as well, checking for worn or loose parts. Damaged toys must be disposed of. Keep foods which might be dangerous away from your baby. That includes pet foods as well, so keep them out of baby's reach. If there's an older brother or sister, put them on guard and explain how important it is that their toys, which might be dangerous to their little sister or brother, stay out of baby's way. One of the main reasons many toys are not recommended for children under a certain age (watch for such designations on boxes and packaging) is because small parts present a choking risk. Please resist the temptation to buy toys labelled for an older child for this reason. Of course, you'll think your infant is advanced and ready for something a little less "baby-ish," but manufacturers place priority on safety first and you should, too. Baby will get to that developmental stage soon, be patient and wait to get that train set (Dad!).

- Drowning

  Babies can drown in just a few inches of water. In addition to being on guard in the bathroom, don't forget that even your pet's water dish may be a drowning hazard for your little one. Don't leave buckets anywhere, if baby fell in headfirst, it might be impossible for her to get out.

- Suffocation

Babies can suffocate if small balloons get caught in their throats. If face-down, a baby can bury his face in an area created by soft-padded mattresses, animal skins or cushioned surfaces and suffocate. Garbage bags are also a danger. Don't let your baby play with a balloon and don't let your favorite restaurant tie balloons to your stroller. Try not to place your baby on softly padded surfaces and put baby to sleep face-up (check with your pediatrician).

- Burns

  Your baby's skin is especially sensitive. Vaporizers and water can scald your baby as can hot coffee or overheated bottles. Biting electrical cords or lamp wires and plugs could cause electrical burns and shock. Go ahead and turn down that hot water temperature to 120°F. Buy a protective spout cover for the bathtub. A cold-water humidifier will be safer, and purchase protective safety devices for your outlets and appliances. Use safety gates for keeping baby out of dangerous areas like the kitchen. Keep your coffee away from your baby and in a covered mug. Don't use your microwave to heat those baby bottles. Store and secure household cleaners and chemicals, and even the dishwasher detergents, out of reach.

Baby-Proofing Your Home

Products to help keep your baby out of harm's way: We were surprised to find only a few manufacturers have ventured into the safety market (for children) but were at least relieved that they seemed to have thought of everything. Safety 1st, First Alert, and Prince Lionheart are the names we found who seem to be doing it right and safely. Order from a catalog like Right Start or One Step Ahead or pop into a store like Toys "R" Us and you'll see more than an adequate range of safety devices and products. We also found a catalog and web site for The Childproofer which has more than a full range of products for safety. Check them out on-line at www.childproofer.com or call for a catalog at 1-800-374-2525.

Baby-proofing your home isn't hard but often it gets annoying. Those safety latches on our kitchen cabinet drawers used to drive us crazy. Despite that, we never once worried that our precious daughter would get access to a sharp instrument. So we suggest you pick up sets of stove and toilet guards, latches on drawers and appliances, fireplace bumpers, and more. Remind grandparents to do the same and as we mention in our Going Places section, pack a mini-bagful of latches, etc. for traveling. These products are not costly, certainly not in the grand scheme of things. Baby's safety is the number one priority, right?

Please remember that even the best baby-proofing is not insurance against dangerous accidents. Your supervision is the best way to protect your child. That said, you need to look around your home from a little child's perspective. Go through the entire house or apartment and look for any possible dangers.

Be sure to have on hand:

- Appliance Latches—We like the Kitch Hitch by Safety 1st. Use on the top or side of almost any appliance to keep your child from opening it. It's strong and durable and can even be removed when baby is older.
- Bathtub spout cover—A soft cover to protect your baby from scalding in the bathtub. There's even a choice of fun and safe animals. Safety 1st makes a good one called "Sof'Spout™" and at only $2.99 you can afford two, one for traveling.
- Cabinet and Drawer Latches—Usually sold in sets, these are typically under $2 for six or seven which is probably enough for your kitchen. Pick up a set for Grandma's house and a set for traveling (put it in your suitcase right away).
- Cord Holders and Cord Shorteners—Remember those dangerous window blind cords? All cords are dangerous, even speaker wires. Pick up these rather inexpensive safety devices—some work like spools winding the wire up inside.
- Corner Guards—These help you keep sharp furniture edges from being a safety hazard by softening the corners. There are a few different styles, some are ends you attach to the corners with double-sided tape but they may not hold well. A bumper guard, costlier, is more like a padded covering going all around the edge of a table. These aren't pretty, you'll have to remind yourself baby's safety comes first, aesthetics second. It isn't forever; just a temporary safety fix.
- Fireplace Bumper Pad—You can cover up to 90 inches straight across the front of your fireplace and 16 inches on each side. Those sharp edges will be covered. It's easy to install, remove and trim. It's ugly, but not as bad as an emergency room visit.

- Outlet Covers/Plugs—Put them all over your house. Outlet plugs are still in service at mine. These will keep your child from sticking her fingers or objects into the electrical outlets. If you're using the simple plugs and take one out to use the outlet, remember to secure it again. The one problem with outlet plugs is that if you have a really curious toddler, she will eventually figure out how to remove them. The outlet cover might be an even better choice. It goes over the switch plate and allows the outlet to remain usable while out of baby's reach. When a plug is removed, the spring-loaded cover will block the opening from investigating little children. The Safe Plate by Mericon is a good choice.
- Oven Lock—Keep your baby away from and out of the stove or the microwave. The oven lock will help prevent burns and scalding and it's heat resistant.
- Safety Gates—We made it through toddlerhood without a gate but we didn't have any stairs to contend with. Basically, a gate will help keep baby from going where you don't want her to. Stairs should be gated at the top and the bottom and also gate off any other dangerous areas. Measure carefully and look at the different types. The Right Start stores and catalogs and A Step Ahead have good selections, as does your local Toys "R" Us.

Gate Safety Savvy Yes, there's an ASTM Standard Consumer Safety Specification for gates. It's F1004 and it involves the finish of parts, type of fasteners, the size of openings, the permanent label advising installation according to the manufacturer's instructions, the warning that gates don't necessarily prevent all accidents and the reminder: never leave your child unattended. When using a gate to block off the top of a set of stairs, be sure to use a hardware-mounted gate screwed directly into the wall. Don't use an accordian gate at the top of stairs, baby can use it as a climbing frame. Don't borrow an older accordian-style gate with crosshatching (they may not have solid tape across the top to keep sharp edges from baby).

- Sliding Cabinet and Window Locks—KidCo® makes one that works on any glass or mirrored surface or any surface you cannot drill into. This lock will easily keep your toddler out of the medicine cabinet or away from your china. Two locks come in the package.
- Stove Guard—There's a good one for $24.95 by Prince Lionheart.

- Toilet Cover Lock—This is one of the devices you may tire of, but it's worth the effort. This keeps the toilet cover shut until you want to use it. Hopefully, your toddler will understand a bit of bathroom safety by the time she needs to be potty-trained. Then you can remove this.
- TV Guard—If only we could lock the TV this easily when baby gets older. The TV guard keeps your baby from getting to the front of the TV with its buttons and switches. It's clear plastic and you can still use the all-powerful remote.
- VCR Guard—Same concept as the TV Guard, the VCR Guard is also a clear plastic shield keeping your little viewer from getting to the VCR buttons, tape slot and knobs. Some even work with Digital Video Discs and Compact Disc Players, too.

Holiday Electrical Safety Each year, more than 2,000 children under the age of four are treated for electrical burns, particularly around the holidays. Young children who might be tempted to chew on cords and explore outlets are at the greatest risk. We know that electrical safety should be addressed all year round but at the holidays parents, particularly new ones, should be careful. These are some tips adapted from the National Electrical Safety Foundation:

- Inspect each decoration. Look for frayed sockets, bare wires, or loose connections.
- Place all cords, indoor and outdoor, out of a child's reach.
- Toddler or infant in the house? Do not place bulbs on the lower branches of your tree.
- Keep saying "Don't touch the lit bulb" and remember what feels warm to you could burn a child.
- No electrical trains if you have a child under the age of seven.
- Remember to re-position those outlet covers on unused sockets.

Battery Basics Your child says "Look at me" and you see a battery sticking out of her ear. Whether it's inside her ear, her nostril or she has sucked on one, batteries can burn. If she swallows one, call your pediatrician and head for the emergency room; batteries can injure the esophageal lining and cause bleeding. Also try to keep your batteries someplace safe and check battery-operated equipment and toys. Be sure the screws are all tightened and as secure as possible.

One last word here. Every home and environment is different and contains objects and events that have the potential to be hazardous for baby. Use common sense and be overly-vigilant in every situation. Prevention is better than cure. As parents, we could possibly have been accused of being a little neurotic in this regard. Far better a little neurosis we think, than to be overly care-free.

Safety Considerations

THE LAST WORD ON RECALLS

We hear about toy and product recalls all the time; on the news, in the papers and in the magazines. Unfortunately, one of the biggest dangers for your baby just might be that fewer than 5% of these are returned or brought back for repair (according to Jayne O'Donnell of *USA Today*). Why are we bringing back 90% of appliances and 60% of child safety seats, but not dangerous toys our children are playing with? Recently, the CPSC (Consumer Product Safety Commission) called for a "recall roundup" at the end of every year to remind consumers about all of these toys and products which might still be in our homes, perhaps presenting a hazard to our children.

The toys range from restaurant toy give-aways (remember to ask for the infant toy with those special meals) to toy chests and even a safety gate. Although we will list some of the big recalls here that had low return rates, we suggest calling for updates regularly. Also check the newspapers and child and baby magazines which often feature such recalls. Some of our favorite chain stores such as Toys "R" Us are also keeping us informed by posting current recalls, so remember to check those out, too.

Fill out your warranty cards and send them in, especially those for children's products. It gives manufacturers an opportunity to reach you in case of a recall. Many of us don't send such cards back, realizing that the information is likely used for mailing lists. As annoying and inconvenient as the subsequent junk mail might be, that mail-in card could be what connects you and a manufacturer who later discovers a defect in a product. A recall letter from that manufacturer is one mailing all of us would welcome.

Remember to contact the U.S. Consumer Product Safety Commission (800-638-2772) about their toy safety roundup and about any complaints, problems and new recalls which might occur. Check out any hand-me-downs or garage sale purchases, too. It's also a good idea to get onto the CPSC's automatic mailing list and do it for some friends as well.

A few recent recalls which might affect your baby are listed below. Our last word on recalls: Have the last word. Call the CPSC, check magazines and the news regularly and report any problems or incidents immediately. If you have a concern about something you buy or receive, contact the manufacturer and the CPSC. And if in doubt about anything, keep it out of baby's way and don't use the product; alert the store about your concerns—most are likely to provide you with a refund or credit.

Toy/Product
What Happens—The Problem
Take Action Now

Soft Walkin' Wheels
Tonka
Choking Hazard: The small wheel hubs separate from the axle.
Call 1-800-524-8107 for free replacement.

Felix the Cat Roller Fun Balls
Wendy's Kid's Meals
Choking Hazard: The roller ball seams may separate causing the release of the small plastic fish inside.
Return to a local Wendy's
or call 1-800-443-7266 for a free replacement.

Weebles Tractor (with red plunger)
Playskool
Choking Hazard: Red plunger can fall apart.
Call 1-888-377-3335 for free replacement.

Wooden Clown Toys
Brio Corp.
Choking Hazard: The clown's small hat is a choking hazard.
Call 1-888-274-6869 for a replacement hat.

Big Storage Chest
Step 2
Strangulation or Injury Hazard: Lids can fall on head or neck.
Call 1-800-347-8372 for a free lid support kit.

Toy Chest
Crate & Barrel
Strangulation or Injury Hazard: Lids can fall on head or neck.
Call 1-800-352-0688 for a free lid support kit.

High Chair Gym Toys (w/clacker balls)
The First Years
Choking Hazard: The clacker balls in the center are a choking hazard.
Call 1-800-533-6708 for a free repair kit.

'Xylophone Mallets
Little Ones
Choking Hazard: The end of the mallet can get stuck in the throat, blocking the airway.
Call 877-725-9935 for a replacement mallet.

Basketball Sets with toy hoops
Numerous Manufacturers including:
Today's Kids, Little Tikes, Ohio Art, Fisher-Price and others.
Strangulation Hazard: Nets can unhook from the plastic rims and children catch their heads in them.
Call the hotline of the Consumer Product Safety Commission for information and details.
Call 1-800-638-2772.

Magic Motion Crib Mobiles
FIsher-Price
The rotating ring and mirror may unscrew as they revolve.
Call 888-407-6479 for a free replacement part.

Fold 'N Go Portable Playpen

Century Product

Suffocation Hazard: The fabric loosens and causes a pocket that could cause suffocation.

Call 800-583-4092 for a free repair kit.

Portable Playpens

Numerous Manufacturers including:

Kolcraft, Graco, Price-Trimble Corp. and others

Strangulation and Entrapment Hazards: These portable playpens which fold in half for storage have rivets protruding up to a half-inch from outside the top rails. They cannot be removed and are dangerous—anything can catch on them.

Call the hotline of the Consumer Product Safety Commission for information and details.

Call 1-800-638-2772

Web Safety Sites

You can also find some information on child safety and product recalls at the following web sites:

Child Magazine
www.childmagazine.com

Consumer Product Safety Commission (CPSC)
www.cpsc.com

Consumer Reports
www.consumerreports.com

The Danny Foundation
www.dannyfoundation.org

Kids in Danger
www.kidsindanger.org

Phthalates

Another issue on the hot burner is that of phthalates, which we first heard about in December, 1998. At that time the CPSC released a study on Phthalates in teethers, rattles and in other children's toys and products. This chemical, diisononyl phthalate (DINP), is used to soften plastic toys and other children's paraphernalia. The study concluded that few if any children are at risk from phthalates—the amount that they ingest doesn't reach a level that would be harmful. Unfortunately, the Commission staff isn't banning the use of phthalates in the United States. Phthalate use is banned from products in Denmark, and several other countries are considering similar legislation.

However, the study did identify areas which needed more conclusive study and so as a precautionary measure, the CPSC requested manufacturers to remove phthalates from soft rattles and teethers by early 1999. Most manufacturers are complying and in the meantime, major retailers have also removed these products from store shelves. CPSC has also asked that a phthalate substitute be found for use in other products for children under three years of age that are likely to be chewed or mouthed.

Only two models of feeding bottle nipple and a pacifier (the Gerber Clear and Soft lines) were found to contain a related phthalate and have been removed from production. If you have any of these, dispose of them. No other Gerber products of this kind are involved.

The danger in phthalates is that existing studies in laboratory animals indicate that in high doses, DINP damages the liver, kidneys and other organs in mice and rats. Other studies indicate that high doses may cause liver tumors in mice and rats. There isn't total agreement on the cancer risk for humans or on how much phthalate a child absorbs while mouthing toys, for instance. Children under the age of one, according to this study, are the most likely to be teething, chewing and mouthing on such products. As a precaution, dispose of any items which have received long periods of such use.

More testing by the CPSC will follow to determine health risks and cancer connections. Manufacturers who have responded by stopping their use of phthalates in rattles and teethers are: Chicco, Disney, Evenflo, Hasbro (including Playskool), Little Tikes, Mattel (Fisher-Price ARCOTOYS, Tyco Preschool), Safety 1st, Sassy, Gerber, Shelcore Toys, and The First Years. The following retailers have removed phthalate-containing teethers, rattles, pacifiers, and bottle nipples from store shelves: K-Mart, Sears, ShopKo Stores, Inc., Target, Toys "R" Us, Walmart, and the Warner Brothers Studio Stores.

If you have any other questions regarding phthalates, contact the CPSC's hotline at (800) 638-2772 or CPSC's teletypewriter at (800) 638-8270. Or look it up on their web site, www.cpsc.gov. Consumers can report any product hazards to info@cpsc.gov.

When Baby Arrives

eeding Baby: The best from bibs to baby food (including making your own and prepared foods), to breast pumps and bottles.

NURSING BABY

We've all heard the adage, "breast is best," but that doesn't mean breast-feeding is easy. Thankfully there are many products and paraphernalia to help. You want to start your baby off right and you're willing to endure those first uncomfortable days; what can help make the process smoother and easier? After all, we figured out that nursing may be natural but that doesn't necessarily mean it comes naturally.

Human milk is the optimum form of nutrition for babies. Research shows that breast-fed babies have less risk of ear infections, diarrhea, respiratory infections, meningitis and even allergies. But did you know nursing benefits moms as well? Breast-feeding releases hormones which help the uterus return to normal and it may also reduce the risk of ovarian cancer. The American Academy of Pediatrics now recommends that new mothers breast-feed their babies for the first year with an introduction of solid foods after the first six months. Not using any formula to supplement breast-feeding is pretty unrealistic for many working moms today, but don't waste your energy feeling guilty. It's still widely believed that any amount of breast-feeding is better than none at all—so if you need to supplement with formula, do so.

Be prepared for breast-feeding. Take a class. Many hospitals, HMOs and large companies offer courses; or, ask your doctor for a referral. Rent video instructional tapes and talk to friends who are nursing. Build a network of people and professionals who can assist you if you run into problems like sore nipples, engorgement, or a plugged duct.

There's a bill being introduced in Congress, the New Mother's Breast-feeding Promotion and Protection Act, which would give working moms time to leave work every day for one hour to nurse or express milk. In reality, research has also shown that breast-feeding moms don't actually end up missing as much work (as non-breast-feeding moms) because their babies are less likely to get sick. Employers should consider offering the time when mom wants off to nurse, realizing its benefits. Unfortunately, many moms will still be fighting it out, both with employers and with Congress. We hope eventually Congress will also recognize the benefits and pass the New Mother's Breast-feeding Promotion and Protection Act.

Nursing Aids

Nursing Aids will help get you through especially those initial tough days and nights. Most moms-to-be have never seen a breast pump before, let alone considered which one to use. How many hours will you be at work? Will you be able to use an electrical outlet, or will you need a battery-operated unit? Will you store your pump or carry it around with you? Determine those things, and then add features such as type and speed of cycling (or sucking action). Many hospitals rent out hospital-grade pumps designed for quick and natural-feeling pumping. However, these units are heavy, most require electrical outlets, and you'll need to buy the accessory kits. But it's still a viable option for you. Or try one of these electric or hand pumps we've listed.

If you think you'll be pumping longer than just the first few months, invest in buying your own. Electric pumps range from just under $100 to around $300. Like hospital-grade pumps, most have adjustable suction levels and double-pumping capability. Only the most costly pumps feature fully automatic systems and quick cycling times. Hand pumps aren't necessarily the most practical for working mothers. They usually require pumping one breast at a time and often require both hands to operate it. Manual hand pumps do come in handy for occasional use at home or if you need to draw out inverted nipples.

Pump Choices

DoubleEase Breastpump

Price: $179.00
Manufacturer: Medela, Inc.
(800) TELL-YOU

This Medela portable pump will let you single or double pump at a suction level that is most comfortable for you. It runs on an AC transformer or two C batteries.

Hospital Grade Pumps

Prices: $ rentals range from $1-3/day (some reduction on monthly rates)

Contact any of the following to rent hospital-grade pumps (or check at your hospital) and don't forget you need to purchase a kit of parts to go with it (price ranges from $25–45 for accessories):

Medela's Lactina Select	(800) 435-8316
White River Concepts Model 9050	(800) 824-6351
Ameda-Egnell Elite	(800) 323-8750

Best Baby Buy

Isis Breast Pump

Price: $50.00
Manufacturer: Avent
(800) 54-AVENT

Here's a lightweight, silent pump that requires no electrical hookups. The Isis silicone diaphragm creates a vacuum while you manually pump it. Five petal-shaped massagers flex in and out to help your milk flow.

Mother's Touch One-Handed Breast Pump

Price: $24.00 approx.
Manufacturer: Ameda-Egnell
(800) 323-8750

This is a one-handed manual pump good for those occasional bottles or when your breasts are engorged and you need a bit of relief. Don't consider this if you plan on very regular pumping.

Cool Classic

Pump 'N Style Breast Pump Kit

Price: $249.95
Manufacturer: Medela, Inc.
(800) TELL-YOU

Here's a full kit from Medela, complete with the only portable hospital grade breast pump on the market. It has an exclusive Autocycle technology which simulates your baby's natural nursing action. The adjustable vacuum control gives you comfort, and everything you could possibly need is in this stylish bag. At the office, you can even leave the pump inside the bag—just plug it in and express, quietly and comfortably. It will work for single or double pumping and has storage space for up to four bottles of breast milk in a special cooled compartment. This is a complete kit and a great pump.

Spring Express

Price: $30.00 approx.
Manufacturer: Medela, Inc.
(800) TELL-YOU

Medela make some great nursing aids; Spring Express is as good as a hand pump can be. Great for occasional bottles.

Nursing Accessories

Breast Shields

Various Manufacturers (Avent, Medela)

Breast Shields help prevent nipple soreness. To help give you some protection while baby nurses, these plastic, circular shields have little holes your nipple extends out of. A pack of two will probably suffice.

Comfort Plus Disposable Nursing Pads

Price: $5.00 for 24
Manufacturer: Omron
(800) 634-4350

Nursing pads will help keep the leakage from being noticeable.

Best Baby Buy

Nursing Bib

Price: $12.95
Available through the: One Step Ahead Catalog
(800) 274-8440

Hate breast-feeding in public? Here's an extra-large bib which will give the utmost in privacy and also provide baby comfort with a mesh panel so fresh air can flow. The mesh also gives you a lone view of baby. It's lightweight and washable and has two large pockets so you can stash nursing pads and pacifiers and more. You can even use it with a breast pump.

Designer's Choice

Nursingwear™

Prices: Vary (dress $52 approx.; long dress $70)
Contact: Nursingwear™
(800) 637-9426

Here's a catalog full of adorable clothing for new moms who are breast-feeding. The clothes have ties or closures around your breasts so there's easy, discrete access, yet flattering designs. This is a line of clothing which is smart and sensible and best of all, very good looking. You'd never know its sole purpose.

Washable Bra Pads

Price: $11 for 4
Manufacturer: Medela, Inc.
(800) 835-5968

Minimize the mess from leaking breasts with these washable bra pads. They're a bit costlier than most but they're good quality.

Nursing Pillows

Best Baby Buy

Boppy™

Price: $30.00 approx.
Manufacturer: Camp Kazoo. Ltd.
(303) 526-2626 also available at many baby stores

The Boppy™ is a very versatile product. It's a great nursing pillow and it's also a great help in propping baby up before she can sit up on her own. The Boppy™ comes in a variety of fabric designs, all of which are machine washable. Who will love Boppy™ more—you or your baby?

My Brest Friend™

Price: $40.00 approx.
Manufacturer: Zenoff Products, Inc.
(800) 555-5522

We saw the My Brest Friend™ pillow in every store we looked. This device allows you to be hands-free to hold baby tight. The My Brest Friend™ is like a giant belt which you can fasten around your waist with Velcro. You get back support and a wider surface for the baby to rest on at breast level while she feeds. It adjusts to any family member's shape or size so Dad can feel close to baby, too. We appreciate how infants and adults with special needs will be supported by My Brest Friend™. Unzip the cotton coverings and machine wash them.

Nursing Stools

Various Manufacturers

Nursing Stools help raise your lap so feeding baby is much more comfortable. Pick one up from a catalog or one from Medela (the Nursing Stool®, which relieves back and shoulder strain, is available in natural or white finish). One of the prettiest stools we've seen is:

Designer's Choice

19th Century Design Nursing Stool

Price: $32.00
Available through: Babessentials™ Catalog
(888) 613-6383

Fashioned out of light pine, this is an attractive nursing stool with a cut-out heart stencil shape. It's fully assembled and provides support for baby and Mom's upper back, legs and arms.

If you're encountering problems or need some extra help getting started, call a supportive nurse, a lactation consultant or a La Leche League volunteer (call 800-LA-LECHE).

Bottle Feeding Baby

We've all read that breast milk is best for babies; however, it isn't best for all moms. For many good reasons, some new moms will elect to bottle-feed. No matter which method you select, feeding your baby is often fraught with mystery—for example, how can you tell if she's getting enough? Baby doesn't come with a handy gas-pump-like gauge, although crying is sometimes an indication of empty, and throwing-up is sometimes an alert that she's full.

Your first two days of breast-feeding or bottle-feeding may be the easiest and most relaxed you'll get. It offers new parents some time to figure out "feedings," some of which you may schedule and some of which will be on-demand feedings. Once you've gotten past those first few days you may find yourself worried that your infant isn't getting enough milk. Obviously, this is important for issues of nutrition and hydration. One indication that baby is getting enough is weight gain. A more immediate measure is to look for milk in baby's mouth after nursing. If bottle-feeding, it's easier to see the milk disappearing—you can get a good read on how much she's taking in. In either case, and whenever you're concerned regarding feedings, monitor baby's milk intake, her weight and her stools; your physician will inform you as to what is right for your baby's health and growth.

Baby Meets the Bottle

When you settle in to more regular feedings, you may decide to get your infant used to a bottle, whether or not you intend to wean her. That way Dad or other caregivers can also help, and it offers them a chance to bond during the feeding ritual. You can get a baby used to a bottle containing expressed milk as early as three to four weeks of age. Remember to incorporate her bottle into the schedule at least once a week. If you forget, or are erratic about the schedule, your baby may refuse to take a bottle—and there goes your big night out!

We think that almost every caregiver should know something about bottles. So, if you're bottle-feeding—or even if you're expressing breast milk—you'll have to decide between the two bottle-feeding systems—standard (plastic or glass) or disposable. And once you've figured that out, you'll still have to choose nipple types. Thankfully, you may want to pass that choice on to your infant: give her a selection and see which seems to work best.

So, should you go ahead and buy disposable? Or is nondisposable (glass or plastic) a better choice? One advantage of the disposable system is that the bottles are ready to use, no pre-cleaning is necessary. They're great for travel, too. One disadvantage is cost, as they tend to be relatively expensive. Also, some problems, such as rupturing if overheated, can occur. And if we think "green," disposables are not environmentally-friendly in terms of sending solid waste to the landfill.

Standard (nondisposable) bottles, on the other hand, can be used over and over and are easily recycled. Set them up like an assembly line for filling (you'll get quite adept at this). When you're filling them, the amounts on the glass bottles are much easier to read than on disposables. So, what's their downside? Standard bottles are a bit of a cleaning challenge; however, some think they really get the cleanest. We went with glass bottles at the beginning. They sparkled when clean and were easier to fill. Now that there are so many affordable options, we might be tempted by the ease the other choices offer. Of course, there is also a considerable amount of energy, water and detergents used in the cleaning of nondisposable bottles. We suggest weighing up both attitudes and balancing it with your own environmental philosophies and practices, as well as considering what is easiest and most cost effective for you.

Disposable or not, pick up four-ounce bottles, especially good for newborns, along with those eight-ounce ones. If you'd rather spend your money on toys than bottles, don't buy any decorative bottles that sometimes cost three times as much.

Here are some of the newer bottle systems we'd try:

Avent

Avent, for example, is a bit costly but claims to reduce colic in newborns due to its patented nipple (which reduces air intake). The Avent system is a reusable one, made by an English manufacturer. It only accepts an Avent nipple, which could be a disadvantage if your baby doesn't like it. Then you'd need to switch from the entire Avent system. Avent is also going to introduce a disposable nurser into the line (complete with their patented nipple). Despite the cost, Avent users swear by it.

Designer's Choice

Johnson & Johnson

We also like the Johnson & Johnson Healthflow® bottle, one of the new breed of "angled nursers" designed to help keep baby filled with milk and not air. This is a much loved product and widely imitated.

Playtex

The Playtex Eazy-Feed™ Drop-Ins® Nurser is as easy as can be. It's sanitary and convenient. All you do is slide in a liner and slide up the built-in burper to remove air. This is a simple and elegant design that we applaud for ease of use.

Playtex Advance is a new reusable bottle advanced in its design. Advance isn't an ordinary bottle—air enters though the Bubble-Free Vent on the bottom, not through the nipple. That way air doesn't mix with the liquid so baby doesn't swallow any bubbles. The Advance bottle system helps prevent gas and spitting up and it's easier to clean than others. The bottom comes off and can be washed completely.

Best Baby Buy

Pür Bottle Set

Price: $19.99

Available through: JCPenney Stores and Catalog

This is a new item and we like being able to purchase this type of selection. Baby can try things out this way, without a huge expense. You get two slow angled and two grip bottles with the patented valves to reduce baby's air intake. Especially handy is that the bottles open on both ends for easier cleaning and there are six additional nipples, varying in size.

Nipples, Hoods, Disks and More

You've decided which bottle system and now you need to pick nipples. Remember if using Avent there's no separate choice. Evenflo, Gerber and Johnson & Johnson (Healthflow®) bottles will accept any nipple you or your baby choose. Nipples are shaped—choose either standard (wider on the bottom and tapering to a rounded tip) or orthodontic (flatter and wider—a bit more like a mother's nipple). Nipples are made of different materials—choose rubber (you'll need to replace these over time) or silicone (lasts longer, gets less sticky, but is also slightly harder). Our daughter really liked the orthodontic nipples and let us know it. It's pretty amazing how quickly your child can make choices.

Gerber makes a standard nipple and also manufactures the orthodontic nipple line called Nuk. Recently they came out with a new One Piece Nipple, where the nipple and the collar are permanently bonded together to form one easy-to-clean piece. Evenflo has quite a variety of nipples available as well, and also produces color-coded ones with different openings for different liquids. Pür, the one our daughter insisted on, makes only silicone nipples. Nipples aren't a high-priced item, so go ahead and try a varied selection.

And what about all of those inevitable little accessories you will need to use with bottles? You'll need some hoods (to cover the nipple when not in use) and disks (to prevent liquids from leaving the bottle and spilling out of the nipple while traveling—you have to remove these before feeding). You'll also want a brush for cleaning those bottles and nipples. A bottle rack is pretty useful too, as is a bottle warmer—we remember getting great use out of ours.

Sterilizers

When we opened our sterilizer for the first time there weren't any directions. Panic set in. How long do you sterilize for? How much water do you use? How often do you sterilize? Today, the rules for sterilizing baby bottles and formulas and heating formula have relaxed, but check with your pediatrician in this regard. Also, be sure to read the formula manufacturer's pamphlets; often they have really complete directions for sterilizing.

Avent Electric Steam Sterilizer

Price: $80.00 approx.

In less than 10 minutes, you can sterilize your baby's bottles with the Avent Electric Steam Sterilizer. Add water and hot steam does the job. It will even shut off automatically. Holds four Avent bottles or six standard bottles plus accessories.

Gerber Electric Bottle Sterilizer Set

Price: $50.00 approx.

Steam-clean those bottles with the Gerber Electric Bottle Sterilizer Set. It holds up to eight bottles at a time. You fill and load according to the simple directions, cover, and press a button to start the sterilizer. When the water boils away, the unit will politely shut itself off. You get all the items you'll need to begin—bottles, nipples, extra accessories and even some tongs. The unit plugs into any standard outlet.

Cool Classic

Gerber Stovetop Sterilizer

Price: $39.99 approx.

We really like the Gerber stovetop sterilizer ($30–40) with its nice tidy rack inside which holds all of your bottles. There are electric sterilizers but the stovetop model is a simple, easy-to-use classic. You can sterilize up to seven bottles at one time. Buy the set and you get bottles, nipples, collars, the works. It's a good value.

Now that you've learned to sterilize, what about formula? Which should you choose? Our daughter came home with an entire case, compliments of the hospital and the makers of Similac. If your child will be using formula, check with your doctor to get a recommendation based on your child's specific needs. We realize many new parents will likely be influenced by the various freebies that you and your baby bring home from the hospital. We don't want to get into the politics of the formula makers—we just want to use good, safe, nutritional formulas for our children.

Most formulas contain the same basic ingredients. As with baby food, balance what you are comfortable with, what your doctor recommends, what you can easily find and lug home and what you have coupons for. We began purchasing in bulk, which is a pretty good way to save a bit of cash (not so great for your back though!). We even tried mixing the powder formulas, which can also save money. Powdered formula might not be the easiest to prepare, although you do get quite adept at mixing and measuring. Think about it like diapering; the more you do it, the easier it gets. Toys "R" Us and other large chain stores often carry formula at very good prices. Compare prices when you shop—our motto. Also, call for coupons—Similac (800-227-5767) and Enfamil Mead Johnson (800-BABY-123 or 800-222-9123) have "welcome baby" programs where you can receive mailings, coupons and more.

Formula Do's and Don'ts

Initially, you'll probably prefer to warm the formula. Later, you'll use it at room temperature (you'll begin to feel comfortable about it) and then eventually, you'll switch to refrigerated formula. No matter what your baby's preference is, refrigerate formula immediately. Don't leave it out. For those middle of the night feedings, you may want an automatic bottle-heating unit, but the easiest way to warm formula is to run warm water over the bottle's lower section for a few minutes. You can put it in a pan of warm water, but be sure to shake the bottle to distribute the warm contents more evenly. We don't ever recommend using your microwave.

Bottle Warmers/Coolers and Accessories

Feeder Set

Price: $39.99

Manufacturer: Playskool®

More expensive than an ordinary warmer, this Playskool feeding assistant is like having an extra pair of hands. There's a removable thermal cooler that keeps two pre-chilled bottles cool and also a steamer to warm them to feeding temperature. No midnight trip to the refrigerator! That alone will make it worth the price to some parents anxious to minimize the complexities of responding to baby's night-time wake-up calls!

Cool Classic

Bottle Drying Rack

Price: $4.96

Manufacturer: Munchkin, Inc.

(800) 344-2229

You've washed those bottles and now the question is, how do you dry them? You try those drying racks that take up way too much room and they don't work well either. Munchkin came up with a fold-up plastic drying rack, really a simple, ingenious (and even affordable) design. The built-in reservoir catches all the drips and you can easily fit the whole drying rack into cabinets or in the dishwasher.

Baby's First Foods

Having a baby is really about making decisions and one of the most hotly debated is whether you will breast-feed or bottle-feed. Talk to your significant other, ask your pediatrician, and then make a decision that suits you and your lifestyle. Six months after your baby is born, you will again make food decisions—vegetarian, home-made food, or other dietary choice.

Feeding baby is often messy, too. You'll need a highchair, bibs and a mat underneath to protect your floor from flying peas. You will not believe the mess—on baby, on you and all around. We speak from experience and observation—there aren't often exceptions. Don't despair, though; there's certainly a funny and charming side to it!

Every single baby is different and every baby is ready for food at a different time. Signs of readiness will appear, such as mouthing or not seeming full from just milk. Speak to your pediatrician about what to start with; most recommend beginning with infant cereals which are fortified with minerals and vitamins. Then each new food should, as your doctor will undoubtedly inform you, be introduced separately so it's easier to see if there's any allergic reaction. Offer these new foods in small amounts, from a bowl—not from the jar. Be patient and at about one year of age, your baby will probably be eating some foods from the regular family meal.

Baby Foods

Gerber is the big name in baby food here in the U.S., while Heinz is the top seller in Canada. Other options are Beech-Nut, Earth's Best, Growing Baby and several smaller companies. We remember being in Europe where we found baby food to be of a totally different palette than we found at home. Our baby hardly noticed, and in fact, seemed to become quite a fan of pureed beans and bacon.

In actual fact, reports have shown that these five major baby food manufacturers are nutritionally comparable. They're even price comparable! Heinz does come in at a slightly lower cost in some areas, but with coupons you can offset any difference. So how will you choose which foods to give your baby? Perhaps you'll select what you're most comfortable with, what you were fed, or your own personal preference (organic foods, perhaps). Try Gerber's Tender Harvest. Yes, Gerber has gone organic with a line of 20 dishes including Chicken and Wild Rice and Spring Garden Vegetables. Gerber is competing with Earth's Best, Organic Baby, Mom's Choice and maybe, you. You could make your own. Another parameter for selecting a baby food is what is conveniently available at your local store or market.

We've seen, in the past few years, baby food manufacturers offer extended age-specific foods for growing children. Single ingredient foods are typically the first foods offered, and then there are two or three more stages available. These graduate into multi-ingredient foods, like dinners and desserts, which help you introduce even more flavors and variety to baby's diet. The older stages include larger-sized portions and foods which are chunkier, encouraging chewing. Always check with your pediatrician about when you can ease off the baby foods and begin more and more table foods. All in all, it may be annoying to purchase all these tiny jars of food, but they don't cost a lot (certainly not as much as diapers). So, watch your baby for signs of readiness and willingness to eat some of what you're having (and confirm it with your doctor).

Read the nutritional information and learn about the ingredients in the baby food jars you're choosing. What's most important ultimately in choosing the best baby food is selecting a wholesome and varied diet for baby that's nutritionally sound.

For information on ingredients, answers to questions (like do you add fillers, such as salt and sugars), and product information—here are some toll-free numbers:

- Beech-Nut 800-523-6633
- Earth's Best 800-442-4221
- Gerber 800-4GERBER
- Growing Healthy 800-755-4999
- Heinz 800-872-2229

Baby Food Safety Savvy

- Check expiration dates. Unopened baby food is good for a year or two. Opened jars should be used within two or three days.
- Don't buy jars that are stained, sticky or cracked. Don't buy any jars where the "button" in the metal screw cap is no longer depressed.
- Listen for the pop when you break the vacuum seal on a jar. If a jar is difficult to open, don't tap it. Just run it under warm water to loosen the seal.
- Taste warmed foods and chilled foods. Are they the right temperature? Getting into a tasting habit is a good idea—then you'll also know if any food has spoiled.
- Don't store food in plastic bags that could become a suffocation hazard if left around.
- Feed from a bowl, not from the jar. Bacteria transfer from baby's mouth to the jar and food will spoil faster.

Where do you put these dozens of baby food jars? This is a Lazy Susan we found that we really like for its space-saving effect:

Food Carousel

Price: $7.50 approx.
Available through the: Baby Catalog of America
(800) 752-9736

Go ahead and organize those big and little baby food jars. Store them conveniently, 24 small jars and 16 junior sized jars, in a space no larger than your dinner plate. Rotates so you or baby can pick out the next meal. Made of durable plastic in three tiers.

Making Your Own Baby Food

Yes, it's less expensive to make your own baby food but parents should be reminded of both pesticide issues and proper sanitation techniques which are involved in its preparation. Blenders, food processors and grinders are all helpful (but not totally necessary) in making baby food. Here are some helpful products:

Compact Food Grinder

Price: $14.95
Ages: 6 months and up
Available through the: One Step Ahead Catalog
(800) 274-8440

The One Step Ahead Catalog has found a compact food grinder that will pureé with just a simple twist. It's an easy to use design, ergonomic, and great for preparing food when the family is traveling. It's even dishwasher safe.

Happy Baby Food Grinder

Price: $10.99
Manufacturer: Marshall Baby Products—A Division of Omron Healthcare Inc.
(800) 634-4350

This grinder is great for making all kinds of fresh foods into baby food. The texture is comparable to the texture of prepared baby foods in a jar. Fill the plastic container with fresh fruit, vegetables or other foods. Turn the handle until the stainless steel blades grind the food and bring it to the top, where it can be served out of the attached dish. Our friends swear by it.

Highchairs and Booster Seats

We think a highchair is a definite, must-have piece of equipment. Like any other piece of baby paraphernalia, the highchair comes in a variety of styles (wooden, plastic, portable, etc.) and with a range of features. Some highchairs require your baby to be able to sit up unassisted (which usually happens somewhere around five to six months). One highchair listed next, the Deluxe 1-2-3 by Playskool®, can actually be used from birth with its newborn recliner. You'll want to choose a highchair that best suits your needs—portability, versatility, usability, and price.

Highchair Safety Savvy

JPMA-certified highchairs are tested for compliance with all sections of the ASTM Standard Consumer Safety Specification for Highchairs. Unfortunately, as we mentioned earlier and in this case, it is only voluntary. So you should know and understand some highchair safety basics. The highchair you purchase should:

- pass load and stability tests—the highchair you'll want should be able to withstand 50 to 100 pounds of weight and it should be stable with a strong frame, joints and a seat which can withstand even the most active toddler (who isn't particularly easy on equipment).
- have no sharp edges or protrusions on any interior or exterior surfaces.
- have a tray equipped with a locking device that will be able to withstand your child's weight against it.
- have protection from coil springs and scissoring. This prevents accidental pinching or cuts.
- have all holes capped or plugged. These should be impossible for your child to remove.
- have passed restraining system tests using a test dummy.
- must have a reliable, adjustable and easy-to-use restraining system (safety belt). If this is designed properly, your child should be unable to stand up in the highchair. It is imperative that a crotch strap be included to prevent your child from slipping underneath the tray.
- display permanent and prominent labeling which informs about the dangers of leaving baby unattended in the highchair and reminds about securing your child with the restraining system.
- come with good informative literature and a manual.

What you really want is a highchair that's stable and won't tip over. The base should be wider than the seat and the legs should slant outward. Safety is always the most important criteria in selecting a product—convenience, budget and comfort should follow.

Highchair and Booster Seat Choices

Our highchair was a foldable one, small, but with a nice wide tray which was great for catching spills and good for small art projects, too. Some tray features you might want are a wide tray, an adjustable tray and/or a removable tray, not to mention dishwasher safe. If you do have a dishwasher, measure to be sure that wide tray will fit inside for easy clean-ups.

A friend of mine with three young boys said recently that her high chair on wheels was the most essential piece of baby equipment she owned. If you do opt for mobility, look for a high chair with brakes and even, a double-locking crotch seat.

There are many combinations of styles and features available. You can purchase by phone, in person, or on-line. Here are some high chairs we really liked:

Baby Looney Tunes Phases Playtop Highchair

Price: $129.99
Manufacturer: Evenflo®
(800) 837-9201

Functional and fun, this highchair does all it should: it has two seat height positions and a large three-position tray. It even converts to a toddler-size play table and chair. We really like the building block desk surface and the Looney Tunes rubbing insert. It can also be used as a booster seat without the tray.

Designer's Choice

Bravo High Chair

Price: $133.99
Manufacturer: Peg Perego®
(219) 482-8191

Bravo! A high chair that's roomy and deep, this one has everything we like in a high chair: a soft, extra padded seat; a washable, hygienic seat cover; and safety straps that are secure but not restrictive. The swivel wheels have a rear wheel braking system. Pick from six height positions for meals and play. The tray is detachable and stores behind the chair. With all of these features, you may not even remember that you can remove the seat from the frame and use it for playtime.

Deluxe 1-2-3 Microban High Chair

Price: $79.00 approx.
Manufacturer: Playskool®
(800) 777-0371

Surprise—a highchair to use in different ways and at different times. Start with the newborn recliner (you use it without the tray), then move on to the standard highchair (with tray) and then for your active little one, use the toddler chair (without tray). Just remember not to use that reclining position when your child is eating foods.

Cool Classics

Hardwood High Chair

Price: $115.95 #638500
Available through: The Natural Baby Catalog
(800) 388-BABY

Here it is, finally, a nice looking, simple, hardwood high chair. It will take some tough use and look great after more than one child. When he's old enough, your child will climb safely in and out by himself. Yet, it's just high enough for you to pull it up to your table and it's not so wide that it takes up too much room! Order the optional wood tray, a good idea for messy eaters, or to introduce some messy activity.

Home & Roam 4-in-1 Highchair

Price: $139.99
Manufacturer: Baby Trend®
(800) 328-7363

It may be a strange name for a highchair, but the Home & Roam is comfortable, roomy and functional. The four wheels come with brakes and there's a one-hand tray adjustment. It nicely converts to a portable hook-on booster chair.

Boosters

Cool Classics

Hardwood Booster Seat

Price: $55.95 #638502
Available through: The Natural Baby Catalog
(800) 388-BABY

Here is an attractive hardwood booster seat, durable and tough, that will hold up well for any growing family.

Safety Booster Seat

Price: $59.99 #660008RED or 660008BLU
Manufacturer: Baby Bjorn®
Available through: Baby Catalog Of America
(800) 752-9736

This booster adapts to either clamp to a table or straps to a regular chair. When baby grows, it even breaks down and can be used up to age 5. Made of plastic (in either red or blue highlights on a granite background), booster gets points for being simple in design, easy to wipe clean, and laden with just the right amount of features.

Bibs, Mats and More

Let's face it. Babies make an absolute mess when they eat! Bibs and mats will really help keep the clean-up down to a minimum. We've never seen so many varieties of bibs—there are disposable, paper, vinyl-backed terry, and now, there's even molded plastic. Disposables are great for travel; they're lightweight and absorbent. The molded plastic bibs with the catch-all rim at the bottom are fabulous but not so easily packed in most diaper bags. For home use, there are plastic bibs that don't ever need laundering; just wipe clean, and despite constant, tough use they look as good as the first day you bought them (well, almost!). The only downside with them is that some crack after constant use. We had a pile of sloppy eating bibs and one special pink terry bib with cowgirl style fringe that matched some adorable socks. That bib was our baby's going-out in-style bib. She looked adorable even with carrot dripping down her cheeks. Fabric bibs like that one are best when they'll be fairly easy to launder (remember they'll get abused and not all stains will come out) and have Velcro closures. Here are some of our new bib favorites and the mats we wouldn't do without:

Designer's Choice

Monkey Bib

Price: $ 5.70
Available through: The Pop Shop
(800) K-HARING

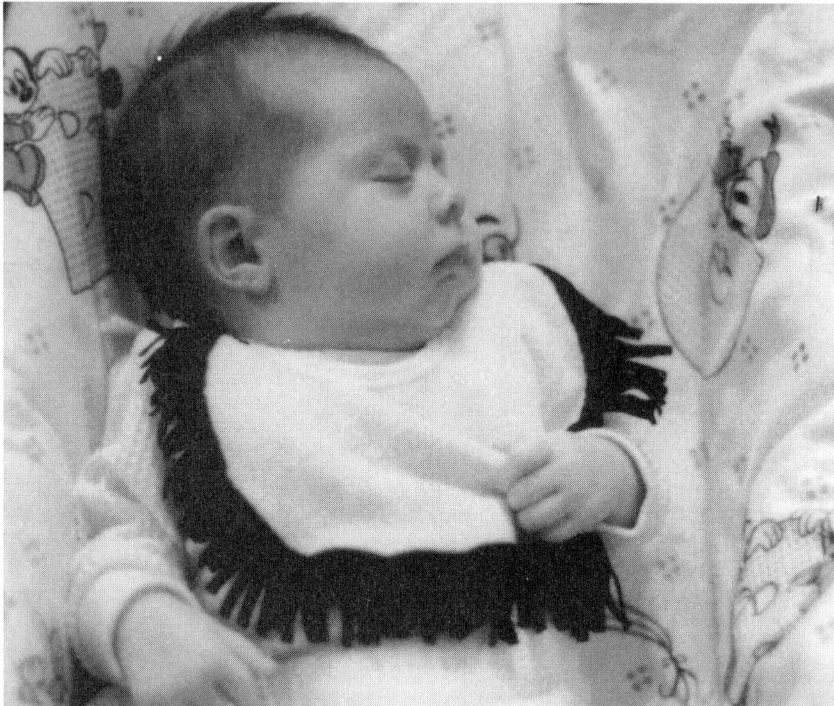

Frills for spills

Keith Haring's simple, child-like drawings are perfect on baby's bibs. These bibs are inventive, humorous, totally adorable and made of 100% cotton. We love them. If little monkeys aren't your thing, order the smiley-faced daisy. It's sunshiny yellow and red.

Petit Prince Terry Bib

Price: $20.00
Available through the: Rue de France Catalog
(800) 777-0998

A little terry bib for your little prince, what could be finer? The drawings of Antoine de Saint-Exupery's book Le Petit Prince with the Little Prince of course, his imaginary pet lamb, the moons and stars—all come alive on the lovely terry bibs (and other accessories).

Feed your little prince

Best Baby Buy

Wonder Bib

Price: $14.95
Available through: One Step Ahead Catalog
(800) 274-8440

At last someone must be listening to moms and dads everywhere! One Step Ahead has come up with a Wonder Bib; long-sleeved and offering lots of coverage for the messiest tot around. Pick your color (royal blue or pink) and even choose your size range (small and medium). The Wonder Bib is a real baby wonder!

Best Baby Buy

Splat Mat Floor Protector

Price: $7.99–9.99 approx.
Manufacturer: Children-on-the-Go

If you think you don't need one, think again. The Splat Mat covers the floor underneath your baby's highchair. It will help contain spills and accidents and even more, it will help keep your carpet and floor clean. Providing 12 square feet of coverage, the Splat Mat also folds for storage or travel. Clean it off easily with a damp cloth. Just one thing about that 12 square feet—there's no guarantee that it'll always be enough!

Dinnerware, Dishes, Sippy Cups and Utensils

27 Piece Feeding Set

Price: $16.95
Available through: One Step Ahead Catalog
(800) 274-8440

Stop buying one piece of tableware at a time. Here is a full set of everything you could possibly need and more (cups, plates, etc.). Each piece even comes with a snug-fitting lid and all are dishwasher safe and even microwavable.

Designer's Choice

Dinnerware

Price: $15.00
Manufacturer: Hoohoobers
(800) 533-1505
Ages: Everyone

Toddlers and eating is one messy event; Hoohoobers can help a bit with their cleverly designed dinnerware. It has four features every mom and dad will be sure to like: a non-tip bowl, the saucer catches spills, the feet keep steady and the straight sides help "corral" food, keeping it on the plate. It won't break, either, when junior drops it on the floor; it's solid polypropylene and dishwasher safe. Pick one set in primary colors and another in pastels.

Designer's Choice

The Little Prince Breakfast Set

Price: $125.00
Available through: Rue de France catalog
(800) 777-0998

Here's a breakfast set for your little prince (or princess). The enchanting pattern is inspired by the drawings of Antoine de Saint-Exupery's classic story, Le Petit Prince. From the little lamb, the moon and the stars,

A royal breakfast set

this is an adorable set bound to cheer your little royal one every morning! (Not in everyone's budget, but a set bound to please for a long time.) Set includes a mug, plate and a bowl.

Cool Classic

Spill-Proof™ Cup

Manufacturer: Playtex

This is the cup that started it all with its unique SipEase™ valve designed to let kids sip with very little effort. It only allows liquid to flow when your toddler drinks. No spills! The cup's one-piece design also makes cleaning very easy.

Designer's Choice

Starter Silverware

Price: $8.00
Manufacturer: Hoohoobers
(800) 533-1505
Ages: 1–3

The Starter Silverware may have been selected into the permanent collection of the Museum of Modern Art in New York, but you'll want to keep them on your table ready for junior. The short handles are easy to grasp and the shortened stainless steel "throats" make it easier for children to guide their fork or spoon to their mouths. For safety, the fork tines are rounded; and my favorite feature, the fork and spoon are different colors. The red fork and yellow spoon can help your toddler learn not only the difference between the two, but also her colors—and maybe, even begin to understand left and right (maybe that's a stretch!).

Best Baby Buy

White Hot Soft Bite Utensils

Age: 3 months and up
Price: $2.97
Manufacturer: Munchkin, Inc.
(800) 344-2229

Feeding utensils that tell baby (and you) when food is too hot! Not only that, but they're well designed and inexpensive, too. A special temperature-sensing material on the tips reacts to heat (that might burn baby's mouth) by turning white—"white hot."

aby's Body—Looking after your baby's body—diapers to powders, ointments to medicine spoons

Moms and Dads want to pamper, groom and primp babies, perhaps because that also provides some marvelous time to bond together. Keeping baby's skin soft and caring for her extra-fine hair and tiny nails takes tenderness, care, and definitely the use of some of these products we all know and love (and maybe some we hadn't heard of before):

Baby Toiletries

You will be sorely tempted to buy many more products for your baby's body than you will ever need. She will need shampoo, oil and probably lotion. Skip talcum powder (not good for babies) and if you feel you need a powder pick an absorbent one, such as cornstarch. Sometimes the simplest, famous brand names are the best—in the case of baby toiletries we like sticking to Johnson & Johnson. However, if you are a natural product fiend, you may wish to try the trendy, made-in-France Mustela® line (available in many baby stores) or the Mama Toto toiletries from the Body Shop. Eco-conscious and environmentally protective? Try some Little Forest products available through the Dr. Possum catalog. Some of these natural products don't contain mineral oil and petroleum by-products. If you are inclined to veer off the standard tried, tested and true path, buy small-sized toiletry samples to try first, and remember to watch for scratchiness or any signs of allergic reactions.

Remember that baby's skin is thinner than yours and is more fragile. It's also less resistant to bacteria and has less protection against sunburn. Heat rash, infant acne, cradle cap, chafing and eczema are not unusual in infants—always check with your pediatrician and ask which products would be best for your child. Here are also a few ways to help protect your baby's skin:

- Detergent residue can be an irritant for baby's skin. Be sure all clothes, toys and diapers are rinsed properly.

- Change diapers as quickly as possible to help reduce the chance of diaper rash.
- When it's warm outside, dress baby in loose clothing and use a hat with a brim. Ask your pediatrician at what age you can apply sunscreen (usually around six months). When you are using a sunscreen, be sure to purchase one with an SPF of 15 or more. Reapply through the day and after going in the water.
- When bathing and washing baby, be sure to rinse and dry thoroughly. Winter weather sometimes brings dryness (often caused by heating systems in your home). To compensate for dry air, ask your doctor about applying moisturizing lotions, oils or creams.

Shampoos

You need to find a shampoo which is gentle, mild and leaves your baby's extra-fine hair soft. You may want to go organic, or classic, or formulated to help with cradle cap. Newborns need their hair washed (probably) only once a week but toddlers who are likely to get food and more smeared on themselves might need more frequent washing. Using a tear-free shampoo like Johnson & Johnson's is a good idea. Botanically based shampoos are also good choices with their low pH (so they won't dry out hair). Here are just a few of the shampoos to suds baby up with:

Botanical Baby Shampoo

Price: $6.75 for 8 oz.
Available through: The Dr. Possum Catalog
Manufacturer: Little Forest

Enriched with chamomile, aloe vera and evening primrose, this gentle (yet costly) shampoo is a special blend of organic ingredients. Safe for sensitive eyes.

Conditioning Shampoo

Price: $8.99–15.99
Manufacturer: Mustela®

Mustela® is the #1 selling line in Europe and has been catching on in Canada and in the United States. For toddlers, this conditioning shampoo is very mild and suitable for frequent use. Tearless and pH balanced, this shampoo has a mild herbal scent and helps make hair easy to comb.

Newborn Shampoo

Prices: $8.99–15.99 for 6.8 fl.oz.
Manufacturer: Mustela®

This is a very mild and tearless shampoo specially formulated to avoid cradle cap. It is lightly scented, pH balanced and hypoallergenic.

Cool Classic

Johnson's Baby Shampoo

Manufacturer: Johnson & Johnson

It's hard not to like this classic. It's inexpensive, gentle, and it smells great. Johnson and Johnson has spent 100 years caring for babies' bodies; it's a name you can trust. With its "No More Tears" formula, the Johnson's Baby Shampoo is truly a classic good buy.

Simple Goodness Foaming Baby Shampoo

Price: $4.50
Available at: Bath & Body Works Stores

Simple Goodness is formulated with aloe vera and Vitamin E and is dispensed from an easy-to-use pump. While you're at the Bath & Body Works store, pick up something nice for yourself.

Soaps

Special soaps aren't really necessary, any mild soap will do. Skip bubble bath (a good thing to avoid for baby's older sister, too—it could result in vaginal irritation). It's too drying for little girls.

Musti-Bear Liquid Soap with Dispenser

Prices: $9.99–19.99
Manufacturer: Mustela®

This adorable, bear-shaped dispenser makes it easy even for your toddler to dispense soap. The liquid soap is hypoallergenic and gentle for skin. With its clean herbal scent, you will want to keep one by the tub and another by the sink.

Musti-Bear Liquid Soap Refill

Prices: $4.99–8.99
Manufacturer: Mustela®

Fill it up again, that cute bear dispenser is empty—so pick up the handy refill size and pour it in.

Therapeutic Tea Tree Baby Soap

Price: $3.95 for 3.65 oz.

Available through: The Dr. Possum Catalog

Manufacturer: Little Forest

A soap for delicate, troubled skin—it includes saponified oils of palm, coconut and olive, natural tea tree essential oil, organic stone ground oatmeal and aloe vera. Little Forest states that it is good for rashes, cradle cap, eczema, etc.

Lotions and Oils

Cleansing Lotion

Prices: $8.99–17.99 (6.8 fl. oz.)

Manufacturer: Mustela®

This is a mild soap-free cleanser that will not sting eyes. Use as a facial cleanser, to cleanse the entire body for a sponge bath. It's also good for cleaning buttocks at diaper changing times.

Hydrating Body Emulsion

Prices: $8.99–17.99 (6.8 fl. oz.)

Manufacturer: Mustela®

A gentle moisturizing lotion that will help hydrate the dry, fragile skin of your newborn. Enriched with avocado oil and vitamin E, this lotion will help protect baby's skin from diapers, baths in hard water, etc.

Johnson's Baby Lotion

Manufacturer: Johnson & Johnson

We can close our eyes and imagine the clean smell of Johnson's baby lotion. Our mothers swore by it and we can, too. It's another classic product by Johnson & Johnson. It has long-lasting protection, it's fast absorbing and it's hypoallergenic. Did we mention it's available just about everywhere and it's also inexpensive?

Cool Classic

Johnson's Baby Oil

Manufacturer: Johnson & Johnson

How could Johnson & Johnson improve on a classic? It's now available in a new formula, that's how. Choose the classic we all know and love or the Aloe Vera and Vitamin E formula we will also love.

Designer's Choice

Tom Kitten Cream for Baby

Price: $15.00

Available at: Crabtree & Evelyn Stores

Scaly skin can be nourished with a thick cream like this Crabtree & Evelyn product, Tom Kitten Cream for Baby.

Other Toiletry Finds and Helpers

Baby Bottom Balm

Price: $12.00

Manufacturer: Origins (800)-ORIGINS

First ask your pediatrician, but this balm might help protect and soothe baby's bottom from diaper rash. It's a rich cream made from shea butter and aloe vera.

Pooh Comb & Brush

Price: $3.60

Manufacturer: The First Years

That extra-fine baby hair does need a special brush and this one is pretty cute, too. Keep those locks or curls in place with the Pooh brush and comb.

Clean Out Your Medicine Chest

Now that your baby has arrived, it is a great time to clean out that medicine chest and stock up on what you will really need. Our biggest surprise regarding medicines was to hear that they should be stored away from humidity. That means *not* in the bathroom or kitchen. Above all, store them safely and locked away from your children.

- Discard all outdated medicines.
- Replenish basic first aid supplies.

With a baby in the house, you might ask, what are those basics that we should have?

- Adhesive bandages and sterile gauze pads.
- Antibacterial soap for washing minor cuts.
- Antibiotic cream or ointment.
- Antihistamine—i.e. Benadryl, for allergic skin reactions and itching.
- Decongestant—i.e. Sudafed.
- Elastic bandages and chemical ice pack for sprains.
- Hydrocortisone cream for minor itches and rashes.
- Ipecac Syrup for forcing vomiting in accidental poisonings (Use only when directed to do so by the poison control center.)
- List of emergency phone numbers, including doctor, pediatrician, fire, police, ambulance, hospital, and poison control center.
- Pain relievers—aspirin, ibuprofen, or acetaminophen.
- Tweezers, scissors, thermometer, disposable gloves and first-aid handbook.
- Wound closure tapes—i.e. Steri-strips.

What else is helpful to have on hand?

- Dosing Dropper or Medicine Spoon—a plastic dropper is best for infants; toddlers can use a dosing spoon. The easiest to use seem to be the dosing spoons which look like a vial or test tube with measurements on the side and a spoon-shaped lip or dropper at the end. Make sure the markings for measurements are easy to see and easy to wash. My daughter is still using hers, ten years later.
- Humidifier—a cool mist humidifier puts moisture back into the air, making it easier for a child to breathe. Dry air irritates respiratory passages, so use your humidifier and be sure to clean it thoroughly every week or you'll put bacteria into the air as well.
- Nasal Bulb syringe—for kids two and under who cannot blow their noses. Use it after some saline drops, squeeze the bulb, gently insert it into baby's nostril and then release. The suction will help you easily clear nasal mucus. There's a nice one available through the Right Start Catalog (800-548-8531) which comes with a nail clipper with an extended wand to grip onto. It's a nice set for only $4.95.
- Petroleum Jelly—yes, classic and simple, it's a multipurpose product. If you're going to use a rectal thermometer, it's a great lubricant and it also heals chapped lips, wind-burned cheeks or sore noses from drippy sinuses.

- Saline nose drops or sprays—(Talk to your pediatrician first.) Saline drops are good for breaking up nasal congestion in infants; use saline sprays when baby is a bit older.
- Sunscreen—even in the winter, sunscreen is a great thing to remember (after six months of age). Protecting a toddler's skin from UV rays is a good idea any time of the year. Pick one with an SPF of at least 15.
- Thermometer—there are so many new types of thermometers out there you may want to check with your doctor. Keeping a rectal mercury one on hand is a pretty good idea as it is best for infants and toddlers. Ear and forehead thermometers provide digital readouts and will give you an idea of whether or not there's a temperature (but the readings are sometimes inaccurate).

Ask your pediatrician about any other items you might want on hand—teething gels, for example.

Some toothbrushing questions you might have:

- When should a baby start brushing? A child should start brushing as soon as her teeth come in. Brush their surfaces for at least two minutes once in the morning and once at night. Help your child until she's at least four years old. She just doesn't have enough manual dexterity to do the job properly on her own.
- What's the right toothbrush? Pick a toddler brush with easy-to-grip handles.
- Should you use toothpaste? Yes and no, not until baby's primary teeth have come through—usually somewhere between one and two years of age. Children don't spit out toothpaste—so really limit the amount you use.
- When should you start flossing? As soon as a child's teeth touch and the brush can't get in between them, flossing is necessary. And until your child is around 10 years old, they probably can't do it correctly by themselves.

Here are a couple of ingenious products you may want to have on hand for looking after baby's body:

Designer's Choice

Boo-Bunnie Ice Pack

Price: $6.95

Manufacturer: Stephan Enterprises

We wanted these for ourselves—the Boo-Bunnie is a clever little ice pack using distilled water. Wrapped into a cute little terry bunny, this is an ice pack your baby will be asking for when those "kiss it make it better" efforts fail.

ComforTemp Thermometer

Price: $70.00 approx.
Manufacturer: The First Years

This thermometer will check baby's temperature under her arm in less than three seconds without any discomfort. It's ideal for the entire family. It comes with an automatic shut-off, a low battery indicator and a 9V battery, included.

Gentle Temp™

Price: $74.95
Available through: The Right Start Catalog
(800) 548-8531

As you can see, these high tech thermometers come with a higher price tag but they also take a child's temperature in only three seconds with no fuss. You can even check your sleeping child's temp. Just place the Gentle Temp in baby's ear and press the button. The audio alert system will tell you when to remove the probe so you don't have to guess. It works by taking five consecutive temperatures of the infrared heat waves which are generated by the eardrum and the surrounding tissue. It's light, easy to use and comes with a three-year battery. Did we mention the easy-to-read digital display?

First Teeth Starter Set

Price: $5.95
Available through: The Right Start Catalog
(800) 548-8531

This is $5.95 well spent. This is a finger toothbrush with flexible bristles. When your baby needs her gums massaged, this will help you. It feels really good on those aching gums and helps stimulate circulation. The toothpaste is made of all natural ingredients and has an apple-banana flavor, tasting pretty good and killing off the bacteria that causes tooth decay.

Safety Toothbrush

Price: $6.95—2 pack
Ages: 6 months and up
Available through: The Right Start Catalog
(800) 548-8531

Here's another ingenious creation—it's a toothbrush that looks more like a teether. It's an award winner but we'd give it an award anyway. The egg shape keeps baby from putting to much into her mouth. The center bar makes it easy for baby to hold her toothbrush herself, encouraging dental hygiene that seems fun. The Safety Toothbrush really can also work as a teether, brushing teeth while baby chews. We love it.

Diapering Your Baby

Diapering becomes second nature; not at first, of course. Most of us initially feel incredibly clumsy, and changing baby's first diapers seems to take forever. The reality is that you'll do more than six thousand changes and by then you'll be an expert diaper changer. By the time Emma was six months old we could change her on a restroom floor, on an airplane seat and frequently on the floor. You'll be doing ten or more changes per day at the beginning, but as baby grows older, thankfully, you'll change fewer diapers.

So it's decision time again, new parents. Will you pick disposables (convenient and expensive), reusable cloth diapers (buy and launder), or a diaper service (pay, pay)? A mixture of these options might work well, too. Some parents like to use the cloth diaper at home, especially for their newborn, and then use disposables when out and about. Later, they may switch over to disposables altogether. Whichever you choose or how you mix use, there are some disadvantages and advantages to each.

Reusable Cloth Diapers

Reusable cloth diapers are more economical and of course, more environmentally sound. Most parents like these for their softness and comfort (why many parents use them for newborns). There's traditional styling (made of gauze for example) or contemporary (looking a lot like disposables). Some of the newest designs come in a variety of quick drying fabrics, and even close without diaper pins (more good news). For those needing diaper pins, choose pins with locking heads (so they don't release and open accidentally).

One downside, as expected, is washing these reusable diapers. They really need to be properly laundered. Residue from soaps could cause ammonia buildup and then diaper rash. It's best to wash them in hot water, low-sudsing detergent, a water softener (not a fabric softener) and a vinegar rinse; all of which could help prevent ammonia buildup in the diapers. Another downside is that the cloth diapers often leak and are often not as absorbent as some of the disposables. That also means almost twice as many changes as disposables. As if you needed another downside, most day care facilities will not allow you to send baby in cloth diapers.

Environmentally, cloth diapers pose a risk as well. We shouldn't forget the use of water and the chemicals we use to launder the diapers, and the fact that we might be releasing chlorine bleach into the environment via the water treatment systems.

Diaper Services

Many commercial diaper services now deliver to your door all the clean and freshly laundered diapers your baby will need. If this is within your budget, you can skip all the work involved with laundering diapers yet have the softness and comfort they afford. Some services will deliver twice a week and some offer the option of using new diapers each time. Remember that you'll still need to purchase diaper covers.

Disposable Diapers

We think disposable diapers keep getting better and better. They have one huge drawback, which is of course how un-environmentally friendly they really are. When you get rid of those disposables, they fill up our landfills. The worst part of it is the poor biodegradability—those diapers sit there for about 500 years! Aside from environmental concerns, disposables now come in a multitude of styles, shapes and designs. *Pampers* came on the market about 30 years ago and even since our Emma wore diapers not so long ago, they continue to improve on the basic design and use. *Huggies, Pampers* and *Luv's* are the big names in Diaper Town, although there are many local and small manufacturers as well.

Some say girls do better with *Pampers* and boys with *Huggies* (better leak protection); we think it's probably another give-them-a-try deal. See what's on sale, what's easily available (you need tons) and what seems to best suit your baby. *Pampers* have introduced the Baby-Dry, a style with a MicroVent cover that lets air in all over (especially good for the heat and humidity of summer days). *Pull-Ups* might help during toilet training, they're comfortable training pants that your toddler will pull on and off herself.

Chain stores like Target, Toys "R" Us and Wal-Mart (plus grocery stores and others) have their own brands, sold at considerable savings. We have heard these are as good as brand name varieties. You may want to try generic diapers and see for yourself.

Tushies® are another option; they're disposables made of natural ingredients (with natural blended cotton for absorbency). While Tushies® are more costly than other disposables, they do provide a "natural" option. According to their manufacturer, other disposables add artificial chemical absorbents such as acrylic acid polymer salts to their all-wood pulp padding. This is done to increase absorbency. However, when these chemicals and moisture react, a gel results which could possibly end up on your baby's bottom. Tushies® have a padding made out of cotton and wood pulp so they're gel-free.

Buying diapers in bulk, at least in 80 or 100-count diaper packs, is a good cost-effective solution. Superstores like Toys "R" Us often stock these larger packs, but grocery stores tend to stick to the smaller sizes like 20-count (ending up costing more). Remember that when your baby is almost into the next size, for example, you may not want to purchase bulk. Wait until she's passed that transition point and is well into the next size.

The "Bottom" Line on Diapers

Financially, diapers are the "bottom"—it's a no-win situation. All diapers, cloth or disposable, cost a fair amount and diapering takes a lot of time and energy. We used to think it's all right, eventually baby will toilet train, and diapering will come to its natural conclusion. The new controversy surrounding diapering and toilet training is that babies are actually staying in their diapers even longer! Toilet-training trends show that back in 1961 (when disposables were coming on the market) only 10% of 2 1/2 year olds were still in diapers. Compare that to the incredible 78% in diapers in 1997. Even the venerable *Time* magazine recently got into the battle over potty training, diapers and questionable affiliations of diapering experts and diaper companies.

For more than a decade, experts like Dr. T. Berry Brazelton have advised new parents to allow baby to decide when to switch from diapers to the potty. The result is that the age of toilet training has risen considerably—and it comes with a rise in related problems such as constipation and bladder-control. John Rosemond, a child-care expert, psychologist, and author of the bestseller *Parent Power!*, published a series of columns in more than 100 newspapers about this trend and whether it is actually the right approach to toilet training. He also felt mothers have switched from taking an authority figure role to choosing one of caretaker, and are therefore, not holding the line with baby over toilet training. Consistency, patience and positive attitudes are what we recommend.

Brazelton professes that back in the 1960's he asked mothers to try something new—allowing children to decide when they were ready to use the potty. This more gentle approach even became called "toilet teaching." Brazelton defends this approach and states that the rise (in age) of non-potty trained children is due to working parents reverting back to the old style of toilet training. These parents don't have the time to properly "teach," and with some day-care facilities refusing non-potty trained kids, the pressure is back on the parents. Penelope Leach, author-psychologist, also agrees with Brazelton that children shouldn't be forced to use the toilet before they're ready.

Leach, however, does agree with Rosemond about Brazelton's questionable affiliation with *Pampers* (he's the chairman of the *Pampers Parenting Institute*). *Pampers* has even designed a diaper for children over 35 pounds and we've seen Brazelton advertising it. To be fair, Brazelton has been giving his advice about toilet teaching for a long time, well before his affiliation with the diaper manufacturer. We may love Brazelton's books and advice, but we're not wild over this controversial affiliation.

For new parents, you just want your daughter or son to use the potty as quickly and as easily as possible. You may not care that Brazelton and Rosemond are hot topics on the news and in print. You simply want your baby out of diapers and using the potty. In that regard, we located some products to help. They can't guarantee potty-training success, however, and whichever approach you take, there'll be some difficult crossroads. But some of these items do seem to offer children a sense of ownership and pride and that can't hurt. We really like a little book and video called, *Once Upon a Potty,* which we were given for our potty-training daughter. Charts, targets and adorable potties and seats will all help ease the process. Try to celebrate it. And when junior does "make" in the potty, make a big deal of it!

Diaper Wipes

Again, you can opt for those brand names or generic wipes. We used brand names at first when we were really overly cautious about baby's skin, and then we switched to a generic version on her second birthday (Walgreen's). We can't say we really noticed all that much difference but you may want to test a few. Some or our friends think generics are not as thick and have less moisture. We really like the generic Walgreen's wipes, (still handy ten years later). Baby Fresh and Huggies are really good brand-name versions. Chubbs come in a cute block container. When empty, you can stack them and fill them with baby's toys. In addition to the brand you'll choose, you have to decide whether to use aloe, scented or unscented. To cut costs, try refillable packages or multibox sets.

Remember to stock up on some travel size wipes. Great for your diaper bag, but unfortunately not so great for your pocketbook.

Diaper Wipe Warmers

This was a totally new innovation for me. I hadn't heard about diaper wipe warmers and couldn't even conceive of its necessity. At three A.M., changing your baby with a cold wipe isn't so pleasant. The wipe warmer wraps around the box of wipes and warms it to 99°. Do you need one? Only if budget isn't an issue—and personally—we remain unconvinced. If you want to add it to your baby registry, go ahead—here's one with the features you'd look for:

Baby Wipe Warmer

Price: $29.95
Available through: The Right Start Catalog
(800) 548-8531

Why would you want a wipe warmer? Especially at night, heating those wipes to a comfortable temperature might soothe baby's skin. There's a thermostatic control which will keep the temperature even and it will shut off automatically in response to any power surge. It plugs into standard AC outlets and conveniently fits on the Right Start Diaper Depot which we recommend in our changing table section.

A Word About Diaper Rash and Diaper Pins

Despite my constant and best attempts at diaper changing and caring for my child's bottom, she still got diaper rash. Her bottom was bright red, had little bumps and was irritated. The doctor suggested she go without diapers, to air her sore bottom. Always contact your pediatrician; sometimes severe diaper rash might stem from a yeast or secondary bacterial infection.

Most diaper rash can, as we learned, be cleared up by going diaper-less between changes and cleaning the bottom gently with a mild soap. Applying petrolatum or zinc oxide might soothe that irritating rash. If that still doesn't do the trick, call your doctor.

Diaper Pins Check your stock of diaper pins often; those with plastic heads may become brittle over time and break. Look for exposed pin rods which could hurt your baby. Also dispose of any pins that have dulled (pushing hard can also lead to an accident).

Diaper Pails

One of the happiest moments in my parenting life was when we got to throw out the diaper pail. Of course, diaper pails have been greatly improved in just the short time since we were using them. The Diaper Genie, for example, disposes of diapers in individual plastic and holds down the odors. We were so enthralled with this when we saw it at a friend's home recently, we spent a half hour checking out how it worked.

Diaper Pail Safety Savvy

The diaper pail is another piece of baby equipment that is essential yet also causes numerous injuries every year. The CPSC has received many reports of young children who ingest the diaper pail cake deodorizers or children who fall headfirst into diaper pails, and drown. All pails, and especially diaper pails, should be out of your child's reach. Choose one with a foot-operated pedal so you can have your hands free. Some of the new diaper pails are especially designed for disposable diapers with their interior plastic garbage bag system which helps with odors. Whichever you choose, remember to put the pail out of baby's reach.

Which Diaper Pail to Select

What you really look for in a diaper pail, comes down to a foot pedal for easy opening, a locking mechanism (obvious) and a charcoal filter or nontoxic deodorizer cake for odor control. Charcoal filters are not the easiest to change, but they do last about three months and control odors. You could use an ordinary garbage can and control the odors with nontoxic deodorizer cakes, but most of the diaper pails we looked at are really affordable. The Gerry and Fisher-Price models are designed for the budget-minded. Be aware that the Diaper Genie that we were so taken with isn't all that expensive, but the refills (those individualized bags) are. We think it's worth it, we couldn't stand our diaper pail and despite constant cleanings it would fill the room with odors upon every opening.

Diaper Genie

Prices: $35.00–40.00 approx.
(800) 843-6430

Our top pick (except for the cost concerned) is the Diaper Genie. It hermetically seals each soiled diaper in its own scented plastic "bag." Open the lid, dispose of the diaper into a small cylinder, and twist the lid. The diaper is forced down the barrel of the Genie. You end up with what looks like a chain of sausages. It's the absolute tops in odor control!

Dispoz-all Diaper Pail Model #3027

Price: $16.00
Manufacturer: First Years
(800) 225-0382

Not that you'd want to, but you could stash up to 25 disposable diapers in the Dispoz-all. Using standard 13-gallon trash liners, the double barrier system locks in odors even when open. A foot pedal opens the lid. To open use the lever on the top—it also locks the diaper and odor inside the bag.

Odor-Free Diaper System Model #9229

Price: $19.00
Manufacturer: Fisher-Price
(800) 828-4000

Use your kitchen-size garbage bags in this diaper pail to keep odors down. This pail also has a lever to seal off diapers and odors. Fill it with up to 20 diapers. The Odor-Free has a foot pedal to open the lid, which also has a child-resistant compartment for a deodorizer.

Odor-Free Diaper Pail Model #478

Price: $16.00
Manufacturer: Gerry
(800) 525-2472

This Odor-Free from Gerry has a double lid system with charcoal filters in each section for trapping odors. It also has the features we like: a foot pedal that opens the flip top lid and an inner ring that holds standard plastic trash liners.

Diaper Bags

We bought an adorable, cotton red and white striped diaper bag. It was useless. The changing pad fell out, the pockets sagged and it got stained. We ended up going through one diaper bag after another. When we saw all the new, tough, durable and (are you ready for this?) *stylish* diaper bags, we simply couldn't believe it. Land's End, Kenneth Cole, Fitigues and more are making great-looking, functional bags to help moms and dads pack everything baby needs.

A diaper bag is like Felix's bag of tricks. It is a portable changing table, a cooling station for milk and drinks, a toy chest, a bookcase and more. It will carry everything you need for junior when you are out and about. It will also need to keep your own items handy (you'll probably stop using a separate bag). You'll keep those keys, sunglasses and wallet in your baby's diaper bag as well. So it becomes a multipurpose, multi-use item, which is why it needs to be strong, functional and aesthetically pleasing. Pick one made from a durable material which is either washable or wipeable.

You can buy diaper bags for less than $10 (but ask if it will hold up to constant use), and there are some that follow the cost-is-no-object ethic. Remember that this is a bag Dad is likely to tote around as well. That's why we really like the Land's End collection of bags. The stylish "black" options by Fitigues and Kenneth Cole are unobtrusive enough that perhaps Dad won't mind. We've also found a backpack version that we like. We don't say you have to have a diaper bag (any bag with a portable changing pad and zippered plastic compartments will suffice), yet, the functionality of these bags we came across make them really useful products. The good ones also help you keep track of essentials and that's one less thing to worry about. Here's what that diaper bag should offer in features:

- inside pockets and compartments to keep necessities handy and to hold diapers, wipes, fresh clothes, books, toys and more. There's so very much to lug around, if the diaper bag can help you organize it all, so much the better.
- a portable, washable, waterproof changing pad so you can change your baby anywhere, anytime. We recommend buying a diaper bag that has

a secure home for the changing pad—it was the first thing we lost out of ours.

- a self-enclosed pouch or pocket for soiled diapers. We know you cannot imagine not finding a place to deposit these, but it happens. When it does, it's essential your diaper bag can hold onto them until you can dispose of them properly.
- compartments for bottles; we think this is essential. If they're insulated pockets for warm and cold liquids, it's even better. Two bottles are usually the minimum, so two pockets would be ideal.

Diaper Bag Necessities

After being stranded on an international flight and waiting over ten hours, we determined what we felt were diaper bag necessities. Some of our friends think you should have two bags geared up—one for small errands and a full-sized one for longer adventures. We worry that's ineffectual and unnecessary, especially with the beautiful diaper bags we found. We'd be the Mom and Dad who pick up the wrong bag and find ourselves short of the essentials. Making sure your diaper bag is well stocked is enough to do for new moms and dads. And speaking of stocking it, the typical diaper bag should have packed in it:

- diapers—a sensible number, more than two and less than twelve (go by current frequency of changes and estimated time out, plus some)
- fresh change of clothes
- travel wipes
- space for toys and books (rattles, board books, mini-manipulative toys)
- comfort items like a "blankie" and pacifiers and teethers
- protective baby gear such as sunscreen, and after 6 months, baby hat and sunglasses
- skin care and toiletries (lotion, diaper rash creams, etc.)
- snacks for you and baby (we didn't go anywhere without our cute little container of Cheerios®. They proved to be a lifesaver many times when we were out longer than we originally thought we'd be)—crackers, juice, bagels—all good choices. We mention carrying some snacks for you as well and we think this is important. If you carry around something nutritious for yourself, too, perhaps you won't fall into that trap of taking great care of baby and neglecting yourself.

- your essentials—checkbook, wallet, and keys (we suggest making an extra set of keys which stay put in the bag just in case you forget that regular set you tote around). Add a paperback—you never know, maybe baby will fall politely asleep and you can actually do some reading.
- camera—my favorite suggestion. How many times will you find yourself saying "If only I had my camera?" If you have a spare, keep it in the bag with some film or drop in a disposable.

A zippered pocket for your wallet or change and keys is also a great help! With all of that in mind, here are the diaper bags we were thrilled to find:

Do-It-All Diaper Bag

Price: $29.50
Available through: Land's End Catalog
(800) 356-4444

This Land's End bag really does it all—you can get going in organized style. The tough nylon fabric is backed with water-resistant vinyl, the removable see-through ditty bag expands to hold extras, the removable changing pad is wider than most and the exterior bottle pockets on each end allow for easy feedings. All of that, and you can get it in "Black," "Navy Blue," "Hunter," "Barn Red" and even "Plum Wine." If this one's not big enough, order the Deluxe.

Little Tripper

Price: $19.50
Available through: Land's End Catalog
(800) 356-4444

You're not going out for long and only need to grab a few necessities. Keep the Little Tripper packed with two diapers, a bottle and a change of clothes, and get going. It looks more like a lunch tote but it'll do the job. It even comes with a small changing pad and water-resistant pouch. Pick your color.

NappySack Diaper Bag Backpack

Price: $72.00
Available through: Fitigues Catalog
(800) 235-9005

Sometimes sophistication costs. This NappySack is pricey, $72, but it's stylish and good-looking. In black nylon, you'll be packing all of baby's diapering needs and a changing pad. The backpack leaves your hands and arms free and balances nicely. Still, the cost is a determinant for some.

Toilet Training

As we mentioned, getting rid of the diaper pail was a great moment—it was also the moment of potty training achievement. The tips we like for toilet training or toilet teaching are pretty much the same. There's success, and there's failure. Parents should be positive, encouraging, enthusiastic and firm!

- Recognize when your child is ready to begin the process of leaving diapers behind. Does junior seem interested or intrigued by the potty or the bathroom? Will your child imitate you? Is your child showing signs of independence"
- Your encouragement should be firm and consistent, positive and enthusiastic. Don't go backwards; once in training pants, stay in them, no matter what the consequences. Your child needs to move forward and you need to be supportive.
- As you have read, the average age of toilet training has risen, so be patient. Perhaps, with encouragement, patience and enthusiasm, your child will make progress earlier.
- Celebrate all successes. It's a great confidence builder. Don't flush away that poop that baby finally makes in the potty; stare at it with wonder. Show sincere appreciation and excitement! Keep doing this.

Toilet Training Potties and Aids Here are just a few toilet training aids we think are pretty helpful. Remember to be enthusiastic and patient.

Cushie-Tushie Potty Seat

Price: $9.39
Available through the: Baby Catalog of America
(800) 752-9736

A cushie-tushie is what every toddler needs! It's an extra-soft potty seat that fits right on your toilet. It's lightweight and easy to clean. It even includes a glow-in-the-dark imprint on the white vinyl so your child will see it at night.

Musical Trainer and Step Stool

Price: $29.95
Available through: One Step Ahead Catalog
(800) 274-8440

An award-winning potty that will make you sing with glee! This potty takes junior through the entire process of toilet training. First the potty is a self-standing one with a removable receptacle and when it's used, your child will be rewarded with the sounds of a waterfall. Then you can use the potty on your toilet and the base becomes a step stool. Music as a reward, and a multi-process potty—a great value. It's no wonder the Musical Trainer is an international award-winner.

Potty Video and Book

Prices: $19.95 Video; $9.95 book
Available through: One Step Ahead Catalog
(800) 274-8440

Part of the Duke University Family Series, this is a video with an entertaining story and music about a birthday party. It just so happens it's also teaching all of the correct steps for toilet training and washing up. It was designed for children two years and up who may need a bit more encouragement or are just starting the process.

Sesame Street Soft Potty

Price: $10.99
Manufacturer: Ginsey Industries, Inc.

This is just the most adorable soft potty seat we've seen. It fits on regular and elongated toilet seats, and is bacteria and mildew resistant. Don't worry—it's easy to clean and really might help shorten that toilet training time.

Splash-Proof Potty

Price: $13.99
Manufacturer: Baby Bjorn

Here's a cute little potty contoured for a toddler's comfort. There's a high splash guard in the front and a wide, stable base so it will stay put when baby stands up. Pick red or blue or better yet, let baby pick the color. This is a simple, uncomplicated potty.

Toilet Trainer

Price: $29.95
Manufacturer: Baby Bjorn

Here's an inventive toilet trainer that adjusts to any size seat, round or oval. The rubber edge grips onto the commode and helps the trainer's stability. It's ergonomically designed (like all fine Swedish design) so toddlers sit properly. The Baby Bjorn Toilet Trainer has all the features you'll need: a splash guard, smooth edges and no finger-pinching joints. It's even dishwasher safe and has a handle. Age two years and up. You can even choose white with blue or blue with red.

ath Time—What's Best for Bathing Baby?

Introduction

Giving baby a bath can either be a rewarding, emotional experience or one of total frustration. The bath-time accessories and equipment listed below will help create a comfortable and more enjoyable bath-time for you and your baby.

Babies don't always want to take a bath; some squirm and wiggle all the way through it. Even if baby likes bathing, the experience can cause wear and tear on your patience. Portable bathtubs, bathinettes, safety aids and accessories can all help you get through it and maybe even enjoy it.

Bathing Safety Savvy

Whatever equipment you choose, and however you decide to bathe baby, remember safety first—ensure your baby is well protected and won't slip or fall. A baby can drown in very little water. Here are our top ten bath-time safety tips, and we place them first, well before the list of items you'll need:

1. You don't need a lot of water to bathe your baby—use only a few inches of water.
2. Never leave baby alone. Let the phone ring. Don't answer the door. If interruptions are a real problem, give your baby a bath when someone else is home to help.
3. Everything you need should be within reach—towels, clean clothes, soap, shampoo, diapers, etc.
4. Test the water temperature—approximately 90 degrees or slightly lower than body temperature. You may be able to adjust your water heater to below 130 degrees, which will help prevent accidental scalding.

5. One hand should be gripping baby firmly at all times during the bath. Support your baby's head and neck on the inside of your left wrist and forearm (left-handed? reverse this). Use the fingers of your left hand to grasp her gently but firmly under the armpit, not under the shoulder blades. Your right hand will be free to do the washing and you will get used to this.
6. Choose a bathtub with a nonslip surface. If using the sink, just add a towel or a rubber mat to the bottom.
7. The room should be warm and free of drafts.
8. When bathing near a faucet, use and shut off the hot water first after filling the bath. Then any drips will be cold water, not hot.
9. Take off your own jewelry to give baby a bath; this will prevent accidental scratches.
10. Empty the bath when finished. Avoid the temptation of the water.

Bathing your baby is a changing program, changing as your baby grows. Your newborn will need no more than a sponge bath at least until the umbilical cord has dropped off (at about two weeks). If you do give your newborn a bath, don't submerge the cord. Use a portable baby bathtub for babies from three to six months of age. How long you can use it depends on the style of the tub and the size of your baby. There are also large, toddler-sized tubs available. You actually may only use this piece of equipment a few times, which is why there are many good, inexpensive ones to choose from.

Which bathtub will be best for your baby? There are some features to look at and some to ignore. Capacity is one to forget about—remember you will be using a minimum of water anyway as a safety precaution. Also, choose one with a nonskid surface on the bottom and rubber grips. Some bathtubs come in a gift package combination—a cost-effective option if you don't already have bath toys and towels. Important considerations are:

- *Size:* Size and shape do matter. They relate to how and where you will be giving baby a bath. If you will be using this portable tub directly in your sink, measure for the best fit. Many smaller tubs are nice fits for standard-sized or standard-double sinks. The larger sized tubs which are heavier might be a bit difficult to work with initially. However, you will be able to use it longer. There is also a nice transition for baby from the bigger tub to the "real" adult tub.

- *Interior Surface:* A foam pad on the inside of the tub helps to reduce slipping—and baby will feel slippery. This pad can be permanently attached or removable. Other tubs have decals of vinyl or rippled surfaces which will do the same. If you have borrowed a tub without such a prevention aid (or are using the sink), add a towel inside to provide a nonslip surface.
- *Storage Compartment:* Totally an extra feature, a built-in storage compartment keeps the necessities handy.

Bathtub Favorites

Here are some of our bathtub favorites and the reasons why we like them:

First Years Pooh Bathtub Gift Set

Price: $39.99

Available through: JCPenney Stores and Catalog

Order this great tub and all its extras. First Years has positioned a great looking Winnie the Pooh on this 2-in-1 tub with its anti-skid foam. Bathe your Pooh fanatic in reclining or sitting positions and then let her play with the bath puppet/washcloth and squeaky toy. When she's finished, wrap her up in the cute Pooh bear hooded towel. Did we mention the brush and comb?

2-Stage Baby Bather Model #3101

Price: $14.00

Manufacturer: First Years

Age: Newborn – Toddlers

This bathtub can be used on a single or double sink (or any flat surface) and is made of rigid, molded plastic. It has a drain spout and a plug on the base. The dual-seats—foam-backed reclining seat on one side for infants, and upright seat for older babies on the other—is an especially ergonomic and useful design. There is also an indented section for storing soap, washcloths or shampoo.

Deluxe Bath Center Model #9326

Price: $16.00

Manufacturer: Fisher-Price

A deluxe model which isn't much more expensive than any other, this tub is deep to keep baby warm (remember still use only a small amount of water).

There is a foam cushion and a drain plug on the base. This tub will work in a multitude of places: sink—single or double, bathtub, or on your countertop. There is a contoured seat, and container sections gracefully hold shampoo, soap, and toys. This is an especially nice bathtub for your baby.

Infant to Toddler Tub Model #466

Price: $18.00
Manufacturer: Gerry
Age: Up to 24 months

A tub within a tub—this clever design allows you to bathe smaller babies with its plastic insert. It even adjusts to two sizes. When baby grows, remove the insert, and the tub provides support for sitting up in the bath. This tub will fit in a "real" adult bath or on a flat countertop. There's even a sensi-temp plug which turns pink if the water is too warm.

Teddy Tub Model #431

Price: $20.00
Manufacturer: Gerry
Age: Up to 24 months

This is another nice tub for your baby by Gerry. It may be bear-shaped for fun, but it is also lined with closed-cell foam for comfort and slip-resistance. The foam and the terry pad can be used to support your baby or used as a drying pad. It also has a sensi-temp plug which turns pink if the water is too warm.

2-in-1 Two Stage Tub Model #41641

Price: $14.00
Manufacturer: Safety 1st
Age: Up to 24 months

This two-stage tub converts for growing babies with its closed-cell foam infant shell and a plastic contour for toddlers. This oval-shaped white tub with carrying rim offers easy emptying with its snap-closed drain. There is also a slip-resistant foam pad.

Bath Seats

The last word on bath seat safety comes from the Consumer Products Safety Commission. With its recorded message, you will hear the dangers of using a bath seat as a flotation device (especially when you leave your baby in it unattended!). Call 800-638-2772.

Bathinettes

So now you know all about baby bathtubs—so what about a bathinette? What is it exactly? Basically a bathtub at mom or dad's hip height, a bathinette today is more of a changing table with expansion into a bath. Generally more popular in Europe, we did find one or two we really like, if you want to spend the extra money:

All-In-One Bathinette

Price: $84.99
Available through: Baby Catalog of America
(800) 752-9736

Here's an all-in-one bathinette and changing table. There's a contoured pad on top which makes a comfortable place for changing diapers and getting baby dressed. Just flip up the pad and you'll find the bathtub underneath. There are two large shelves for storage and a bin across the front to hold all baby's toiletries. Bathtub has a drain plug with a hose so emptying into your sink is easier.

PrimeBolle Bathinette

Price: $400.00 approx.
Manufacturer: Peg Perego
(219) 482-8191

Okay, when you can bathe your baby for less than $20, why purchase this high ticket item? It is an ultimate space saving device—combining a dresser, changing table and baby bath all in one. It is made of lightweight injection-molded plastic on casters, so it can be easily moved about. There is a shelf and a built-in towel rack which hides away when not in use. Peg Perego makes ergonomically designed products, expensive but inventive.

What we don't like There are a lot of to-do's and not-to-do's for bathing your baby. There are also some items to avoid whenever possible. We don't like suctioned bath seats as the suction cups could suddenly release—your baby and the seat could tip and fall over. Also avoid foam bath sponges which can be picked apart and eaten, causing choking hazards.

Bath Safety Products

There are some bath accessories which will help make your bathroom a safer place.

Bath Pal Thermometer

Price: $2.49

Available through: Baby Catalog of America

Yellow Ducky or Tug Boat—either choice is a good one. A floating bath toy and an easy-to-read thermometer in one. You can measure the water temperature in 30 seconds, in Fahrenheit and Celsius.

Bathe'r Save'r Comfort Pad and Bath Organizer

Price: $11.68

Available through: Baby Catalog of America

This plastic cushioned pad is for mom and dad. It will help save your knees and elbows. It folds around the side of your tub. Remember kneeling on that hard tile with elbows on the hard porcelain tub can get very uncomfortable. Hang it up to dry, then fold it easily for storage.

Safti-Grip™

Manufacturer: Rubbermaid

The Safti-Grip™ bathmat has many suction cups on the bottom. They help anchor the mat to your tub and that will hopefully help anchor your child's bottom to the tub.

Sof' Spout Faucet Cover

Price: $2.59–3.49 approx.

An inflatable spout cover to protect your child from head injuries in the tub. This one we like to pack for traveling—it's easy to install and easy to remove. Made of nontoxic plastic.

Tubbly Bubbly

Price: $12.95

Manufacturer: Kel-Gar, Inc.

Available at: Toys "R" Us, Wal-Mart, Target and through most catalogs

Go ahead and put this cheerful elephant on your faucet as a cover that also doubles as a liquid bubble bath dispenser. It fits all standard faucets and the water flows right through the elephant's mouth. Its fun, soft and safe molded plastic/rubber. If elephants aren't your favorite, pick up the hippo or the dolphin.

Sprayer Nozzle

You just might want a sprayer nozzle attachment on your sink or tub, wherever you're bathing baby. Just be sure to test the water first.

Bath Towels, Robes, Hooded Towels and More

Bath Towel and Mitt Sets

Price: $22.00
Contact: Land's End Catalog
(800) 332-0103

Land's End has a fabulous array of bath towel and mitt sets to choose from. You can pick from the appliquéd (hockey, football, bows, fire trucks, space explorers, ballet slippers and more) to the monogrammed. Towels and mitts are 100% cotton and the towels measure a generous 27" x 55." Your child will definitely know her own towels.

Petit Prince Bath Collection

Price: $52 (Bath Towel and Mitt Set)
Available through the: Rue de France Catalog
(800) 777-0998

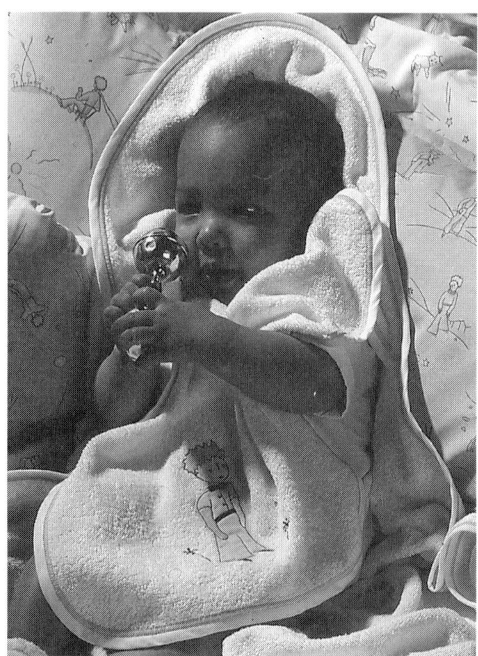

Wrap your Little Prince up royally—Courtesy of Rue de France

If you love Le Petit Prince and have a little princess (or prince) of your own in the bath, wrap her up in this terry towel. It has the little prince pictured on it and it comes with a mitt to wash your little royal one.

Bath Toys and Books You Will Like

There are so many items to choose from. We like products that are both useful and designed well. Here are some of those we wouldn't do without:

Bath Book—Fun-Fax™ Series

Price: $4.95

Publisher: Covent Garden Books

Learn the alphabet while bathing! Baby will enjoy flipping the pages of her new bath book and she'll certainly be able to recognize "b" is for "baby" when she sees the pictures of real children, animals and more. It's all part of Fun-Fax series of books, for the bath and more.

Bath Pal Thermometer

Price: $2.19

Available through: Baby Catalog of America

(800) 752-9736

Inexpensive, useful and fun, this is a floating bath toy and easy-to-read underwater thermometer all in one! It's a great way to prevent scalding with its 30-second measuring. Shows Fahrenheit and Celsius and you can pick either a yellow duck or a tug boat.

Brio Chunky Car

Price: $11.99

Available through: Baby Catalog of America

(800) 752-9736

We just adore Brio but baby will have to be age two for this great chunky car. It works on the water and on land and features wind-up action. There are some adorable big paddle wheels for water play. There's a cute car face, too, and your toddler can immerse this chunky car totally as it's made of durable plastic.

Scoop and Squirt Fun Pack

Price: $18.75
Manufacturer: Lego Shop at Home Service
(800) 453-4652
Ages: 6 to 36 months

We're so happy Lego decided to make some bath toys. The Scoop and Squirt Fun Pack is definitely fun. It comes with a frog that squirts water, a lily pad that floats and an adorable, swimming turtle. We especially like the way the nine pieces mix and match and fit together in unexpected ways. Watch out in case junior squirts you!

Stack 'n Build Boat

Price: $9.99 approx.
Manufacturer: Fisher-Price
(800) 432-KIDS
Age: 6 to 36 months

Smooth sailing from now on. Baby will love this happy little boat for her bath. Check out all the other Fisher-Price bath toys, too. They're inexpensive and a lot of splashing fun.

lothing Baby

The Layette—Baby's First Wardrobe

When we began shopping, we were asked about our baby's layette. A layette? We didn't even know what it was. Did we really need six layette gowns and two unionsuits—whatever they were? There really isn't a mystery: a layette is your baby's first wardrobe, the clothes your baby will grow out of so fast your head will swim. What you will want in a layette is quality, comfort and value. How do you know what you will really need and how much?

Most baby clothes come in a range of sizes. If budget is an issue, skip the newborn size and use the three to six months range. For premature babies, you'll need special sizing. Remember you can always add to your layette, so going with a conservative guess of how many shirts, gowns and the like you'll need is a good approach. A layette is a beginning wardrobe and is only intended to keep your baby clothed for the first three months.

Underwear and Everywhere

Although most manufacturers call all of these underwear, our baby was quite happy sitting around in her side snap shirts. You will love all of these layette pieces. They are functional, easy to wash and very sensibly designed. Here's exactly what they are and some of our picks for each.

Shirts, onesies, side snaps, creepers—you'll catch on pretty quickly. The names differ slightly as do the designs. Rapidly, you'll discover through personal preference what's best for the way you'll dress your baby and as you buy replacements, you'll purchase more of your favorites. Our favorites were the easiest items to put on, take off and wash. Here are some wardrobe clues:

- Side Snap Shirts—allow you to snap baby up on the side and make it a cinch to change your baby without fuss and without having to remove the whole outfit.

- Bodysuits—pick the 100% cotton ones. They're the most comfortable, especially when they also have an expandable neck opening (allows mom to dress baby with ease). Reinforced snaps are a necessity. Even though baby will only be in each outfit for the first few months, you'll feel like you've done and undone a million snaps. You'll soon discover (and be replacing) any layette items with poor snaps.
- Layette Gowns—it's a nightgown with elastic or ties around the bottom. Pull to keep baby snug or open for easy changes late at night. We prefer the elastic ones (ties seem like a hazard). Carter's makes some great, simple gowns and the elastic doesn't get all knotted up in our washing machine, another plus.
- Pullover Shirts—like your Gap basic "T," the pullover shirt is the basic baby T-shirt. Look for that expandable neck opening again.
- Unionsuits—one-piece garments, usually with long sleeves.
- Sleepers—these will keep baby warm and cozy. Sleepers are adorable to look at and lovely to hold (usually of fleece, flannel or other soft fabrics). To make dressing easier, be sure to buy those with snaps all along the inseams and down the front.
- Sleeping Bags—When cooler weather hits, sleeping bags will keep your little baby warm and cozy. They're a cross between a blanket, a sleeping bag and a sleeper. Patagonia makes one which is especially nice. When your baby is a newborn, you can use it as a "bag" where it blankets around your little one. When she gets a bit older, the sleeping bag converts (the snaps reconfigure) to make pant legs. That's very clever and very good design. Patagonia makes it out of its famous fleece and in wonderful colors. You'll like sleeping bag buntings a lot. There are a couple of outfits you'll discover for baby that you'll wish came in your size! The sleeping bag is one of them.

Baby Clothes or Baby Wear

What should your baby wear over her underwear? Creepers, overalls and maybe a jumpsuit or two. Need some definitions? These garments are for going out or playing in. A creeper is a one-piece garment, rather like a bodysuit. Jumpsuits are one piece, overalls sometimes one, sometimes two pieces. To complete the ensemble, don't forget some caps and booties. Depending on your climate, lifestyle and the time of year, consider the types of fabric that'll be appropriate to make baby comfortable. If you are planning to purchase clothing ahead of schedule you may want to think about layering natural fabrics and be sure to consider size. How big will baby be in the wintertime, and what kind of clothes will be appropriate? Plan carefully and insist on comfort before fashion—remember that your baby will look cute in pretty much anything.

Different manufacturers often have different names, even clever ones, for these garments. It's good to remind yourself how long your baby will wear this layette. From experience and observation, we know the answer is "not long." A Carter's layette gown, for example, comes in one size and fits a newborn up to 11 pounds. We happen to think that you can get many of the clothing basics for a pretty reasonable price from Carter's, Gerber or from JCPenney (catalog, too). We aren't at all convinced you need that Gap Baby cashmere sweater, although it's adorable. For those special occasions pick up a special jumpsuit at Gap, a Fitigues romper or—to top it off—pick up that fabulous Ralph Lauren Polo Sport Cap!

Our favorite basics can be found conveniently at Dayton Hudson (Marshall Fields), Gap, JCPenney, Kmart, Macy's, Sears and Target stores. Our favorite manufacturers also include the very cost-conscious Gerber Childrenswear Sleep 'n Play line (800-4-GERBER), Carter's (770-961-8722) and the very affordable Baby B'Gosh.

We were really excited to hear the news that Sears and Benetton USA are joining forces. The result is sure to be a great line of basic children's clothing. We hope this new venture features the great details and super good looks of the original items carried in the Benetton stores we sorely miss. Since it's happening at Sears we're likely assured of better pricing as well. We can't wait. For everyday layette wear, we're still not sure about the upcoming new Donna Karan line for kids. It makes us wonder if we really need a sweatshirt outfit with a prestigious logo for our little trend-setter. Maybe, maybe not. We'll have to wait until it arrives on the scene to see.

We do think it's nice to splurge on one or two special items for baby. For the first photo, or a big family event, certainly, the memory and pictures of baby making a fashion statement will be fondly recalled in future years. So, as long as you don't expect to get many wears for the dollar, don't feel guilty about some of those less-than-practical purchases. Baby is only a baby once and not for long. A little hint—such items are great opportunities for grandparents to spoil!

Until then, we wanted to mention some specific layette favorites:

Baby Bunting

Price: $64.00
Available through: Patagonia Kids Catalog
(800) 638-6464

This is just about the cutest, warmest and most environmentally conscious bunting we could find. Made of easy-care post-consumer recycled Synchilla® fleece, this little cocoon conveniently switches from bunting bag to zippered up legs. That's great for going from car seats to backpacks, too. If you're inclined to stick to the bottom line, this piece may not fit your budget. However, it's versatility and longevity make it a great choice (especially if you're planning on having more than one child to pass it down to). Colors and adorable patterns seem to change seasonally, but there's always a bright, cheerful selection of buntings in the Patagonia catalog.

Basic Beginnings® Body Suits

Price: $18.00 package of 6 (short sleeve #R 344-0120D)
$21.00 package of 6 (long sleeve #R 344-0013D)
Available through: JCPenney Catalog
(800) 222-6161

Basics are often the best and these bodysuits, we wouldn't have done without. We really loved baby wearing these under sweaters and they made for great layering opportunities. The snap leg openings are a cinch and make diapering a breeze. The rib knit binding and lap-shoulder neck openings also make dressing much easier. Pick up prints for girls or boys or just stick to basics and buy the assorted colors.

Baby Midweight Capilene® Underwear Set

Price: $36.00
Available through: Patagonia Kids Catalog
(800) 638-6464

This moisture-wicking base layer is baby's defense against winter chills. The two-piece set, designed just for baby's little bodies, is easy to put on and easy to peel off.

Best Baby Buy

Bright Future® Hooded Pramsuit

Price: $9.99
Available through: JCPenney Catalog
(800) 222-6161

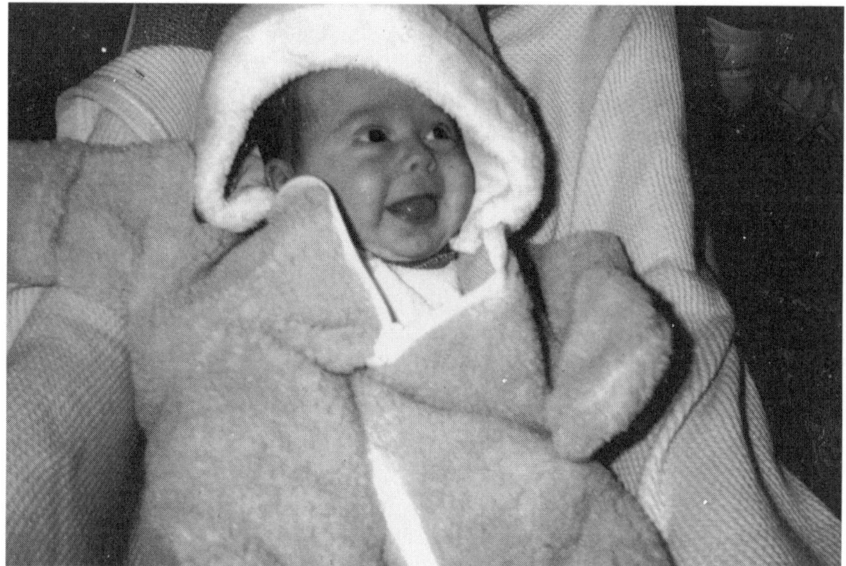

A baby with a very Bright Future®

We brought our daughter home in this good-looking pramsuit—we loved its lushness and its low price. It comes in white, blue and pink and is made in the U.S.

Carter's Cotton Cardigan and Pant Set

Price: $24.00 set

Available through: JCPenney Catalog (800) 222-6161

Hint to Grandma about this great little buy! Gift boxed, Carter's has put together items they do best: a white cotton cardigan with checked trim, checked pants with elastic waist, a little cozy hat and even a 3" x 3" picture frame to complete the set. No yellow unfortunately, but you or Grandma can pick blue or pink and dress baby up for a few memorable snapshots.

Critter Cape

Price: $24.95

Available through the: Natural Baby Catalog

(800) 388-BABY

#157552 One size fits 1 to 4 years

What a great name for a great little poncho! It has these adorable ears on the hood which help make the bath or pool fun. This poncho helps mom keep baby dry and warm after the chills set in. It's easy to put on and take off with its simple neck snap and it's part of a natural knit basics collection we really like a lot. There are playsuits, day saques, booties and more. Get one, get two, get them all.

Denim Overalls

Price: $25.00 embroidered
Manufacturer: OshKosh B'Gosh
(414) 231-8800

Those first denim overalls are so darn cute! OshKosh makes the cutest of them all—and they're tough, durable, and very washable. Get your camera out when baby models these denim overalls.

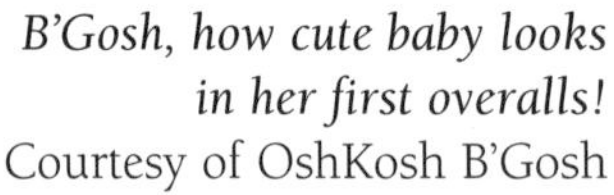

B'Gosh, how cute baby looks in her first overalls!
Courtesy of OshKosh B'Gosh

Land's End Kimono Shirt #3889-12D1

Price: $14.00
Available through: Land's End Catalog
(800) 356-4444

Easy dressing and sophisticated styling make the kimono shirt one of our favorite layette items! Land's End makes a really nice one which does a cross-over, snapping in the front. Pick from this season's colors: "Rosebud," "Ice Blue," or "White."

Land's End Polartec Bunting and Cuddly Fuzzy Bear Hat

Prices: $44.50 bunting #5347-12D6; $21.50 hat #5548-52D1
Available through: Land's End Catalog
(800) 356-4444

There's actually a whole Polartec collection for your baby, but we really adore the bunting and little bear hat. Polartec really pampers your little one and keeps her warm. This bunting even unzips all the way so diaper changes are easy. The little fuzzy bear hat just caps it off! The colors are really soft and lovely; choose "Soft Teal," "Honey Gold," "Soft Sage" or "Dusty Plum, among others.

Thermal Romper

Price: $84.00
Manufacturer: Fitigues
(800) 235-9005
#1BOO (Sizes: 6, 12, 18, 24 months)

Fitigues make some great clothing pieces out of thermal 100% cotton which has been prewashed to prevent shrinkage. Their line changes almost every season. This year the romper is in a lovely mulberry color with trim at the sleeves and ankles. Machine washable, these rompers will become instant favorites! Fitigues makes excellent quality items for all ages; their simple, elegant fabrics and designs are consistent through all age groups, so it's very likely that Mom and baby, yes and even Dad, could find themselves in coordinating, or even matching outfits. Great cuteness potential here.

Veggie Long Sleeve Long Leg Romper

Price: $29.95
Available through the: Natural Baby Catalog
(800) 388-BABY
#705558 Sizes: 6, 12, 18, 24 months

These are the cutest of rompers (a jumpsuit style) with snaps, especially if you're a vegetarian. We don't know which we like best—eggplant, pumpkin or pea—the veggies are silk-screened using a water-based ink on 100% natural organic brushed French terry. Environmentally sound and garden gorgeous, these rompers are a real hit! Don't forget to order the topper hat to go with it (#705559)—your baby will look adorable in it.

Special Clothing for Premature Babies

We discovered a wonderful source that produces clothing for premature babies (with a pretty wonderful owner—the mom of two preemies). Pat Cotter's, *For a Special Baby*, even makes isolette clothing—an isolette being the little plastic box that babies are kept in to keep their temperature regulated. There are also really adorable, precious outfits for preemies in sizes of one to eight pounds and even more choices in slightly larger sizes to hopefully

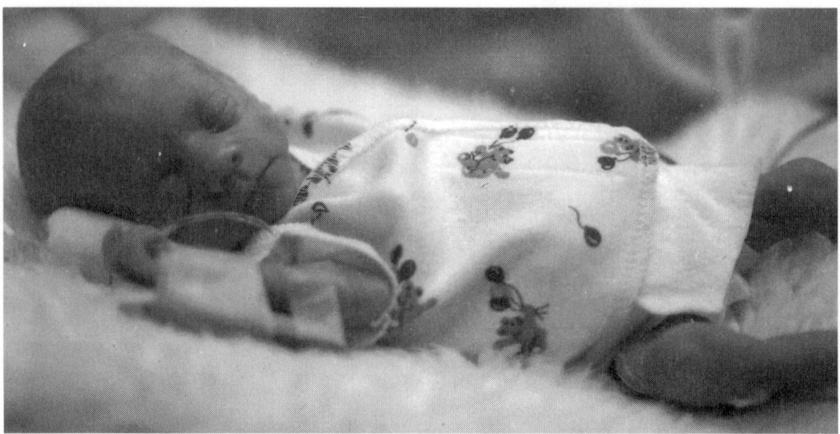

For a special baby

wear home. The clothes are well made, and extremely reasonable in cost. While no one wants to consider the implication of needing special clothing for special babies, *For a Special Baby* can handle the most urgent needs of many exceptional parents. View the collection on the web or call for a catalog (http://foraspecialbaby.itool.com & 651-631-3128). We're pretty proud of this collection. It offers optimism and fills a tremendous need.

The Layette–How Many, How Much?

How many, how much? How many do you need of all the basics in a layette? A few of each and more of what you'll use the most, like bodysuits.

The answer of quantity really varies and will depend on you. Some manufacturers recommend larger quantities of each layette item than others. Is it a ploy to have you buy more than you need or an accurate assumption? How often will you be doing the wash? That figures into the quantity figure as well. For those who are budget conscious, pick items which can do dual duty—like versatile side-snap shirts to be worn as underwear and baby wear or sleeper bags that convert into pants.

Since every layette guide we came across seemed to offer differing opinions on how many you need of each item, we think you could be safe having three of four of each of the basic items to begin with. Stores and clothing companies provide little layette checklists and while helpful, remember they are pitching product. If you fall in love with the ease of side snap shirts, for instance, than you can easily pick up some more. We actually found we needed at least four of the following: side snap shirts, layette gowns, sleepers and pullover shirts; but start small, and give hints to relatives when you find your supply is low.

The Layette by Catalog and On-Line

You can easily pick out baby's layette totally by catalog shopping (and web shopping). Return policies are better than ever, and many companies offer unconditional guarantees for exchange or return. Look for at least a 30-day guarantee for returns. Do check out sizes carefully, they seem to vary widely (refer to each company's size charts). Imagine doing all of baby's shopping while you listen to some pleasant music, smell some aromatherapy candles and put your feet up. It's more than possible—get on-line, get-set and order. You can have the best dressed little model without ever leaving home! Check out our internet shopping guide and our list of toll free numbers for sources.

Layette Receiving Blankets and "Blankies"

How do you keep your baby warm and comfortable? Receiving blankets will do the trick, and if you didn't know what they were before, you will soon. Keep several on hand, and depending on the season, you can pick either thermal or nonthermal types. There are still a couple on hand in our house that have done wonderful service for baby, as a comforter for a little girl, and now, at playtime with her stuffed animals!

With all that polar fleece around, your baby may easily think her "blankie" is more than a blanket. Indeed, some are even part toy. All of the ones we love will help you provide your baby with soothing comfort, a sense of security and perhaps, more than a few snuggles.

Baby Blanket

Price: $29.95
Manufacturer: CherryTree®
(888) BABY-021

A marvelous blanket in high quality non-pill fleece. We can't ever decide between the baby blue with ducks, the cream with snowflakes or the baby pink with bunnies. The Baby Blanket is machine washable and made in New England. A great gift for your baby or your friends, it comes beautifully wrapped.

Designer's Choice

Benny Blanket

Price: $24.00

Manufacturer: Rumpus

Call 888-rumpus-1 for store information

We think it's awfully cute—a security blanket that rolls into a smiley character with bushy, fringed hair. After taking a nap, your baby will want to play with Benny. He's 15 inches of soft polar fleece. Pick up one or two in your favorite colors—available in red, purple, pink and of course, baby blue. There's even a story book you can get to go along with your blanket, called "Benny Blanket," so you and your little one can find out all about Benny.

Dutch Knotty Doll

Price: $18.00

Manufacturer: Biobottoms

(800) 766-1254

Is it a doll or a "blankie"? No matter, baby will likely love it. The doll's body is made of cotton flannel and had knots for teething in its corners. The doll's face is finished in either pink or tan (nontoxic paint) and doubles as a rattle. Thoughtfully, the Dutch Knotty Doll is machine washable—an essential attribute.

Baby Bear Baby Hugs–"Luvies™"

Price: $39.95, personalized

Contact: Maple Springs

(215) 234-0812 and www.maplesprings.com)

Our friends at Maple Springs take the adorable Luvies™ bear (or is it a blanket) made by Dakin and they'll personalize it for your baby. It's an heirloom, a blankie and a cuddly bear. You can have it embroidered with name and even birthdate. Pick pink or blue and you'll have an irresistible friend for your little one.

Polar Fleece Baby Blanket

Price: $24.00

Available through: Land's End Catalog

(800) 356-4444

Is it a bear to cuddle or a blankie to hold tight? Photo courtesy of Maple Springs.

Another very nice and soft polar fleece baby blanket in a variety of soft colors. Match it to your nursery decor. This is a slightly larger blanket, 30 by 40 inches and for an additional charge can even be monogrammed (with your baby's stats—go ahead and add her first name, birth date and weight). Nine colors to choose from: rhubarb, powder blue, soft rose, royal blue, soft green, sunlight, red, ivory, and periwinkle.

Baby and Toddler Shoes

What do you put on baby's feet? In nice weather, probably not very much. When baby is bundled up you may want to check out some Okie-Dokie® suede chukka booties in great colors (available through JCPenney), Reebok® Momentum's—a cross trainer for infants (available through JCPenney), and even some elegant patent leather Mary Janes (Striderite Children's Group, 800-955-5510).

Can you buy shoes too early, too cheaply or too late? Not really. The best indoor foot covering is really none at all. A soft shoe when it's chilly is fine if there's room for the foot to move and grow. Good shoes don't need to be expensive—look for flexible shoes with bendable flat soles that won't be slippery. You might want that first "real" pair of shoes somewhere around 8 to 18 months.

Shoes were the worst thing we ever shopped for. Our daughter would much rather run barefoot all of the time than put her two feet into shoes of any style. We found every children's shoe store we could. Some major department stores also carry kids' collections but may not have the same fitting expertise as specialty shops. At first, you'll really want to check baby's size and be sure of properly fitting shoes. Then you can ease off a bit and check out many of the wonderful selections available by catalog and discount stores.

Nike® makes some great baby and toddler sneakers, also now called "cross trainers." They're good for multipurpose activities and for new walkers. Pick the "Baby Perishette" or the "Baby Swoosh Crib Shoe." Do keep in mind how quickly shoes will be outgrown. We never liked spending more than $30.00 for shoes and that's maybe gone up a hair but not much more than that. Save those expensive Michael Jordan's for when your child is grown a bit and can really get some wear out of them. Reebok makes a cute "Classic Leather Jogger," although we aren't sure where baby is off jogging to. But it might look just like mom's pair and that might be sufficient reasoning to purchase them.

Then there are also those soft shoes that look an awful lot like slippers. They're really fine for infants when it's chilly. But check with your physician about shoes. Ours really stressed going barefoot. She felt it was great for our baby to learn how to use her toes and feet, first for crawling and then for walking. Try these.

Joshi's Booties

Price: $16.00
Available through: Babessentials™ Catalog
(888) 613-6383

Handcrafted out of soft fleece, these little booties are easy to put on and easy to take off. They have nonslip soles to prevent bruises and they're designed to grow right along with your baby. They close with Velcro and come in three sizes. We really appreciate the choice of winterweight or lightweight fabrics in a multitude of adorable patterns.

Toasty Toes™

Price: $17.95
Available through: Colorado Kids Clothing Company
(800) 500-4182

Baby can have the toastiest toes around—just order a pair or two of these. The cuff is designed to be rolled up to protect baby's leg right up to the knee. These soft booties are perfect for crawling infants or for extra protection outdoors. The medium and large sizes are designed with nonslip surfaces and soft soles perfect for babies who are learning to walk and crawl.

Toddler Clothing

Layering Up Your Toddler for Winter

We all know layers are the key to dressing right for wintertime. With toddlers it's tough to find the right balance of layers which don't restrict, yet are enough to keep him warm and dry. Try a two-layer or three-layer approach for your toddler.

Layer One This layer, also called the wicking layer, is the closest one to baby's skin. Always begin with a clean diaper (or training pants). Add some long underwear in two-pieces, like cotton thermal leggings and a cotton T-shirt. Skip one-piece underwear because the moment she's fully dressed your baby will probably have to go to the potty or have a diaper change. Now add some cotton or wool socks (put the wool over the cotton so it's not itchy).

Layer Two The warming layer is what comes next. Add some pants; sweatpants are great choices. They're comfy and soft. Now add a turtleneck or sweater with long sleeves. Other good options are fleece tops and bottoms.

Layer Three Now, on to outerwear which forms the outer or weather layer meant to protect your child from the elements. Look for choices which waterproof, windproof and insulate. Parkas and snowpants are pretty great choices to keep your child's body from exposure to wind and cold. Test the zippers as they'll be used often. Ribbing at the wrists and ankles also helps keep snow and wind out. Boots should be water-resistant with an insulating liner. We really like the ones with the removable liners and we usually buy ours a tad bit big—big enough for two pairs of socks. Don't forget to add a hat or band around the ears and some gloves before your toddler's off making a snowman. Again, consider climate and time of year when coordinating with size or planning ahead. And for those of you in those warmer zones, you can probably stop at layer two, most of the time. Infants don't move around enough to warm themselves up, so 15 minutes out in bitter cold is plenty.

Don't forget baby's feet. Layer cotton or thick wool socks over thinner cotton socks. Top off with lined, waterproof boots, best with a drawstring which really helps keep out snow. Scarves will keep a child's neck warm and can even cover the lower part of her face; just keep them from dangling. If you want more information about dressing baby warmly, there are some comprehensive guidelines in *What to Expect the First Year* by Eisenberg, Murkoff and Hathaway (Workman Publishing). The authors stress the importance of hats, especially for infants.

Keep a winter weather kit by your door. That might keep gearing-up time to a minimum. If hats, mittens, scarves, sunglasses, waterproof boots, tissues, petroleum jelly, and sunscreen are always by the door, you just might get out in time to enjoy yourself.

Some cold weather winners.

Baby Midweight Capilene® Underwear Set

Price: $36.00
Available through: Patagonia Kids Catalog
(800) 638-6464

This moisture-wicking base layer is baby's defense against winter chills. The two-piece set, designed just for baby's little bodies, is easy to put on and easy to peel off.

L.L. Bear™ Fleece

Prices: $40.00 jacket; $25.00 hat and mittens
Available through: L.L. Kids by L.L. Bean
(800) 221-4221
#HG27078 jacket
#HG27046 hat and mittens

Your little bear will be all bundled up in the Bear Fleece jacket. The skiing bear and snowflake print is full of winter whimsy. It's even machine washable. The chin-strap hat comes with two little ears—you'll have to supply the grandmother and wolf yourself.

Sun Glasses

Prices: $6.00–12.00
Manufacturer: Riviera Kid's

These plastic frames will help protect those little eyes from UVA/UVB rays. They even bend to fit really small heads. Do not underestimate the sun at any time of year, whether you are on the beach, on the slopes, or just running around. Baby's skin and eyes must always be protected, no matter how resistant you feel your own skin and coloring is to harmful UV rays. If in doubt, be over-protective and ask your pediatrician for his/her recommendations and guidelines.

Thermal Hooded Top and Leggings

Prices: $54.00 Hooded Top; $24.00 Legging
Manufacturer: Fitigues
(800) 235-9005
#1B73 Top #1Bo4 Legging
Sizes: 6, 12, 18, 24 months

More of Fitigues wonderful thermal gear which is great for layering up. This season's hot color is sage. These thermals are great basics and remember, they're machine washable. Gray is a perennial favorite—a great choice for Mom and Dad, too. Fitigues do wonderfully in the wash, too.

Toddler Rough and Tough Play Gear–Dressing for Fun

Flapdoodles (800-220-FLAP, and available at specialty stores and department stores) are more than a cute name. There's real style and sensible, washable fabrics being used (and abused) by toddlers everywhere. The Little Arizona Jean Company (available through JCPenney stores) makes a line of durable, well-designed jeans, fleece and tops. There are adjustable denim and twill overalls for boys or girls, fleece tops and jeans of all kinds which might look like Mom and Dad's jeans, too. Little Arizona's clothing (and shoes) for toddlers are sensible, washable and very cute. Did we mention affordable? Mickey & Co. and Pooh 100-Acre Collection (available through JCPenney stores) will keep your toddler dressed in all of her favorite characters. Pick Minnie in fleece, Mickey and company on jeans and Pooh embroidered on cotton denim jeans. If your little one likes Bugs Bunny, Tweety and Sylvester, head off to the nearest Warner Brothers Store. (If there isn't one near you, call for information). "Baby Looney Tunes" also appears on the newest Gerber Childrenswear line for baby. They're covering babies in everything from sleepwear to underwear to playwear. K Mart has the new Sesame Street line with lots of fleece and creature comforts for newborns, infants and toddlers. What we really like about all of these collections is that they are cute, durable and budget-conscious.

Sporty kids will like the Nike® for Kids Collection. There are Kinderfleece® hooded tops, windpants with the famous embroidered "Swoosh," and even, "Swoosh" turtlenecks. Toddlers can look like professionals. The Nike shoes are good buys too, just stay away from the overly-expensive models. If Dad (or Mom) is hooked on pro sports, check out the NFL and NBA collection available through JCPenney. Your little cheerleader and pro-baller will look the part in windsuits and drop-waist jumpers with team logos of course. Not every team is available, but there's plenty to cheer for. Don't forget to order the little sports cap to go with, one size fits most toddler fans.

Swim Gear

Little Swimmers

Price: $6.99 for pack of 9
Manufacturer: Huggies

Taking your baby swimming poses some problems as disposable diapers keep absorbing water. They weigh her down and ultimately fall apart. Rubber pants struggle to keep the diaper underneath dry. So what can you do when the temperature soars? Pick up a pack of Huggies Little Swimmers. This nice pack of disposable swim pants offer the diaper-like protection baby needs without swelling or falling apart. Little Swimmers are available in sizes for children between 16 and 36 pounds. Get out that sunscreen and use it—very important. Baby is not interested in a tan; she already is too cool for words.

Sun Glasses

Prices: $ 6.00–12.00
Manufacturer: Riviera Kid's

Yes, again we mention putting some plastic frames on baby to help protect those little peepers from UVA/UVB rays. Remember to ask your doctor about protective warm weather guidelines.

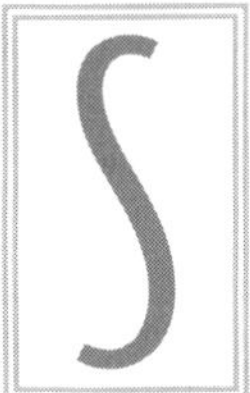

oothing Baby—From lullabies to white noise. Swings and rockers are old time favorites, not to mention great music for young children.

INTRODUCTION

Are you ever ready for the first time that your baby is inconsolable? You try everything—changing her again, feeding her, burping her, hugging her, singing to her, walking around with her, and no matter what you try, she cries louder and louder. What can you do to soothe your baby and are there any products which can help? You probably already do most of what works and you do it instinctively. Here's some of what might help soothe your baby:

- Touch

  Touch is so important. It helps your baby feel secure and safe, so cuddle her, hold her, and caress her. Research shows that babies who are touched and held often sleep better, are less fussy and even have stronger immune systems. Try gently massaging baby's scalp as you shampoo, or after a bath, apply baby lotion in long, gentle strokes. If bottle feeding, rest her cheek against your bare arm.
- Sound

  Babies respond to soothing sounds. They like rhythmic, repetitive sounds that are reminiscent of the sounds they heard in the womb. Sounds like a ticking clock, a fan whizzing around or the ocean might be relaxing to your baby. Lullabies and soft, lilting music can also ease baby. Sing away, baby will love to hear you and they don't care how well you can sing. Purchase some baby tapes and CDs. Check out our recommendations for lullabies.
- Movement

  Rocking, strolling and gentle movement are all soothing to baby. Babies in utero are used to mom being in motion and so repetitive, rhythmic movements are very soothing. When your baby needs some comfort dance cheek to cheek, carry her about, pop her into a reclining swing—all will help.

- Sight and Scent

  Babies are very familiar with odors such as perfume or shampoo associated with their mom. These become comfortable because they become familiar.

- Routine

  Routines are very comforting to your baby. They can sense a predictable pattern of their needs being met. The same lullaby tape played every evening might begin to frazzle your nerves but to your baby it will be very soothing.

Baby Massage

How do you massage your baby? Gentle strokes and a small amount of baby oil can be massaged into baby's skin. Johnson's Baby Oil is fine to use, it's a classic. Go easy though, apply oil in a soothing, circular motion. Start at baby's feet, calves and thighs working up to her tummy and shoulders, arms and hands. Keep going just as long as your baby is enjoying it or is soothed by it. Massage relaxes muscles, increases circulation, and encourages bonding. Ask your pediatrician for more information on baby massage and check into some of the new Baby Massage classes popping up everywhere. You can also contact The International Association of Infant Massage which will provide you with a list of instructors. Call 800-248-5432. If you want to read more about baby massage and its physical and emotional benefits, here are a few suggestions:

Baby Massage: A Practical Guide to Massage and Movement for Babies and Infants

Author: Peter Walker
List Price: $16.95
Publisher: St. Martin's Press

Walker's written a how-to guide for understanding baby's movement and muscular development. Learn all about the practical benefits of massaging your infant. We really like the last chapter called "A Healing Touch," about massage for children with special needs.

Loving Hands: The Traditional Art of Baby Massage

Author: Frederick Leboyer (Photographer)
List Price: $15.95
Publisher: Newmarket Press

Dr. Leboyer teaches how mothers can use baby massage to communicate affection, love and strength to their newborns. The author's own photos illustrate his guide.

Soothing Products

From lullabies to white noise, not to mention cuddling and massage, and a lexicon of "baby talk," here are some of our favorite soothing products. Give a few of these a try:

Lullabies and Peaceful Sounds

If the lullabies don't soothe baby, they might just soothe you and either way they might be of help. For even more musical selections check out our Music and Video Section. The first listing isn't a lullaby but "heartbeat musical therapy"; you might want to give it a try.

Baby-Go-To-Sleep Tapes:

Stops Crying! Heartbeat Musical Therapy (CD1 & CD2)

Price: $12.95 each tape

Available through: Audio-Therapy Innovations @ 800-678-7748 or the nursery department at JCPenney Stores

Terry Woodford was a driving force behind such musical groups as Alabama, The Temptations and Barbara Mandrell. He left a 20-year career in the music entertainment industry after discovering heartbeat music therapy. For over a decade, Woodford's been studying the principles of sound and music which can calm children. He recommends, and so do we, that you try these recordings—which include an actual human heartbeat—as the rhythm of traditional lullabies. Combine that with good bedtime routines, Woodford advises, and you have a natural way to stop a baby from crying and even helping children sleep though the night. We know it sounds peculiar but we never knock anything that works. It's a fairly inexpensive solution to at least try. Over 8,000 hospitals and special care centers are using Woodford's tapes.

A Child's Celebration of Lullaby

Price: $16 CD; $10 cassette

Music For Little People

(800) 346-4445

Age: Birth and Up

How else can you tolerate Raffi except in a sampler recording? A little bit of this and a bit of that, this is an eclectic musical collection with Lena Horne giving her all on the Gershwin standard "Summertime." Samplers are great ways to introduce different strains of music. You'll appreciate hearing some of your favorites like Linda Ronstadt, Aaron Neville, and Ladysmith Black Mambazo. It's a delight for you and your baby.

Designer's Choice

Return to Pooh Corner: Kenny Loggins Sings to His Son

Price: $14 CD; $12 Cassette

Sony Music

Children will love it but so will you. Kenny Loggins is most appealing in this gentle and soft album. With versions of Paul Williams's "Rainbow Connection," Jimmy Webb's "The Last Unicorn" and John Lennon's "Love," mom might be listening more than baby will. Grab your old Pooh bear and baby's new one, and cuddle up together. You'll remember what you liked most about Kenny Loggins—the silky-smooth vocals and beautiful harmonies—and you'll find it all in Return to Pooh Corner.

Moondreamer–Priscilla Herdman

Price: $15.00 CD

Redwing Music (773-463-8184)

Moondreamer is unusual. Priscilla Herdman provides the relaxing vocals for lullabies for a dog in "Howl at the Moon" and for a toy rabbit in "A Velveteen Love Song." The elegantly arranged "Dreamland" (a Mary Chapin Carpenter song) and (Billy Joel's) "Lullaby" keep you wanting more. Sometimes unusual is just what you need.

Pacifiers

You may not believe in pacifiers but some find themselves changing their minds when baby won't quit crying (after hours on end). Keep in mind that early use of pacifiers might interfere with breast-feeding. So it's best to consult with your pediatrician about the use of pacifiers, if you're unsure or if you have questions.

You decide you want to use a pacifier and there are many, many brands to choose from. Two of the most popular are Nuk made by Gerber and Mini Mam by Sassy. Both of those are orthodontic pacifiers, shaped flat and wide like natural nipples. Two pacifiers usually cost between three and five dollars. That's a lot of peace for little cost. You'll need extras, since they get lost or mislaid, and you'll want to have baby preferring a brand you can replace without difficulty. Unfortunately, our little one got hooked on a pacifier made in England and Grandma had to ship them to us. Until those replacements arrived, we tried all sorts of alternatives, none of which sufficed. At first, bring home one or two different ones. Let baby decide.

When it's time for baby to stop using a pacifier, check with your pediatrician for advice. We went cold turkey. After two rough nights she really didn't ask for it again, except for a few rare occasions of being really overtired. Your doctor will be able to point you in the right direction. You can start by using the pacifier only at bedtime and try to offer a special blanket or a teddy bear as a substitute. You can even try the Pacifier Fairy who will leave a present under your toddler's pillow in exchange for baby giving up her pacifier. Be patient, but firm and taper off. You don't want any resulting dental problems, so as she learns to crawl, eat solids and drink from a cup, sucking may become less necessary. That's the time to ease off. Remember your baby won't go off to college with a pacifier in her mouth.

Pacifier Safety Savvy

- Never attach a pacifier to a crib or any part of her body with a long string or cord. She could strangle herself.
- Keep those pacifiers clean. Wash them off before use and if baby drops them, wash them immediately. We still need to remind some parents not to use their mouths to clean a pacifier.
- Inspect your baby's pacifiers and throw away any with signs of deterioration.
- Inspect the shield between the nipple and the ring of the pacifier. Is it wide enough to keep your infant from fitting it into her mouth? Does it have holes for ventilation—(it should).
- Never, ever dip a pacifier into liquor or any sweet liquids like honey. Alcohol will disrupt sleep and honey can cause botulism poisoning (in children under the age of one) Sugary, sweet substances can contribute to tooth decay even at the earliest ages.

Give some of these a try:

Avent's Newborn Silicone Pacifier

Price: $7.00 for two

For all of you Avent fans, here's a newborn pacifier with a taste-free nipple that's also dishwasher safe.

Evenflo's Soft Top Pacifier

Price: $1.80 each

The Soft Top by Evenflo has an ultra-vent shield allowing air circulation which helps ward off skin irritation.

Mini Mam Pacifier

Price: $2.50 for two

Designed for newborns through about four months, the Mini Mam has a latex, orthodontic nipple.

Designer's Choice

Nuk Orthodontic Pacifiers and the Nuk Nite Time Pacifier

Price: $1.50–3.50

Nuk (from Gerber) are great orthodontic pacifiers similar in shape to mom's nipple during breast-feeding. They come in various sizes for different age ranges, and there's even a glow-in-the-dark one (Nuk Nite Time) so it's easy to find at night.

Playtex Binky Gel-Filled Pacifier

Price: $2.30 for two (approx.)

The Binky by Playtex has an extra-firm latex nipple.

Safety 1st's Mini Buddy

Price: $1.49 each

Here's a cute, cow-print pacifier in a one-piece design that won't pull apart.

Ulti Mam Pacifier

Price: $3.50 for two (approx.)

This pacifier has a soft, orthodontic nipple and raised dimples for increased air circulation. The Ulti Mam has a latex nipple and is for babies 4 to 36 months.

Skip pacifier clips. The convenience of having the pacifier snapped to baby's clothes does not trade off of baby's safety. When attached to your baby while she's in the crib, there's a strangulation hazard. We say skip them altogether and get used to picking them up (over and over). When that starts to happen, it might just be time to ease off their use.

Teethers, Rattles and Toys

Sometimes teethers are the only thing to soothe fussy, teething babies. Teethers today are incredible—they're fabulous, multi-sensory toys which also provide much needed physical relief. Rattles, too, are often forgotten as soothing toys. Babies love the sounds of a rattle and some of the best new ones offer manipulative challenges as well. Here are some we adore:

Teethers

Designer's Choice

Brain-Teether

Price: $10.00
Manufacturer: Wimmer-Ferguson
(800) 541-1345
Ages: 6 to 12 months

We like everything about this teether, especially the name! The Brain-Teether is a super combination of a toy with great graphics, a rattle, and a teether. It stimulates an infant's developing senses (sight, sound and touch). Your baby will use it to provide relief from teething or just for fun, shaking it and playing with it. The Brain-Teether comes with a rattle with colorful balls inside and two, interchangeable fabric attachments (in black and white or color graphics) and encourages visual and gross motor activity (great for babies!).

Grip & Grab Rattle

Manufacturer: Lamaze Infant System
(800) 704-8697

The name of this rattle is a perfect description as baby can really grip and grab it. It's an intriguing rattle, with see through tubing and sounds which are pleasing to everyone's ears.

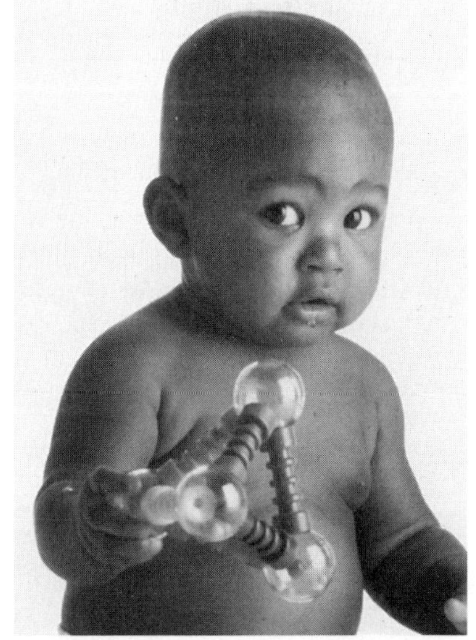

Baby can grip and grab this rattle all by herself

Rattlebug

Manufacturer: Lamaze Infant System
(800) 704-8697

Baby can rattle this little bug and have a great time. It's ergonomically designed for baby's grasp and has a smiling face and pleasant sounds.

Best Baby Buy

Sensory Teether

Price: $9.00
Manufacturer: Manhattan Baby™
(800) 541-1345

Manhattan Baby has made the Sensory Teether terribly sensible and terribly cute. We like the purple monkey best, but they've all sorts of animals, shapes and forms. The sensory teether soothes, and encourages development and self-awareness. You'll like it so much you'll want the purple monkey, the sunflower and the cloud. Baby will like it so much (it eases the pain of incoming teeth) she'll want to squeak, squeeze and shake it, too.

Sensory Teether makes teething almost fun!

Rattles and More

Giraffe Wrist–Ankle Rattle

Price: $6.00
Manufacturer: Manhattan Baby™
(800) 541-1345

Baby can wear this giraffe rattle on her wrist or on her ankle. Just a gentle movement and the smiling giraffe will make the most pleasant rattling sounds. It's soft and friendly and the adjustable band all help make this rattle a favorite toy. Stick one in the diaper bag and keep another at home.

Rattle & Roll

Price: $15.00
Manufacturer: Manhattan Baby™
(800) 541-1345

Baby will rattle and roll all day long with this soft, fun discovery rattle. Will she find all the hidden sounds while she spins and slides the movable pieces? The Rattle & Roll is designed for little hands to hold onto and play with.

Sweet Slumber Bear

Price: $29.95
Available through: One Step Ahead Catalog
(800) 274-8440

This is a cuddly, baby-safe, battery-operated teddy who plays soothing womb sounds. Hugging the bear, listening to the sounds or cuddling up together in the crib—any or all can calm fussy babies. The little bear comes in his own p.j.'s and looks ready for bed. Pick pink, mint or blue velour.

Swings

Swings can provide a wonderful, soothing motion for your baby. Automatic ones will keep you from having your arm ache. This type of swing usually hangs from a collapsible, free-standing A-frame. Some have reclining seats or hanging bassinets so small infants can enjoy them. The two types available include mechanical wind-up and battery-powered.

A swing is a great thing to borrow but try to find a newer model. Call the manufacturer to make sure the model has not been recalled. Also be sure to check the metal frame and the rods which hold the seat—are they secure? Be sure the swing is sturdy and that it has a working seat restraint.

Many argue about the necessity of having a swing. Others say nothing calms their little one like a swing. If you decide to purchase one, remember the many safety warnings. Swings have no stringent standards for safety, so be sure to:

- Stay with your baby when she is in the swing.
- Always use the restraining belt.
- Stop using the swing when your baby reaches the weight limit (16 to 25 pounds depending upon the model selected).
- Don't use a broken, damaged or incompletely assembled swing.
- Don't swing for long—no more than half an hour and not for naps.
- Don't let an older sibling play with the swing, as a head entrapment hazard does exist.

For those tight on space, the automatic swing might not make it on the purchase list. The tubular legs usually have a wide stance for stability. If space is an issue, check for one with a smaller base footprint.

The two types of models are those which run approximately 15 to 30 minutes (manual wind-up) and those which can run for many hours on a set of batteries. New models run more efficiently and are quieter than previous models. New models are also rid of many earlier mechanical problems and are more durable.

We don't really like models which swing baby from side to side in a cradle attachment. More natural motion is swinging from head to toe. Choose a sturdy model and ask how long it will swing on a single winding or on a set of batteries. Once baby has reached the weight limit or can sit up, the swing will be outgrown—put it out of reach and sight.

Here are the swinging models we like:

Designer's Choice

Advantage

Price: $65.00 to 100.00

Manufacturer: Graco

Our Designer's Choice, the Graco Advantage is the best we could find. It's a battery-operated model with a removable and washable liner. With three swinging speeds and an adjustable seat, from a reclining position to upright, this swing has many features. With its side mounted motor, you can put baby in and out without bumping her head. This design removes the typical overhead bar. It even comes with a lifetime warranty on the swing motor (to the original owner).

Cradle Rocker Seat Model #9273

Price: $75.00

Manufacturer: Fisher-Price

Although it rocks side-to-side as a cradle, we prefer to use it as a head-to-toe rocker. Base locks upright as a feeding seat. Handles help make it portable. (Remember not to place swings on table tops).

Freedom in 1 Swing

Price: $120.00

Manufacturer: Century

This battery-operated swing offers a natural arc with head to toe motion. The base accepts an infant car seat and there is an upright and reclined position. The base footprint area is about 2 by 2 feet. There is a variable speed control. Access is from the top and all sides.

802 Easy-Sit Swing

Price: $90.00

Manufacturer: Gerry

Glide swing motion is battery operated. Base footprint is about 2 1/2 by 2 1/2 feet; This swing is open from all sides and the top for easy access. It also features a side motor and a pivoting tray for ease in putting baby in and taking him out of the Easy-Sit.

arental Peace—How to get it when you need it. The best products to keep you sane from tranquillity tapes to family activities.

Introduction

Sometimes peace of mind comes when you know what to expect, or you feel prepared to handle whatever may come about. If you don't know already, very soon you'll realize that expecting the unexpected is the norm with children (often this can be a source of great delight, too). Most of the time, someone has already experienced what you are going through. If the unexpected leads to anxiety, sifting through some great baby care guides or speaking with the doctor or friends can help. This will help you feel prepared, confident, reassured and most of all, not alone.

When your baby is asleep and all is well, you should also feel relaxed and peaceful. Often, new parents are too exhausted or too stressed to calm down. We'll take a look at some products that might help put you in a better state of mind, body, and even spirit. Our baby doctor said quite simply that when our newborn slept, we should sleep. Easier said than done; sometimes we were so overtired we couldn't sleep. When you get there, you'll relate, too! It's a good idea to try concentrating on something else—perhaps catching up on the latest baby magazines, burning some aromatherapy candles, curling up with a good book (not about babies), or practicing some yoga. Whatever it is that works for you—that gives you some parental peace of mind—keep doing it. In those "baby-free" moments, make sure you do some things for yourself, with a partner, or with a friend. If this is a stretch and you just can't imagine any "peaceful product" or activity that would help, we've listed a few of our favorite things which just might inspire you. We felt better just reading some of the descriptions. Some made us laugh with their "peaceful prose," but we all know laughter is also good medicine. You can find balance with humor, too.

We also want to mention that when asking friends and family about "parental peace" they very often mentioned specific moments that included their child. When your little one curls up in bed with you, when you ignore the telephone, when you get on your hands and knees to build something together, or when you're conjuring up something imaginative with your toddler—those are special, peaceful moments, too. Peaceful for mom and dad because it's that "quality time" we hear bandied about a lot. Yet, it's true. To help new parents find that quality time, we suggest reading the section on "Organizing the Nursery and Your Life." It'll hint about some products and services like voice mail, answering machines and Caller ID. Find that time together, and make the most of it.

Parental peace is also about renewal. You can take this new role of mom or dad and renew your membership to a museum, the gym or sign up for a class. Start small and start right away. Try to experience life like your little one is—with open eyes and ears and with passion and vigor; explore the unfamiliar. The best parents we know are those who are growing right along with their babies. Renew. You might find that parental peace we mention. Don't underestimate or dismiss the importance of your own well being—your baby really needs a happy, healthy parent.

We'll start with some great books for your library. Names you will know or come to know are of course, Dr. Spock, Dr. T. Berry Brazelton, Howard Gardner, and Dr. William Sears.

Touchpoints, by Dr. T. Berry Brazelton, is a great book and you should put it in your library. To see and hear about everything a new parent needs to know, the new video series, *Touchpoints,* is another intelligent purchase. It's a three-volume series at a reasonable price, covering a multitude of parental problems, situations and even tantrums (800-829-7797 to order). Brazelton's goal is to help you understand and advance your child's development. Volume I guides you through the pregnancy and bringing baby home, Volume II through the first year, and Volume III straight into toddlerhood, toilet training and more.

Cool Classic

Dr. Spock's Baby and Child Care

Authors: Benjamin Spock, Stephen J. Parker

List Price: $34.95 ($7.99 paperback)

A true classic, *Dr. Spock's Baby and Child Care,* was the most sensible, compassionate advice we read as new parents. We give this often as gifts to our friends. This edition has all the advice and how-to's in it that Dr. Spock has always been famous for. It covers common medical questions about diaper rash, diarrhea, dental care, and more, and it also touches sensibly on parenting issues, too, like school and learning problems, and raising nonviolent children.

Dr. Spock used to say to trust yourself, meaning many new parents know more than they think they do. Know enough to buy this invaluable book.

Best Baby Buy

The Baby Book: Everything You Need to Know About Your Baby from Birth to Age Two

Author: William Sears, Martha Sears (Contributor)

List Price: $21.95

Publisher: Little Brown & Co.

This hefty, yet totally comprehensive guide will provide new parents with information about caring for baby. William and Martha Sears are child-care experts who offer a unique approach to parenting, called "attachment parenting." They stress bonding with your child and give advice on responding and caring for your child. *The Baby Book: Everything You Need to Know About Your Baby from Birth to Age Two* focuses on a baby's five needs: eating, sleeping, development, health, and comfort. There's a wonderful blend of professional and personal experience presented here (they're parents of seven). This is a good guide for a growing family.

Complete Book of Mother & Baby Care

Author: Canadian Medical Association

Price: $39.95

Publisher: Readers Digest Association of Canada

Another very good guide to caring for baby put together by the Canadian Medical Association. It also covers mom herself which is really nice to see included.

Best Baby Buy

What to Expect the First Year

Authors: Arlene Eisenberg, Heidi Eisenberg Murkoff, Sandee Eisenberg Hathaway

List Price: $13.95

Publisher: Workman Publishing Company

Those creators of the bestseller, *What to Expect When You're Expecting,* are at it again. This time, the three authors, all mothers, encourage and calm in their rather large (all 671 pages) guide to that first important year of baby's life. It moves along chronologically, is easy to digest and is broken down into informative sections. We like the recipes, the useful charts and remedies, and the complete index. If this book has a weakness, when we used it as fledgling parents, we sometimes felt it divulged more than we wanted to know. However, if you like to have complete information at your fingertips and liked their other books, than this would be a great resource for you to delve into.

Advice for Moms and Women

There are also some books for moms and women who take on too much or who contemplate too much. For those of us who are like that, we heartily recommend: *Meditations for New Mothers* by Beth Wilson Saavedra (Workman Publishing—$6.95) and *Meditations for Women Who Do Too Much* by Anne Wilson Schaef, Ph.D. (Harper San Francisco—$6.99). Both of these little books are filled with common sense advice and sensible thought.

Aromatherapy, The Bath, Candles and More

You're tired of diaper smells and food smells, and your baby is asleep. Give in; lounge about and try some aromatherapy. You can use incense, candles or a techno-approach like the Norelco Aromatherapy System. Just be sure to keep these products out of toddler's reach.

Aromathology Romance Bath Salts

Crabtree & Evelyn

Soak up the serenity these bath salts with rose oil provide. Pampering yourself with these Crabtree & Evelyn Aromathology Romance Bath Salts might help you think of something besides baby (just for an hour or so).

Budget Buy

Calgon Home Collection

This collection of candles and other home scents at a reasonable cost will help "take you away," away to wherever you can dream of. Calgon is a name many trust and this line of home products, candles, linen and room spray, scented sachets and gel potpourri, allows you to have a scentsational experience. Pick your comforting scent from "Water Lilies," "Morning Glory," "Turquoise Seas" and "Vanilla," among others.

Designer's Choice

Diana Candle

Price: $25.00

Available at: Neiman Marcus Stores

Why not do something nice for yourself and others at the same time? A portion of the proceeds of the sale of the Diana Candle, created in memory of the Princess of Wales, goes to the official charity sanctioned by the late Princess' family. The soft, lovely pink candle burns about 50 hours and gives off the scent of English garden roses, her favorite.

Earth Therapeutics Terry Covered Bath Pillow

Price: $8.00

Available at: Pier 1 Imports

Taking a bath break? Lean back on your terry covered and terribly comfy pillow, it's as simple as that.

Designer's Choice

Healing Garden

(800) 400-1114

We really like the name and the product. Healing is what new parents should be doing. The Healing Garden has introduced what they call "Cold Comfortherapy," holistic fragrances and products infused with eucalyptus and enhanced with botanicals like echinacea and goldenseal and even Vitamin C. Find comfort and relief with bath crystals "Chills Chaser," a vaporizing balm "Unstuff," "Breathe-Deeply" pillow and room sprays. There's even a "Restful Candle," light it and go have a rest. It may be new on the "cold front," but Cold Comfortherapy seems to warm the chills and lets you feel its healing power.

Perfume Isabell's Shimmering Bath Lights

Call 800-ISABELL for stores

Bathing by candlelight is magical. It will invigorate, relax and feel incredibly special. Perfume Isabell's Shimmering Bath Lights are lightly scented votives to put all around your bathroom when baby is asleep and you can feel and smell the magic.

Budget Buy

Simple Escapes™ Aromatherapy

Glade

Pick up some aromatherapy candles and sprays which will help you feel more calm and tranquil. If it doesn't move you to a different state of mind, at least the house will smell delightful. The Simple Escapes™ come in citrus, soothing vanilla and sensual rose and at such a reasonable price, you can afford to keep them all on hand.

Designer's Choice

Pier 1 Aromatherapy Products

Prices: Vary

Available at: Pier 1 Imports

Pier 1 Aromatherapy products are more sophisticated than some of the supermarket brand products, but at a price that's more reasonable than many other exotic-sounding ones. Under the Pier One label there are candles (scented, pillars, columns), incense, room sprays and lots more. There's a Spa Elements of Pier 1 line we really like, too. Walk into any Pier 1, sniff all the different varieties of candles, and bring something soothing home. We really like the Pier 1 Sensual Fragrance Cones and Sensual Candles, a blend of ylang-ylang, sandalwood and jasmine. Of course, cones and candles should be kept away from children, but you'll really appreciate changing the aroma and attitude around your home.

The At-Home Spa and Massage Products

How do you relieve the physical body stress you face after carrying around baby all day? We mention baby massage for soothing your baby but what about soothing you? You and your husband could give each other a nice, relaxing massage. And if you're on your own, don't worry; there are some great products to help massage you.

Homedics Body Basics™

Available at: most Beauty Supply Stores and Drugstores

Body Basics are just what new parents need. Try the Homedics Foot Rejuvenator (Price: $49.99 approx.) because what could be better than a foot massage? Not much, we guess, and this one doesn't disappoint. Homedics makes one of the best—it's easy to use, easy to rinse and very easy to enjoy. The Rejuvenator does just that.

The Muscle Therapist Deep Kneading Massager is a great buy. The Rotating Shiatsu Massager has nine rolling knuckles which simulate the skilled hands of a masseur and two speeds to help soothe those tired parent muscles. It's ergonomically designed for an easy grip and adjustable use. Those skilled masseur hands (simulated) will only set you back $49.95, approximately. Other products include the Homedics Percussion Massager (Price: $49.99 approx.), which is cordless and easy to use. It's a great personal massager. Or try the Heat Wave Thermal Massager with all sorts of attachments (Price: $54.99 approx.) or the Chiropractic Massage Cushion with invigorating powerful massage action.

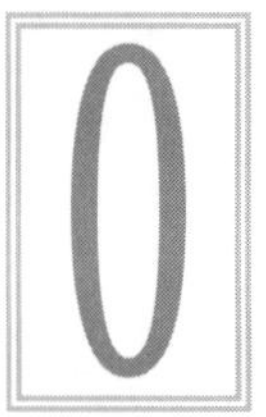rganizing The Nursery and Your Life—Top products to help you organize baby, yourself and your growing family. From calendars to closet organizers and more.

Certainly, not everything in this book is an essential purchase. Your baby is likely to grow and develop because she receives your love and care, not because she has the most stuff. There is something to be said though for your own peace of mind and a well organized, efficient life that gives you some personal time for yourself and alleviates some of the stress occasionally inherent to the addition of a new family member. Here are some of the top products to help you organize your baby, yourself, and your growing home. You'll know what kinds of things will suit you. Some of the things here may or may not be right for your needs or personality. But we recommend that you sift through this list of calendars, closet organizers and more. In all likelihood, you'll see something that will inspire you into a mode of thinking or organization that will be a godsend in what may be a chaotic time in your life. If you are more at ease with the organization of the nursery and family life, it's likely that you'll enjoy and appreciate parenthood and yourself even more.

You work from 9:00 A.M. to 3:00 P.M. everyday; your mom will take baby on Tuesdays if you drop her off; baby has swim class every other Thursday; your partner takes baby to the office on Monday, Wednesday and Thursday afternoon, but you need to get her to the babysitter on those mornings. Life will never be the same. Scheduling for three or more can become a nightmare if you don't get organized. We've found some products to help you do just that—things to help you organize your baby, yourself and your growing family. Check out this myriad of paper and electronic organizers and calendars, and storage solutions and closet organizers. Get into an organizing frame of mind. We bet you'll be able to make some suggestions of your own, too; let us know your favorites.

Managing Our Time and Baby's

We've read a lot lately about time management. We need to learn how to do that for our families so we manage our time and don't waste it. Time is a precious commodity. Steven Covey writes about this subject often. His book, *The 7 Habits of Highly Effective People,* is one of the best-selling self-help books to come about in years. He followed it up with *The 7 Habits of Highly Effective Families.* Buy both and start reading about this common sense approach. Covey's seven habits include being proactive, think win-win and putting first things first. There's even more there; there's a philosophy rooted in the importance of family, which is why we heartily recommend Covey's books.

Planners and Calendars

Now to manage our lives even more effectively, and to motivate ourselves into an organized world, Steven Covey has developed planners and planner systems. Sold through the Franklin Covey stores nationwide, these planners claim over 15 million believers, or users, however you decide to look at it. Purchase the basic "planner" and then customize it for yourself with the additional inserts. If you garden, you can record your planting schedule, and moms with older siblings will especially like the "Child's Play" insert which contains games to occupy little ones.

The staff at Franklin Covey seem knowledgeable and ready to help you plan away stress and organize your life. With 128 stores and counting, you'll probably find one close enough for you to engage in a "counseling session." Employees will assess your needs and determine which inserts, etc. will best suit your lifestyle. And if you're the nervous type, not wanting to put all of your crucial information in one little book, Franklin Covey will assist in your Palm Pilot purchase geared up to make copies of your records. So go ahead and prioritize.

Another planner that might be focused on your needs is the Feminine Focus™ calendar organizer, sold at many bookstores.

Software

Address Book 6.0

Price: $19.95

Manufacturer: Broderbund

Stop losing all of those important phone numbers and addresses! You can access names, addresses, phone numbers and more with the ease of a click of the mouse! The Address Book 6.0 is really family friendly—you can input up to six children's names. Imagine how easy it is to do a mailing for that first birthday party with the smart data entry and mail merge. You'll be keeping in touch and doing it with ease.

Calendar Creator 5.0

Price: $29.95 (CD—Win95)

Manufacturer: The Learning Company

Calendar Creator 5.0 is a calendar making software program which will help you organize, manage and track those dates and appointments you keep forgetting. You can even add graphics, video and sound easily with drag-and-drop. There's an address book, event lists you can print out and you can even download web events adding them to your own schedule. Go ahead and create your own calendars, any size and any style.

MemoirTRACKER

Price: $24.95

Manufacturer: Lean Software

(888) LeanSoft

MemoirTRACKER is an award-winning PC software solution to help make your personal and family life run smoother. Lean Software likes to say it's been designed for "Mom." Most people can get it up and running in only a few minutes and without a manual. It even won a National Parenting Center Seal of Approval (1997). Lean Software seems to understand that perhaps no one has more appointments, commitments and scheduling nightmares than today's parents. MemoirTRACKER was designed to handle and organize all sorts of home record-keeping information. It's really an ideal family information management tool. A downside we found was that it's only PC friendly, but hopefully this is something that will be developed for fanatics of the Macintosh, especially as the iMac computer is becoming the most popular computer for families.

Organizing Home

Even kids learn the word "chore" really early. If it's not part of their vocabulary, they certainly understand the concept, as housework odds and ends deprive them of the quality time with Mom or Dad that they crave. They also learn the feelings we seem to associate with that word—"avoid," "dislike," and "responsibility." Try to introduce chores to even a toddler (with lots of help and love) and aim to display a more positive image when doing that third load of laundry. Remember you're laying some "chore" groundwork for the future. If the family shares appropriate household and family responsibilities, then there'll be more quality time together—and if you've never tried it, doing those unpleasant jobs around the house can sometimes be fun when everyone pitches in. Has your partner learned the word "chore"? Are you both sharing the responsibilities? Do you feel overwhelmed? There are some really good, common sense books which might help you learn how to cope with organizing your household. Try a few of these:

Chores Without Wars: Turning Dad and Kids from Reluctant Stick-in-the-Muds to Enthusiastic Team Players

Authors: Riki Intner and Lynne Lott

Publisher: Prima Publishing

We don't assume that Dad isn't always a help, but aside from the title, this book offers some nice team approaches to getting the chores done and without too much struggle.

Organize Your Family! Simple Routines That Work for You and Your Kids

Author: Ronnie Eisenberg

Publisher: Hyperion

Eisenberg's goal is to help you get your family's physical and psychological clutter under control with simple, common sense routines.

On to your home—you need it to run more efficiently and be tidy and organized. You're finding storage a problem and your closets are totally out of control. Where do you start? What do you do with all of baby's belongings?

Here are some products and companies geared up to help families get themselves organized and efficient:

Storage Solutions—Closets, Shelves and More

Some of us seem to work more efficiently and more productively when our workspace is clear and organized. The same holds true for the home. A few trips to stores like Office Depot and the Container Store and we came home with all the organizing gear we needed. Just make the time to get it done—organizing takes some guts. You need to dig deep; the more shelving and storage solutions you can come up with, the easier it will be to put things back into place. So do that spring cleaning and organizing any time of year you have the energy and enthusiasm. Here are some other helpers:

California Closets®

(847) 541-8666

www.calclosets.com

Call in the experts! California Closets® will come into your home, survey your needs, maximize your available space and come back to install your custom storage systems. California Closets® builds storage for pantry, laundry rooms, nurseries, home offices, and more, and does it using quality materials and good design principles.

The Container Store

(800) 733-3532

Hopefully there's a Container Store near you, especially if you are a "do-it-yourself-er." The Container Store has more gadgets, gizmos, boxes and, of course, containers than we've ever seen before, all of which will help put you into the spring cleaning mode. As for closets, they also have in-store consultants ready to help you use every inch of closet space effectively.

Eames® Hang-It-All

Price: $135.00
Available through: The Museum of Modern Art Catalog
(800) 447-6662

Hang it all, where do you put all of baby's stuff? The Eames, the famous designing pair, knew. They designed this playful, functional rack back in 1953, yet it's fresh and colorful and perfect for today's nursery. It's made in the U.S. of painted steel-wire rods capped with large and small painted maple balls. The hardware is included and it's easy to hang.

Hold Everything®

(800) 421-2264

Call for a catalog right away! Hold Everything does—it has containers and storage solutions for just about anything we might collect, own and pile up. There are storage two-ers, taborets, desk accessories, trunks, closet organizers and much more. The prices are reasonable and the quality fine. We are constantly finding pieces of equipment to make maintaining our home easier.

On-Line Organizing Visit these sites which offer advice for organizing kids' spaces as well as other areas of your home:

1,2,3 Sort It
www.123sortit.com/RO

The Dollar Stretcher
www.stretcher.com/stories

The Get Organized! News
www.tgon.com

Has the Clutter Bug Got You?
www.web-oats.com/clutterbug

The Blossoming of Baby

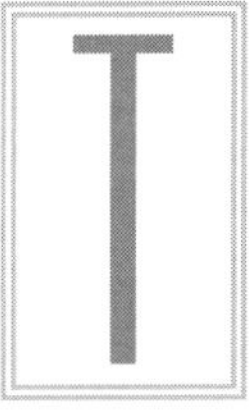

oys—The best learning toys, the best new toys, the classics.

Are toys arriving for baby already? Have you received lots of black and white toys? What is an "educational" toy? Should you pick classic, constructive, or familiar toys? Are your baby's toys age-appropriate, not to mention safe and durable? Should you be collecting Beanie Babies or Barbie dolls? How do you choose between Playskool and Playmobil?

The selection of toys is far from child's play. There exists an ever-increasing plethora of choice. Although we all know in our hearts that playing with our baby will be far more important to her development and well-being than any toy, the selection of that first teddy bear is an overwhelming decision. (We went with Winnie the Pooh, a sentimental decision).

The most important guide we can provide is that toys should fit your infant and toddler's interests and abilities, not your own. Good toys can help develop problem-solving skills, nurture creativity and build fine motor skills. Provide a variety of playthings and materials and rotate them, keeping them fresh and interesting. Be sure you don't shy away from a musical toy just because you cannot carry a tune. Your baby won't mind, by the way, for she likes the sound of your voice.

Also remember to provide the right toy at the right time. Most toys come with age-appropriate recommendations. Use them as a guide, but remember baby just might not be ready for that next step. Don't rush your child—she will be the best judge of readiness for a new challenge.

Your baby is already exploring and delighting in the use of all of her senses, and is also slowly learning to control her body. Baby will proudly learn to stand. Play is constant as baby is becoming more and more aware of her world. The very foundation of baby's intellectual, social and physical development is play. So keep in mind our basic criteria for good toys for encouraging play: variety, fun, learning, value, durability, and of course, safety.

What about those black and white toys? Just what is an educational toy? While we all want to give our children a head start, the American Academy of Pediatrics has issued a warning regarding deceptive advertising of toys as "educational tools." The best early education you can offer your baby is your time. Play with her often and teach her how to explore, to discover and to create. After all, who hasn't seen a set of pots and pans pulled out from the kitchen become a symphony of fun and learning? So look instead for opportunities to provide and establish educational variety with your baby—just don't forget to have fun.

Best Toys for Babies

- have bright colors, smiling faces, and lots of patterns and textures
- are sturdy and lightweight
- are washable
- play music, soft melodies or lullabies
- allow teething but are too large to fit into baby's mouth
- are tactile, providing a variety of experiences (i.e. soft, furry, shiny, smooth, rough)
- are easy to grasp
- are responsive, showing basic cause and effect. Baby interacts with toy and something happens.

For crib and car toys, look in "Gearing Up—Crib Toys" and in "Going Places With Baby—Car Seat Toys." Pacifiers and rattles can be found in "Soothing Baby."

So why have we included these so-called "developmental, educational" toys on our list of favorites? They do offer your baby multisensory stimulation and they do encourage learning. They have been developed with all of baby's senses in mind, as well as baby's developing physical and intellectual skills. So go ahead and pick up one or two of these. Just don't make it the only type of toy available.

Here are some of the toys for babies we admire and why:

Developmental Classics

All of these are classic toys and those you really don't want to forget about including. Drop some hints to family and friends and try those new on-line registries at many web sites.

Baby's First Blocks

Price: $7.99 approx.
Manufacturer: Fisher-Price
(800) 432-KIDS

An essential is Fisher-Price's Baby's First Blocks—they're simple, elegant, ergonomic and not fancy. The bright yellow canister with a lid for sorting is filled with over twenty blocks in three basic geometric shapes. Baby will sort, stack and drop blocks inside over and over again.

Best Baby Buy

Bobo Ball© D. Silverglate

Manufacturer: Pappa Geppetto's Toys
(800) 541-1345
Ages: 6 mos. and up

Silk, stretchy, musical—this spiral is easy to grip, pull and chew on. Buy one in stripes or one in dots, or double your baby's pleasure and explore both. The Bobo Ball is a never-ending circle of fun.

A never-ending circle of fun!

Cool Classic

Double-Feature Mirror®

Manufacturer: Wimmer Ferguson
(800) 541-1345
Ages: Birth to 24 months

We love the Double-Feature Mirror® with its durable graphics display. Curiosity is a wondrous thing and your baby will find the Double-Feature Mirror® curiously satisfying and stimulating. The large mirror on the front will encourage your baby to develop a sense of self while the stimulating black and white patterns on the back will encourage all sorts of visual activities. Developmental value aside, we also like how easy it is to clean and take along, so baby can investigate and play with it often. Oppenheim Toy Portfolio Blue Chip Classic Award Winner and the Canadian Toy Council's Highest Rating.

Seeing Double? The Double Feature encourages visual activities.

Best Baby Buy

GymFinity

Price: $40.00

Manufacturer: Today's Kids

Available through catalogs like: the Baby Catalog of America

In its eighth year and imitated widely, the GymFinity is a classic in our books! This 2-in-1 activity center comes out of one of the oldest toy companies in the U.S., Today's Kids. The colorful, hanging shapes with black-and-white animal characters will attract your newborn's attention and keep her amused. For growing baby, transform the gym into a play center, complete with puzzle pieces, movable gears and shapes to sort. An exploration and activity not to be missed!

Measure Up! Cups

Manufacturer: Discovery Toys

(800) 426-4777 U.S.; (800) 267-0477 Canada

Stacking cups are a perennial favorite—fill them up, stack them, knock them down and do it over and over. Any good colorful, sturdy set will do, but our pick is Discovery Toys Measure Up! Cups. This set of twelve can be stacked, fit inside each other and are easily emptied.

Best Baby Buy

Pattern Pals®

Price: $10.00 each
Manufacturer: Wimmer Ferguson
(800) 541-1345
Ages: Birth to 24 months

Our daughter had a taxi and a cow many years ago as Pattern Pals®. Now the colorful multisensory collection includes a boat, a snake and a fish. Take them anywhere and everywhere. Baby will love the graphics, the fun textures and the surprise sounds. They're cute as is, but did you know they encourage visual activity, eye/hand coordination, gross motor skills and simulate tactile and auditory senses?

Cool Classic

Rock-A-Stack

Manufacturer: Fisher-Price
(800) 432-KIDS
Ages: 6 to 36 mos.

A rainbow of stacking fun, these teethable rings fit over a cone with a rocking base. Classic fun!

Soft Sorter

Price: $19.99 approx.
Manufacturer: Lamaze Infant Development System
(800) 704-8697
Ages: 6 months and up

Sorting and matching are great activities for baby. We've all watched infants sort and then empty out a sorting container and start again. This time the dumping is hushed because all the parts are soft and cushioned. The Soft Sorter is brightly colored and patterned and will attract baby's interest. Gently chiming, squeaking and crinkling, the Soft Sorter is a big award winner—*Parenting Magazine's* 1997 Toys of the Year Award, and *Parent's Magazine* Top Toys of 1997 Award—and we can figure out why.

Baby can sort softly over and over and you won't mind the noise!

Lamaze has taken a truly classic toy and activity and made it developmentally even more appropriate for your infant.

Designer's Choice

Skwish Classic ©1988 Intension Designs Ltd.

Price: $17.00
Manufacturer: Pappa Geppetto's Toys
(800) 541-1345

Hard to describe and hard to put down, the Skwish Classic© has, for over a decade, been a toy that is a must have. The interconnecting rods "skwish" flat and bounce back when baby pushes, prods and pulls. We like it for its simplicity in design but complexity in activity. Babies will find it irresistible and maybe mom and dad will, too (it also relieves stress for adults). Although Skwish© is based on a structural principle of "tensegrity," baby doesn't have to know that. It's a Canadian Toy Council Highest Rating Winner and one of Dr. Toy's Best Classic Toys 1997.

Soft Star

Price: $11.99 approx.
Manufacturer: Lamaze Infant Development System
(800) 704-8697

Out of the Lamaze Phase One set of developmental toys (for babies 0 and up) comes the cutest, happiest star we've ever seen. The brightly colored side smiles back at baby and the flip sides are those black and white and red patterns complete with a mirror which stimulates inquiring little eyes. Soft Star is so very simple, baby will adore it. National Parenting Honors Award Winner.

Star Soft—will you smile down on me tonight?

Cool Classic

Stacking Rings

Price: $19.99 approx.
Manufacturer: Lamaze Infant Development System
(800) 704-8697

The Lamaze Infant Development System Stacking Rings by Learning Curve are beautifully designed. The five cushioned, brightly patterned rings can be slipped on or off the soft post. Watch your baby as she discovers the hidden sound in each ring. We love the patterns and colors (even on the post) and stacking is a classic developmental activity for babies.

Best Baby Buy

Whoozit ©1994 André Sala

Price: $20.00
Manufacturer: Hoopla by André
(800) 541-1345
Ages: Birth to 24 months

What is it? It's a Whoozit!

Fanciful and cheerful, this multi-sensory toy is a winner, an award winner to be exact. This imaginative creature will captivate your child through a variety of different activities. Fun noises, a cheerful mouth that can bend, a hidden mirror and hide-and-seek legs will keep your baby or toddler busy. Whoozit© can travel anywhere baby goes; on the crib, the stroller or on the high chair. For infants, the black and white target is stimulating while the bright and wacky colors and patterns will delight toddlers. There's also a Baby Whoozit© size!

Pretend and Role-Play Toys For Baby

Cool Classic

Chatter Telephone

Price: $8.99 approx.
Manufacturer: Fisher-Price
(800) 432-KIDS

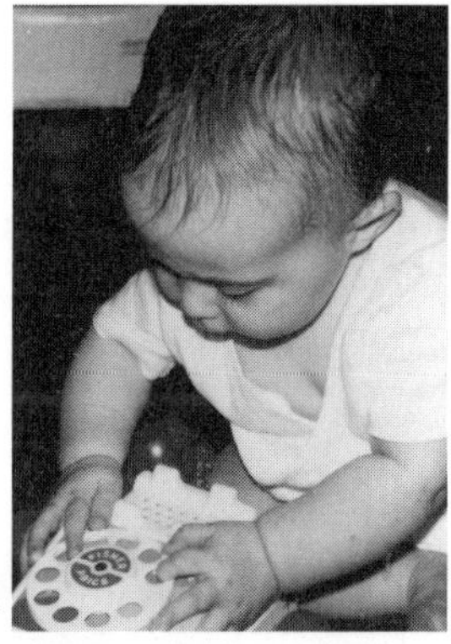

Baby will chat all day.

Baby will chat away on this classic pull toy! No one does a telephone better than this simple, intoxicating Fisher-Price version. And it's the same classic *you* made calls on, with moving eyes and a ringing dial!

Inchworm

Price: $14.95
Manufacturer: Lamaze Infant Development System
(800) 704-8697
Ages: 0 to 36 months

The little inchworm puppet helps parent and baby engage in pretend play and what a delight it is to find the hidden rattle. It can double as a tape measure to determine baby's early growth too. Simple, cute and well designed, this little worm will inch its way into baby's heart.

Lights 'N Surprise Laptop

Price: $19.99 approx.
Manufacturer: Fisher-Price
(800) 432-KIDS
Ages: 6 months and up

Fisher-Price's Lights 'n Surprise Laptop teaches a playful, colorful lesson in cause and effect. Help baby identify her 1-2-3's and A-B-C's on a light-up screen with a "roller" mouse and clicking cheese. Microban antibacterial protection helps keep those germs away. Lights, sound and music—baby's computer does as much as yours!

Peek-a-boo Puppet

Price: $14.99 approx.
Manufacturer: Lamaze Infant Development System
(800) 704-8697

Here are two of our favorites things—a puppet, and a chance to play peek-a-boo. What could be better than that? Winning *Child Magazine's* Best Toy of the Year Award 1997 isn't bad. But this is one great high-contrast puppet—the rabbit reverses into a turtle and you can play peek-a-boo with your baby over and over.

Peek-a-boo! Where did Mr. Rabbit go?

Soft Keys

Price: $7.99 approx.
Manufacturer: Lamaze Infant Development System
(800) 704-8697
Ages: 3 months and up

Even at the earliest ages, children want to imitate—our daughter was fascinated with keys. That's probably why we really like the soft keys by Lamaze. They're simple and soft for baby to grasp and play with, and you can help her begin to recognize and understand names and uses of objects. Just wait until baby unlocks the hidden sounds of each key!

Stuffed Toys—"Plush" for Baby

We walked through FAO Schwartz recently and the salesperson came over to tell us all about the "plush" toys we were looking at: collectibles, pillow pals or buddies, bean bag style, plain old stuffed animals in every shape, form and style. By the time your baby is two, you'll have more "plush" around than you'll know what to do with (we hint about that in "Organizing the Nursery"). Stuffed toys are friendly, comforting and help baby feel secure. Just remember that when your baby is a newborn, keep them out of the crib—they are a suffocation hazard. Be sure to check age ranges, which are indicated on the toys tags.

Best Baby Buy

Gloworm

Price: $9.99 approx.
Manufacturer: Playskool®
(800) PLAYSKL

A true friend to light the way to bed, Gloworm will be a baby's best friend. Mom's best friend, too, because its body is made of cuddly soft nylon fabric that's easy for baby to hold. With a big friendly reassuring smile, Gloworm will light up when baby gives it a little squeeze.

Mommy Bear

Price: $17.95
Manufacturer: Dex Baby Products
(800) 546-1996
Ages: Newborn +

Mommy Bear is a soft friend for baby. Soft rhythmic sounds (from real recorded sounds of the womb) will help baby to relax and sleep. Mommy Bear is hypo-allergenic, and runs on a battery that plays for 40 minutes and then shuts itself off. The adjustable loop allows you to hook Mommy Bear to the crib, or even on the diaper bag (we know baby will want her near).

Powder

Price: $11.00
Manufacturer: babyGund
(732) 248-1500
Ages: Birth and up

Infants love to snuggle up to this scented (baby powder smell) teddy bear. Someone to cuddle who smells just like baby!

Big Baby Play

Activity centers, playmats, push and pull toys and large scale constructive toys are all great additions to baby's toy collection. The different scale offers new challenges for your infant and new opportunities to grow, develop and succeed.

Activity Centers, Playmats and Pillow Props

Best Baby Buy

Boppy™

Price: $30.00 approx.
Manufacturer: Camp Kazoo. Ltd.
(303) 526-2626; also available at many baby stores

The Boppy™ is a very versatile product. It's a great nursing pillow and it's also a great help in propping baby up before she can sit up on her own. The Boppy™ comes in a variety of fabric designs, all of which are machine washable. Who will love Boppy™ more—you or your baby?

Who will love Boppy™ more—you or your baby?

Designer's Choice

Busy Garden

Price: $40.00
Manufacturer: Hoopla by André
(800) 541-1345

Plant the seeds of the joys of gardening; the Busy Garden is quite the imaginative activity center. Fresh fruits, vegetables and flowers grow in this portable plot of fun. Your little gardener will love using the soft tools to water, rake and hoe. You may not get baby to eat her vegetables, but the busy garden will teach her which ones are which and how much fun gardening play is.

Best Baby Buy

$ Discover and Go Playmat®

Price: $45.00
Manufacturer: Wimmer Ferguson
(800) 541-1345
Ages: Birth to 12 months

For families on the go, this Discover and Go Playmat® combines fun activities with travel capabilities in one versatile toy. Typical of the Wimmer Ferguson line, this mat features all sorts of developmental activities. Baby will love finding the hidden noises and looking at her reflection in the unbreakable mirror. Attach it to the back of the car seat for a traveling activity center. The Discover and Go encourages all sorts of visual and tactile experiences as well as being a mat filled with fun. Folds right into its pouch and is hand washable.

Discover and go with this traveling playmat.

Designer's Choice

Enchanted Garden Playmat

Price: $60.00 approx.
Manufacturer: Manhattan Baby
(800) 541-1345

A garden playmat with bumblebees, butterflies and smiling sunflowers adorning it. Baby will be enchanted by it.

Junior Activity Garden

Price: $54.99 approx.
Manufacturer: Little Tikes Co.
(800) 321-0183
Ages: 9 months to 3 years

Too late for my daughter, now ten, Little Tikes has now designed a wondrous garden of delight with its Junior Activity Garden. This circular play station has a swinging door, a squeaky doorbell and even a tunnel for baby to crawl through. Vegetables in the garden are soft, squeezable, and can be sorted by shape. The chirping birdhouse is an added delight. Made of brightly colored molded plastic, the activity garden is a cinch to wash and tidy.

See & Sleep

Price: $49.99 approx.
Manufacturer: Lamaze Infant Development System
(800) 704-8697
Ages: Birth to 12 months

Round up your baby in the See & Sleep.

Baby can nap or spend some time looking at all the visual treats on the See & Sleep. It's a soft little corral with all sorts of encouraging activities to keep baby interested and stimulated. The black and white graphics reverse to brightly colored animals on the other side. See & Sleep comes with a carrying bag in case baby becomes hooked on it (we think she will).

Large Constructive Toys

Best Baby Buy

Build & Store Block Table & Chair

Price: $35–45.00 approx.
Manufacturer: Step2
(800) 347-8372

Here's the perfect place to deposit all those blocks your little builder has collected. Much better than stepping on them, purchase this inexpensive Build & Store Block Table. It provides the perfect building surface and is sturdy. The side doors fold down for easy access to even more storage below.

Cool Classic

Duplo Baby X-Large Stack 'N' Learn Set

Manufacturer: Lego Systems, Inc.
(800) 453-4652

A great constructive toy is the Lego Duplo Baby X-Large Stack 'N' Learn Set. Your baby will delight in building with this set, which includes animals with rattles inside, a mirrored block, a special spinning piece and a base to pile it all on. A good basic builder.

Push and Pull Toys

Cool Classic

Melody Push Chime

Price: $7.99 approx.
Manufacturer: Fisher-Price
(800) 432-KIDS
Ages: 1 to 3 years

Remember when you pushed along your Melody Push Chime? This cool classic's been around for over 50 years, and it's a great toy despite its age. When kids push it, the Melody Chime's roller spins around, showing off the whimsical animal characters and making those delightful sounds you'll recall instantly.

Cool Classic

Primo Caterpillar

Price: $10.00
Manufacturer: Lego Systems, Inc.
(800) 453-4652
Ages: 6 to 24 months

This little caterpillar will inch along when your baby gives it a push. Stripey Bee and Spotty Ladybug can go along for a ride. This caterpillar is part of the fine Lego Primo line designed for little contractors aged 6 to 24 months. We were so excited when Lego made Primo, since the Duplo collection starts at 1 1/2 years. This new series allows younger toddlers to really explore and build, just like big kids. Transitionally this is fabulous, kids will be hooked on Lego, moving up to the different collections geared for their age! Lego is a classic we admire—our 10-year-old is still playing with hers, and with all the high-tech competition, that's saying an awful lot.

Baby Bouncers

Your infant wants to bounce, bounce, bounce and you can't spend every single minute with her on your knee. Baby bouncers are a good alternative—they save the wear and tear on your own body and baby will really be entertained.

Bouncer Safety Savvy

- Don't put a bouncer near the stairs or on top of the counter or on any vibrating surface.
- Don't put a bouncer on a bed or any piece of upholstered furniture—there's a suffocation threat if the infant topples over.
- Don't move your child when she's in a bouncer—it is not a carrier.

Read more in our toddler section about walkers and saucers and safety hazards.

Deluxe Soothing Bouncer Seat

Price: $24.00
Manufacturer: Fisher-Price
(800) 432-KIDS

This is a colorful, busy bouncer, with a removable toy bar. It's also soothing (a battery-powered vibrator powers up a car ride feel).

Cool Classic

Exersaucer Baby

Price: $40.00
Manufacturer: Evenflo
(800) 432-4453

This unusual styled saucer can rock baby or be braced to stand still. One of the best features is that once your baby outgrows the saucer (at around six months), take out the gym bar. Baby can be entertained while lounging around.

Outdoor Toys for Baby

Penguin Sled

Price: $20.00 approx.
Ages: 9 months to 2 years
Manufacturer: Step2

Even baby wants to sled along, pulled by mom and dad. The Penguin Sled will allow baby to have a safe, snowy experience. It's lightweight and easy to manage with a sturdy cord. The high sides, back support and safety belt all help hold your baby. After all, everyone wants to play In the snow.

Take your snow baby sledding.

Toddler Toys

Your toddler is suddenly mobile. She wants to push, prod and pull. She likes to shake, bang and drop her toys. Your growing child adores playing peek-a-boo and will begin to wave good bye. Provide toys that will inspire, activate and support both her physical and intellectual advances.

What toddler doesn't want to play pretend? Toys where tots can mimic mom, dad or sibling will help them in role-playing, which is great for building self-esteem. Toddlers are perfect candidates for this type of imaginative play. This can be enhanced through the use of puppets, dolls or other role-playing toys. Dolls, soft animals and puppets will be great companions for your child and are good to take on outings. These props and puppets can also help you work on your child's vocabulary and help her develop storytelling skills.

Toddlers love to listen as they make music. Creating sounds is so much fun, you may want to pick up some aspirin along with some instruments like drums, bells, and tambourines.

Simple, easy-to-grasp toys, toys that open and close, fill and spill toys, blocks, and clutch-style dolls are perfect for your toddler at this age. As your child gets older, you might want to share in the construction and design of such toys. Delight, amuse and teach your baby with these wonderful toys:

Best Toys for Toddlers

- will grow and challenge your toddler as she grows
- inspire imaginative play
- offer opportunities for pretend play
- are washable
- play music
- feature pop-up buttons and parts
- are tactile, providing a variety of experiences (i.e. soft, furry, shiny, smooth, rough)
- are easy to grasp, easy to hold onto
- create a space to climb, crawl or slide through or on
- have objects or components to hide, sort, stack, match, and even toss about

- are responsive, showing basic cause and effect—baby interacts with toy and something happens

Some of our ready-to-go favorites for your toddler are:

Little Builders–Constructive Sets

Designer's Choice

Builder System: Racing Car Set

Price: $30.00
Manufacturer: Brio
(888) 274-6859

Easy to grasp, these chunky and delightful pieces (with great illustrated instructions) will help your little one build, assemble, take apart and reassemble all sorts of sturdy wood roadsters. We love the little hammer.

Cool Classic

Duplo Tubes

Price: $18.00
Manufacturer: Lego Systems, Inc.
(800) 453-4652

We couldn't be more delighted that Lego has begun to make really unusual and exceptional Duplo sets for toddlers. These curving tubes and roving ball add a new twist to construction for your little worker. This is a 33-piece set, brightly colored, for junior to connect and construct block creations with all sorts of tunnels. This a great toy to help build learning and motor skills.

Manipulatives

Bigger Family Roller Coaster

Price: $20–30 approx.
Manufacturer: Step2
(800) 347-8372

A full 2 feet high and 4 1/2 feet long, the Bigger Family Roller Coaster isn't for tight spaces but it's toddler high-speed heaven. Sending cars, balls, anything at all down the Roller Coaster is sure to give thrills! It teaches your go faster child how different objects move and reinforces cause and effect. We know the cause, and the effect is thrilling.

Hammer and Nails Bench

Price: $24.99

Manufacturer: Kid Classics—Learning Curve ™

(800) 704-8697

An updated classic cobbler's bench, the Hammer and Nails Bench by Kid Classics is made of beautiful hand-crafted, high quality wood. Your carpenter can hammer one nail in and another pops up so the work and play will go on and on.

Little Shakers

Price: $12.98

Manufacturer: Discovery Toys

(800) 426-4777

Shake, rattle and roll! Your musical toddler can really shake things up with this duo of colorful noisemakers.

Tangiball

Price: $10.00

Manufacturer: Discovery Toys

(800) 426-4777 U.S.; (800) 267-0477 Canada

Sometimes simple things are the best! Pick up one or two of these Tangiballs and squeeze away. Textured activity ball helps toddler develop her grasp.

Pretend and Role-Play Toys (puppets, dolls and more)

Busy Camera

Manufacturer: Gerber Products Co.

(800) 4-GERBER

Smile! The Gerber Busy Camera will keep your little one busy with its spinning balls, sounds, squeaking button, peek-through lens and easy-to-grab handle. Made of cheerful red plastic, this camera is bound to develop into fun.

First Shot Basketball

Price: $20.00–23.00

Manufacturer: Step2

(800) 347-8372

Ages: 1 1/2 years and up

What little superstars wouldn't adore the chance to dunk a brightly colored ball through the hoop! It's nice to see some fitness inspired activities for little ones with big dreams. This Step2 basketball version avoids some of the problems other children's basketball sets had with the netting—First Shot Basketball has a molded plastic hoop, thoughtfully designed and safe. It includes a basketball, and rings a bell when you score. Watch out M.J., junior's at the line!

Little Knotties™

Price: $2.50 each
Manufacturer: Lamaze Infant Development System
(800) 704-8697
Ages: Birth to 24 months

Little Knotties solved a knotty problem: Most bean bag style toys are not appropriate for little tots, but these were designed specifically for young babies. They're made from a variety of textured materials so baby can touch, cuddle and even chew. Encouraging visual activities, these little creatures are machine washable and double-bagged for safety. There's an entire menagerie to choose from, all with a signature knot. We're fond of Marley the Lion, Bumbles the Bee, Whiskers the Rabbit and Patches the Elephant.

Knot for anyone but baby!

Little People School Bus

Price: $14.99
Manufacturer: Fisher-Price
(800) 432-KIDS
Ages: 1 1/2 to 5

You'll spend a lot of time singing "the wheels on the bus go round and round" to your little bus driver. She can drive around town to pick up realistically detailed Little People friends, (a diverse group). Any Little People toy is fun—a garage, a house, the farm—and baby can discover the world through her Little People friends.

Push About Fire Truck

Price: $23.00
Manufacturer: Step2
(800) 347-8372

Your toddler will love these firefighting heroes in their oversized truck (with removable kid-sized handle). It's junior to the rescue!

Teach Me Elmo

Price: $20.00
Manufacturer: Tyco Preschool

We couldn't resist Elmo. Your toddler can squeeze his hand, nose or tummy and hear his sweet giggly voice identifying body parts. Best of all, pucker up when you squeeze his lips, Elmo will give your child a kiss!

Puzzles

Puzzles challenge children and help them strengthen their abstract thinking. As they puzzle over the solution, they will learn how to visualize how it looks completed. Your child will have fun and gain quite a sense of accomplishment when they put that last piece in the right place.

Changing Pieces Puzzle

Price: $11.00
Manufacturer: Small World Toys
(310) 645-9680

Your baby can have so much fun mixing and matching these see-through pieces. She'll create all sorts of silly combinations like putting a monkey on a raft. Get her to tell you some stories about them.

Madeline™ Puzzles

Price: $10.99 each
Manufacturer: Kid Classics—Learning Curve ™
(800) 704-8697

In an old house in Paris . . .

Madeline is a classic, a one-of-a-kind. Here are some fabulous puzzles which capture the beautiful illustrations of your toddler's soon to be favorite stories (if they aren't already). Madeline and her adventures are pictured in these new puzzles which will get your child puzzling over the possibilities. You'll enjoy them, too.

Miss Spider™ Puzzles

Price: $10.99 each
Manufacturer: Kid Classics—Learning Curve ™
(800) 704-8697

These Miss Spider puzzles will catch your toddler in their challenging web.

There are five puzzles available with Miss Spider (based on those award-winning books by David Kirk) and each and every one will entertain and challenge your toddler. These are based on favorite scenes from the Miss Spider stories, and you can even get Miss Spider as a colorful pull toy. Puzzles are toys which offer an educational challenge while entertaining, too.

Thomas the Tank Engine & Friends™ Puzzles

Price: $10.99 each
Manufacturer: Kid Classics—Learning Curve ™
(800) 704-8697

Come aboard with another set of Learning Curve puzzles. This series is based on the award-winning television show, "Shining Time Station." There are five kid puzzles available with Thomas the Tank Engine and his friends, and like Miss Spider, there's even a Thomas pull toy. Sit down with your toddler and help her put Thomas in the right places; it's fun and challenging, too.

Shapes and Sorters

Everyone seems to remember sorting toys. They help toddlers reinforce their basic developmental skills while having great fun, and they play with these toys over and over again. Here are some we think are classics:

Cobbler's Bench

Price: $7.00
Manufacturer: Playskool®
(800) PLAYSKL

Imaginative and constructive play sewn into one cobbler's bench—this is a classic toy and one we always recommend.

Turtle Shape Sorter

Manufacturer: Learning Curve ™
(800) 704-8697

This beautiful purple turtle can stick its head out or push it down and the wooden shapes pop right out of his shell! Your toddler can have fun popping them back in. Matching triangle to triangle, star to star, your little sorter will have a good time learning how to make things fit and just enjoying his new animal friend.

Qubix™

Price: $30.00
Manufacturer: Hoopla by André
(800) 541-1345
Ages: Birth and up

This modern, soft shape sorter looks totally wonderful, and is. Qubix™ is filled with hidden surprises, and new activities and different sounds. Each of the 12 panels has a unique feature like a mirror or a tying lace, and Qubix™ can collapse for traveling. It might not look serious with its wacky colors, but Qubix™ is a serious toy filled with challenging activities and many opportunities for success with sorting and matching.

Hidden surprises!

Stuffed Friends and "Plush"

Hug 'n Wiggle Pooh

Price: $24.99 approx.
Manufacturer: Mattel
(800) 524-8697

Hug Pooh and baby will find Pooh is very responsive. He's plush and cuddly. Squeeze his tummy and Pooh will touch his nose and giggle. He also speaks several phrases. Did we mention Pooh also wiggles? Baby will adore him, hugging and giggling right along with Pooh.

Peabodies

Price: $20.00 approx.
Manufacturer: Manhattan Toy
(800) 541-1345

Soft and cuddly, Peabodies are award-winning creatures your little one will hold onto. The names match the personalities—pick Campbell Camel, Drayton Dragon, Hickory Horse, Gilligan Duck and Gigi Giraffe. The 20" size is nice for hugging and loving, and mom will like their washability.

Every child needs good friends like Peabodies.

Sing Along Blue

Price: $14.95
Manufacturer: Tyco
Ages: 18 months and up

Blue is really adorable, yet most of the Blues Clues products we found were for three-year-olds and up. The little friend is perfect for a toddler—soft and huggable. Press Blue's right paw and she'll play right along, barking in tune.

Toss & Tickle Me Elmo

Price: $38.95
Manufacturer: Tyco
Ages: 18 months and up

We couldn't put Elmo down—we giggled each and every time he did. We know it's silly, and that's exactly why we adore him. Elmo talks and laughs and when your toddler bounces him around, new phrases are activated. Toss & Tickle Me Elmo really helps encourage your little one to speak and interact with Elmo. Caring for a friend like Elmo is really terrific for little Sesame Street fans.

Ride-On Toys, Cars, Saucers and (Hopefully) No "Traditional" Walkers

Toddlers are very interested in being mobile. These toys will meet that need and more. Although walkers are designed to also keep your child upright and help him move about, we haven't found any of the "traditional" style to recommend. Instead of the circular frame and X-frame walkers with all their inherent dangers, we have selected, instead, pushcart styles where the child walks behind, or a saucer style without wheels.

If someone does buy or lend you a "traditional" walker, be sure the brakes work and never leave your child unattended. Let your child use it just for short amounts of time and only until she's walking on her own. Keep checking for exposed points or sharp edges especially on screws and locking devices and be sure the wheels are large enough to help prevent tipping.

Because of the number of injuries in the more traditional, mobile walker and its popularity, some new standards are coming about. Manufacturers will have to meet at least one of the following:

- The walker must be too wide to fit through a standard doorway (of 36 inches).
- The walker must have features which help stop it when it is at the edge of a step.

If we were doing the shopping, we'd select one of the following instead—still offering baby an opportunity to move, ride and be mobile, just in another fashion.

Cozy Coupe II

Price: $40.00
Manufacturer: Little Tikes Co.
(800) 321-0183

Just like the real automotive industry, Little Tikes has just given their best-selling car an overhaul. The new model has been updated with vanity plates, fatter tires, and a remote key with four sounds. The Cozy Coupe II, like its predecessor, is a foot-powered plastic ride-on toy. For $40, this toy will give your toddler a first rate ride and nothing to recharge except junior.

Primo Baby Walker

Price: $25
Manufacturer: Lego Systems, Inc.
(800) 453-4652

Let your baby take some first steps with this lightweight pushcart filled with oversized, colorful Lego Primo pieces. When she tires of stretching her legs, she can empty the cart out and build something really wonderful. This is great fun for a beginning walker and junior construction worker!

Soft Rocking Cow

Price: $39.99

Manufacturer: Little Tikes Co.

(800) 321-0183

Also with a wide stable base and a low center of gravity, the Little Tikes Soft Rocking Cow is a delight for your toddler. It has easy to grip handles and offers a smooth rocking ride. We love that the cow's soft spotted body can be removed easily for machine washing.

Spot's Fire Express

Price: $80.00

Manufacturer: Manhattan Toy

(800) 541-1345

Spot's Fire Express is ready for any emergency. This toddler-sized fire truck rocks gently while taking your little hero off to save the day. There's a clicking steering wheel, a play telephone and an attached water hose. Spot can come off to play and the fire express is hand washable, so Mom likes it too. Sound the bell—here come Spot and Junior to the rescue.

Volkswagen Beetle

Price: $425.00

Available through: Neiman Marcus Stores

We all know the bug is back and now there's an exclusive (translates as expensive) child-sized beetle to drive around in! From Italy, this import has an iron chassis, strong plastic body and automatic transmission. When baby and beetle tire, there's a rechargeable battery (for the car anyway). This isn't for everyone, just for those kids who have to accelerate and whose parents can afford it. Buy just before that big second birthday.

Trikes, Bikes and Wagons

Best Baby Buy

$ Ready Steady Ride-On

Price: $19.99

Manufacturer: Playskool®

(800) PLAYSKL

Playskool has transportation covered with its Ready Steady Ride-On. Your toddler can push it along, ride on it or use it as a first trike. Baby is not always steady—so the wide base in front and the narrow one in back helps keep the Ride-On steady and easy to hop on or off. A great purchase.

Cool Classic

Radio Flyer Classic Red Wagon

Price: $ 56.99 approx.
Manufacturer: Radio Flyer
(800) 621-7613

Over 80 years old and looking great, the sturdy red wagon we all know and love is a classic. Radio Flyer was founded in 1917 in Chicago by Antonio Pasin, an Italian immigrant and cabinetmaker who made his first wagons out of wood. The auto industry prompted the change in 1928 to steel, and Pasin named his toy according to the times—"radio" was for the new, fascinating invention and "flyer" to symbolize the excitement of the airplane and travel. The classic Radio Flyer is always new and exciting. Radio Flyer has also introduced "My First Wagon," perfect for toddler to pull his toys along all by himself.

The Right Start® Safe Trike

Price: $99.95
Available through: The Right Start Catalog
(800) 548-8531
Ages: 2 and up
Weight Limitations: up to 55 lbs.

The only thing we didn't like about this trike is the price, but it does have style and safety features. It has a one-piece, strong tubular steel frame and a low center of gravity for added stability. Those fat tires won't sink into the grass and the scratch-resistant paint will keep the trike looking good even through hard wear and tear. Lots of height adjustments and thoughtful design will help your little rider learn quickly and safely.

Wagon for Two™

Price: $50–60.00 approx.
Manufacturer: Step2
(800) 347-8372
Ages: 1 1/2 years and up

A wagon built for two.

You can pull baby and a friend (real or imaginary) along easily in Step2's great little wagon. If that's not enough space, add on the Tag-Along Trailer.

Outdoor Play Toys and Equipment

Take a careful look at what space you have to devote to big outdoor play areas and equipment. Then look at what's available—we looked at Little Tikes, Step2, Fisher-Price, Hedstrom and Backyard Escapes; they all have some innovative and appropriate outdoor toys and equipment. You will need to decide on the aesthetics of the equipment as well—traditional (i.e. wood) or contemporary, colorful plastics? Whichever you end up with, consider safety first, age appropriateness next and then filter in price, budget, and availability. Here are just a few of our favorites:

8-in-1 Adjustable Playground

Price: $279.99 approx.
Manufacturer: Little Tikes Co.
(800) 321-0183
Ages: 2 years and up

Set this up for baby's second birthday and she'll be thrilled! It's actually eight different playgrounds in one, featuring a swinging door, two slides and a crawl-through-tunnel. Absolutely no tools needed for assembly—isn't that amazing? And it's easy to assemble!

Climb & Slide Playhouse

Price: $49.99 approx.
Manufacturer: Little Tikes Co.
(800) 321-0183
Ages: 1 1/2 years and up

With its easy to climb stairs, your little tot can play and slide all afternoon. There's lots more, too. The Climb & Slide Playhouse has some tunnels and a molded-in mailbox.

Dinosaur Sandbox

Price: $49.99 approx.
Manufacturer: Little Tikes Co.
(800) 321-0183
Ages: 1 year and up

A Triceratops sandbox with four built-in seats for your toddler and friends (real or imaginary). You can empty out all of the sand and easily convert the dinosaur into a pool.

My First Swing Set

Price: $89.99 approx.
Manufacturer: Hedstrom (Available at Toys "R" Us Stores)
Ages: 1 to 3 years

Baby will be swinging away in no time with Hedstrom's My First Swing Set. It has a two-level adjustable deck, slide and ladder. The swing has a seat belt and gliding action. It's fairly portable, too.

Sun and Shade Sandbox

Price: $60.00
Manufacturer: Little Tikes Co.
(800) 321-0183

A beach and cabana right in toddler's own backyard! The water-resistant canopy snaps-on and then becomes a cover when play is over. Your tot can dig to China and stay in the shade.

Best Baby Buy

Tuggy 2 Sandbox & Splasher™

Price: $60–70 approx.
Manufacturer: Step2
(800) 347-8372
Ages: 1 year and up

Baby can chart her course with the Tuggy 2—she's sea-worthy, so to speak. As either a sandbox in a special toddler size and scale, or as a pool, baby will love playing with the steering wheel and more. There's a protective storage cover and it's strong enough to keep 300 pounds of sand clean and dry.

Smocks and Making a Mess Gear

Scribble Center

Price: $20.00 approx.
Manufacturer: Step2
(800) 347-8372
Ages: 1 1/2 years and up

Go ahead and let baby scribble away! Scribbling is great for a child's development and every child has the heart of an artist. It comes fully assembled, folds flat for storage and is inexpensive. It features a chalkboard with a clip for a 12" x 18" paper pad, and a molded-in chalk tray to collect the chalk and dust. The Scribble Center is the perfect size and scale for your budding Picasso, and it's perfectly easy for you to contain and clean.

For budding Picasso's.

Smock

Price: $20.00 ($5.00 for personalizing)
Manufacturer: Hoohoobers
(800) 533-1505

Sometimes good clean fun is messy, so pick up a few of these artist-style smocks from Hoohobbers. The small toddler size will work until age four. We like the leak-proof vinyl front, the long sleeves which will cover clothes and the unique, attached chest pocket. Choose a Jungle Patch, Scottie, Pastel or Primary one and remember to have an extra on hand for neighboring artists who may drop by.

Play and Buy Safe Toys—For Infants and Toddlers

How do you know if toys are safe, especially if toy safety standards are voluntary?

Examine your baby's new toys to be sure they are in sealed packages, and check them for potential hazards. Look for loose or small parts or bolts, wheels, buttons, trim, any decorations which might fall or come off easily and find their way into your baby's mouth. Take a toilet paper roll test: anything that passes through that roll is probably too small for a child under the age of three. Don't forget to do periodic checks, too. Check for cracks, splits and any broken parts or sharp edges. Measure those strings; nothing should be over 12 inches long (a strangulation hazard). Remove packaging immediately as it poses choking and suffocating risks as well. Electric toys have their own hazards so be sure they are stamped UL or ASTM approved.

Don't ignore recalls. Return or repair any toy if it's recalled. Usually you will hear about recalls on the news or they're featured in the newspapers or children's magazines, but if you are concerned about a specific item, call the Consumer Product Safety Commission (CPSC) at (800) 638-2772.

Toy Chests and Boxes

There are so many injuries associated with toy chests—fingers get trapped, lids smash down or children climb in and the lids fully close. Recently, the Consumer Product Safety Commission announced a repair program for over 350,000 toy chests. The Step2 Company will send out a free repair kit to help keep the lid from fully closing on the Big Storage Chest—call (800) 347-8372.

Not only are toy chests problematic, but they aren't really very good for organizing. Almost always the toy your toddler wants will be at the bottom, and everything will come spilling out. So, how can you teach your child to put their toys away without a toy chest? We've found some substitutes we like—all without lids. Toys arranged on low, open shelves will be easy for your little one to get, and maybe even put back. Try storage units with baskets. Or try plastic laundry baskets, which let your youngster see what's inside and are ideal for items like toy trucks or stuffed animals. They are also helpful in those beginning efforts at sorting.

Bigger Family Hamper Toybox™

Price: $20.00–25.00
Manufacturer: Step2
(800) 347-8372
Ages: 1 1/2 years and up

The Bigger Family is part of a series of adorable toys made by Step2. They feature recognizable, cute family members your child will engage in all sorts of role-playing activities. Here in their enlarged state, the boy or girl Bigger Family members help your child keep their toys tidy or their clothes ready to be washed. The head or top lifts off giving easy access to the storage space. They're so cute and so much fun your child will really want to use them.

Baby's Bigger Family friend will help her put her toys away.

Safe and Soft™ Toy Box

Price: $58.00
Manufacturer: Hoohoobers
(800) 533-1505
Ages: Everyone

What this toy box doesn't have makes it one of the best we've seen—no lid! Another nice feature is the stable, trapezoidal shape. Wider at the bottom by 11"; your toddler can pull-up on the sides without pulling this toy box over! There's more, too, as it's generously sized and made of the tough, see-through fabric usually seen on outdoor furniture. It's rugged and water-safe, so go ahead and hose it down. Did we mention it comes in a palette of primary, pastel or all white colors to choose from?

Toy Town or Toy Overload?

Our final thoughts about toys is that eventually your child will have way too many toys. No matter how little or how much you purchase, there's Grandma around the corner getting one more beanie baby to be kept for junior's future. Or yet another give away from a fast food restaurant! Birthdays, holidays, aunts and uncles, reward, treats, and more, more, more until your baby's room is overloaded.

Here are some suggestions to unload, clean out and pare down.

- Send some off to Grandma and Grandpa's house—create a toy heaven away from home.
- Rotate. Often children neglect toys (good toys) because something new has come along. Try to rotate the selection. We used to set out a good constructive toy we didn't think was getting enough attention and sure enough our daughter would sit down and play with it. She never asked why it was out.
- Donate, pare down and be generous to those who might really be in need of toys.
- Select some toys which have longer lives—toys that are additive. Examples are Lego and Brio sets that you can continue to add on to. If there's a zealous family member, it's often good to suggest another Playmobil set, for example.
- Limit. Learn to limit gifts and your generosity. As time goes on, it's delightful when a child has learned that a great gift is a magazine subscription or having a pizza delivered. For birthdays, perhaps baby gets an educational present, a book and just a wacky, wonderful toy. Keep things in balance.

usic, TV and Video:
Music—the best CDs and tapes for baby and you.

Introduction

Music is the stuff to soothe little souls; and often mom and dad, too. Baby begins to recognize her parents' voices while she is still in the womb. Whether conscious of this or not, most parents begin to have a "special voice" for their child even before she's born. There's a vocal intimacy that is a wonderful part of the parent/child relationship. Babies love the sound of voices and music, and they especially love singing (even the ramblings of tone-deaf dad!). Lullabies are wonderful pacifiers and can be magical moments between parent and child as waking hours give way to sleep. Music with rhythm and beat is perfect for dancing and movement with baby. As soon as she discovers how, your baby will love to clap as an expression of joy; the gleeful clapping accompaniment of a child moving to the rhythm of music is an event every parent will cherish. And if there's one thing any young child loves more than clapping to a tune, it's the universally popular sing-a-long. Perhaps you think that some music intended for children is hard on the ears—think again; the joy that music gives your baby will be the source of much delight for you, too. Don't worry that you can't hold a tune; your baby loves your voice. Enjoying music with your family is something that can last a lifetime. From sharing nursery rhymes in early years to attending concerts later, the joy of music is something that can never begin too early.

Here we have recommended some tapes and CDs that are timeless in their appeal to young families. They encourage interaction and expression between parent and child at every level (sometimes it's appropriate to soothe, and then sometimes there's nothing better than a boisterous, bouncy dance!). In addition, we also encourage you to listen to the music you like with your baby (you can even listen to the Beatles or Bach, played for babies—so don't feel badly about having to listen to children's music; musicians have your tastes in mind, too!). An appreciation of music is a fabulous thing to share, whether it be of a chamber orchestra or rock music; just as you share baby's music, she can share yours as well. Don't worry though, as she grows, she'll have very definite musical opinions of her own (trust us on this one!).

Children's Tape Players and More

What will you play these tapes on? There are many tape players designed specifically for use with children, with battery-safe compartments and simple controls. Once again, we always encourage you to keep electrical appliances well out of baby's way, and to be particularly sensitive to baby's hearing when you crank up the stereo (if you are unsure about appropriate volumes, talk to your pediatrician). It's very convenient to have a small portable player that can move about your home, car, playground, beach or wherever you might be. Many of the musical titles come as both CDs and cassettes (sorry, but we couldn't find any 8-tracks!), so you can go with your personal preferences. If you drive a car, music can be the savior of many a trip, taking your baby's attention and allowing you to concentrate on safe driving, particularly on a long journey. Determining whether you should buy a CD or a cassette might depend on the kind of equipment you have in your car. Don't ever forget to have music in the car—and if you do forget, well, you can always sing something yourself. Baby will love it!

Pick out one or two of these players specifically designed with young children in mind. Some have specific purposes:

Crib Cassette Tape Player and Crib Light

Price: $29.99
Manufacturer: The First Years
(800) 225-0382

What a delight! You can easily attach this cassette player to your baby's crib rail, and it's loaded with features you'll appreciate: a 10-minute timer, a soft night-light, and both light and music will shut off. It's child resistant—there's a safety lock on the controls and the buttons. It's a great piece of equipment for the price.

Mother Goose Storyteller Lamp

Price: $70.00
Available through: JCPenney, Baby Catalog of America, etc.

Is it a lamp or a cassette player? It's both, and the adorable goose will lull your child to sleep and then politely shut off. It even includes a 60-minute tape of lullabies and nursery rhymes (it is Mother Goose, after all). As the tape ends, the lamp dims and then turns off. Added features we appreciate are the flexible lamp neck, and the control switch so you can use the cassette only, the light only, or both.

My First Sony

Price: $69.00 approx.
Manufacturer: Sony

The Sony range of electronic equipment is more than suitable for children. It also has the technology and sound of big people Sony stuff. My First Sony screams "I am for you" to a child—it's brightly colored, very strong and it sounds great. It will keep you and your child happily singing along.

Nurserytronics Crib Cassette Tape Player and Light

Price: $30.00
Manufacturer: The First Years
(800) 225-0382

Here's a tape player that easily attaches to baby's crib rail. Soothe baby to sleep with some lullabies. Nurserytronics is thoughtfully designed. Especially appreciated are the night-light and the 10-minute timer for automatic shut-off. There's a child-resistant safety lock on the controls and the buttons. All of that, and it still sounds good!

The Musical Notes

Now that you have the equipment to play some music, what shall you choose? These albums rarely make the charts, but at least one of them will certainly make your top-10 list of favorite things to listen to with your baby. In addition to commercially available releases, we also recommend making your own tapes. When a parent has to go away on a trip, take time to prepare some good-night messages, tell a story or sing a favorite song and record them on your cassette player. These can be great soothers when someone feels far away from your child (and spouse, too). Have grandparents sing on a tape, too. That's a magnificent way to have your entire family feel close together all the time, and music is a wonderful vehicle for doing that. These tapes make wonderful treasures and keepsakes alongside photo albums and other memories.

Classical

Listening to certain classical music, according to research, helps enhance spatial abilities, or so they say. Whether it does or doesn't we don't know for sure, but it gives you and your baby some wonderful listening moments together.

Best Baby Buy

Baby Mozart

Price: $12.95 CD
Available through: The Right Start Catalog
(800) 548-8531
Ages: Birth and Up

This exclusive collection, selected and orchestrated especially for young listeners, will bring musical discovery and enjoyment to your family.

Classical Cats—David Chesky

Price: $10 cassette w/book; $12 CD w/book
Manufacturer: Chesky Records Kids
Ages: 2 to 8 years

Composer and concert pianist David Chesky has created some felines with cartoonish voices to guide young listeners through the orchestra. Kid-friendly excerpts from well-loved works by Tchaikovsky, Grieg and Copeland will add classical music to your child's repertoire. The coloring book reinforces the educational musical experience.

The Mozart Effect: Music For Children, Vols. 1-3 [BOX SET]

Various Artists
Price: $39.00

Two hundred years after Wolfgang Amadeus Mozart's death, French physician Dr. Tomatis discovered a relationship between listening and learning. Remarkably, he found that children develop their listening ability in the womb.

Lullabies and Peaceful Sounds

Ah, the stuff to soothe baby's soul. Here are some that put us to sleep.

A Child's Celebration of Lullaby

Prices: $16 CD; $10 cassette
Music For Little People
(800) 346-4445
Ages: Birth and Up

How else can you tolerate Raffi except in a sampler recording (just joking, Raffi)? A little bit of this and a bit of that, this is an eclectic musical collection with Lena Horne giving her all on the Gershwin standard "Summertime." Samplers are great ways to introduce different strains of music. You'll appreciate hearing some of your favorites like Linda Ronstadt, Aaron Neville, and Ladysmith Black Mambazo. It's a delight for you and your baby.

A Child's Gift of Lullabies

Prices: $16.95 CD; $13.95 cassette
Available through: One Step Ahead
(800) 274-8440
Ages: Birth and Up

These are Grammy Award winning lullabies full of original, beautifully orchestrated music. One side has those soft, lilting vocals to calm baby and the other is instrumental. If you like this one, pick up a few more. The others include the Snuggle-Up Collection, Rock-A-Bye Collection Volumes I and II, Love Songs or Lullabies for Daddy's Little Dreamer.

Dedicated To The One I Love—Linda Ronstadt

Price: $12.99 cassette

Aimed at new parents and their little newborns, Ronstadt can certainly handle the standards in this lovely collection. She delivers with Devoted to You, Angel Baby, Be My Baby and more. *Dedicated To The One I Love* is sweet and airy and isn't it nice for parents to be able to listen to someone of Ronstadt's caliber?

Best Baby Buy

Lullaby Berceuse—Connie Kaldor and Carmen Campagne

Prices: $9.98 cassette; $15.98 CD
Available through: Amazon.com and many children's catalogs

The voices are soothing and the songs, in English and in French, are sweet and familiar. With tender sounds, Kaldor and Campagne have created a memorable lullaby collection for parents and babies. Several of our friends had loved it so much, they kept re-purchasing it for gifts.

Designer's Choice

Return to Pooh Corner: Kenny Loggins Sings to His Son

Prices: $14 CD; $12 Cassette
Sony Music

Children will love it, but so will you. Kenny Loggins is most appealing in this gentle and soft album. With versions of Paul Williams's "Rainbow Connection," Jimmy Webb's "The Last Unicorn" and John Lennon's "Love," mom might be listening more than baby will. Grab your old Pooh bear and baby's new one, and cuddle up together. You'll remember what you liked most about Kenny Loggins—the silky-smooth vocals and beautiful harmonies—and you'll find it all in Return to Pooh Corner.

Moondreamer–Priscilla Herdman

Price: $15.00 CD
Redwing Music
(773) 463-8184

Moondreamer is unusual. Priscilla Herdman provides the relaxing vocals for lullabies for a dog in "Howl at the Moon" and for a toy rabbit in "A Velveteen Love Song." The elegantly arranged "Dreamland" (a Mary Chapin Carpenter song) and (Billy Joel's) "Lullaby" keep you wanting more. Sometimes the unusual is just what you need.

Sleep, Baby, Sleep- Nicolette Larson

Price: $14.95

This selection features the wonderful voice of Nicolette Larson for baby's ears (and thankfully, for yours too). This collection is full of soothing lullabies that mom and dad will enjoy as much as baby. Everyone will be singing along, until everyone falls asleep.

Fun, Entertaining, Jazzy and Other Musical Magic

What do Carly Simon, Susan Salidor, Joannie Bartels, Raffi, and Bananas in Pajamas have in common? They will musically entertain both you and your child and they'll do it in style. Here are some of our favorites:

It's Singing Time: A Collection Of Nursery Rhymes–Bananas In Pajamas

Price: $15.97 approx.
Emd/Capitol
Ages: All Ages

This collection is pretty darn good, upbeat and fun. Bananas in Pajamas, in case you're wondering, is a group from Australia and their songs are just like them—lively, entertaining and energetic. The collection includes all the favorite nursery rhymes from "Humpty Dumpty" to "Hey Diddle Diddle," "Alouette" to "Yankee Doodle."

Cool Classic

By Heart–Susan Salidor

Prices: $10 cassette, $14 CD
Available through: Susan Salidor
(773) 271-5568
Ages: All ages

Music for children and their families is what Salidor says "By Heart" is. And what delightful music it is. You and baby will be singing and humming along to favorites "If I Had A Hammer," "Shortnin' Bread," and "My Father's Song." This album won a Parent's Choice Award—the Rosa Parks song is a stand-out. It's music your toddler will grow into and grow up with.

You and your baby will know these songs by heart!

Cool Classic

Happy Baby Beatles for Babies

Prices: $9.99 cassette; $14.99 CD
Available through: The Baby Catalog of America
(800) 752-9736

The Happy Baby Series has been specially orchestrated for tiny ears. Here's George, Ringo, Paul and John especially for your baby. You'll get used to it!

Designer's Choice

Color Me Singing

Prices: $10 cassette; $14 CD
Available through: Susan Salidor
(773) 271-5568
Ages: All ages

We just had to put all of Susan Salidor's recordings in. This is the newest, and it's bound to hit baby's

Color your baby singing.

top of the charts! We still can't get "At the Resale Shop" out of our heads and classics like "One Potato, Two Potato" and "Skip To My Lou" will keep you singing along. Salidor is a master at putting together an eclectic repertoire which entertains and also empowers young listeners. As an added bonus, there's a fold-out poster of Susan, her friends and her musical instruments to color. When your toddler's ready for crayons, he can fill in the cover art while he sings along.

Cool Classic

Little Voices In My Head–Susan Salidor

Prices: $10 cassette, $14 CD
Available through: Susan Salidor
(773) 271-5568
Ages: All ages

"Little Voices In My Head" will stick in your head! You and your toddler will be singing along to "I Love My Sister," "Tubby Time Medley" and, my personal favorite, the "Boo Boo Blues." It's full of catchy and uncomplicated songs structured around a toddler's day, from rising and finding time to talk to people ("Hello") to playing ("Hambone") to bedtime ("Hannah's Lullaby"). This appealing collection won an Oppenheim Toy Portfolio Award for Best Audio, and *Sesame Street Parents* magazine said it was one of the year's top five children's recordings. (I could have told you that.)

Best Baby Buy

The Best Of Elmo–Sesame Street

Price: $15.00
Sony Music

Cleverly written and just plain fun, this CD of songs sung by Elmo and friends is entertaining and exciting. Tap to the Sesame Street beat! Your baby will love it!

Cool Classic

Walt Disney Records : Children's Favorite Songs, Vol. 1–Various Artists

Price: $9.97 approx.
Disney/Buena Vista Blisterpack

Disney at its best—classic children's songs are brought to life in this collection. You'll enjoy everything from "Home On the Range" to "Pop! Goes the Weasel." If you're a big Disney fan, you'll also want Volumes 2, 3, and 4.

Audio Tapes (Books on Tape)

We wanted to mention books on tape (audio tapes) because they are a good way to encourage reading. Most of the ones we like are geared to three year olds but you might want to begin your collection and have a few on hand. The best way, as we mentioned, is for you to read every day to your child, but we know sometimes you might just run out of steam. Books on tape should not be a substitute for you, but a supplement. They can help encourage good listening skills that toddlers are just beginning to develop. The variety is pretty enormous—everything from Dr. Seuss to Disney in Spanish. We purchased many of the Disney collections because we liked the little booklets that came with them—our daughter could easily follow along with their page turning hints. We added in a sprinkling of classics, some Seuss, some nursery rhymes and even Mother Goose, and pretty soon we had a library of books on tape. At the beginning, practice listening skills with your little listener; sit together and see how she does. If she is so squirmy she can't sit through any of it, she might not be ready. Try a little bit at a time and before you know it, she'll be listening on her own (of course you'll want to know how it all turns out, too).

Television and Videos

Having a baby leads to many decisions, and one to think about now is television, music and videos. How much? How little? You might already be concerned with how much your child should watch TV, and what shows to select. There is a lot of good TV out there with the increase of children's programming on network, cable and independent stations. Look for an educational icon (different for each station) to flash on the screen before a show starts, indicating that the station rates the program educational. Your child will also be creating viewing habits (which may last her entire youth) so keep that in mind when you plunk her down in front of Sesame Street. As for the violence, guns, war etc. on television, remember if we pay close attention to what our children are watching, our children will be fine. After all, we like TV ourselves. The key would seem to be in monitoring and selecting appropriate, both age and content, television and videos. To judge a show's educational or "teaching" value, watch it first and ask yourself if it teaches a lesson, has diverse characters, doesn't stereotype, doesn't demonstrate violence, doesn't use slang and doesn't show unsafe behavior.

According to the American Medical Association. excessive television watching among our children can lead to insomnia, increased violence, poor school performance, decreased attention span (except perhaps to TV) and increased use of tobacco and alcohol. Think hard about these studies now. Then create a wonderful, entertaining video library and most importantly, monitor television time and content. Make this a habit for you and your child.

Whatever your personal choices lead you to—no television except for public/educational viewing or limited watching options—try to watch TV together. Keep in mind that no television at all might produce adverse reactions, particularly when children are older. Some families have no TV times and also set viewing schedules such as our Friday evening sessions. A recent school project taught my daughter that there were as many as 40 commercials in one half-hour show (she thought mostly for "stuff" she didn't need). Average American children watch too much, this we know; an average of three hours a day (240 commercials and we wonder why our children ask for all sorts of "stuff")!

Adventures in Wonderland

(Disney Channel)

You may wonder about the portrayals of Lewis Carroll characters in this show, but it is a show children respond to. The music is fun to listen to.

Bear in the Big Blue House

Ages: 2 to 6 years

Disney Channel

A seven-foot-tall honey of a bear is the charming host of this Disney series. He'll engage your little viewer with read-alouds, songs and animal facts and figures. From the time your child enters through a large open door, she'll feel comfortable and welcome.

Pappyland

The Learning Channel

We like the encouragement of art as Pappy (Michael Cariglio) guides his little viewers through coloring a drawing.

Sesame Street

PBS

We know Sesame Street is a classic, fast paced and educational. It also came first, now there are over 400 children's shows. To compete in this ever enlarging and increasing market, Sesame Street is being revamped. This year with Big Bird turning 30, the show debuted "Elmo's World," a little show-within-the-show. It's 15 minutes of fun and energy and is perfect for toddlers. Sesame Street now has fewer video clips and more story lines. There's more time spent with the ever-adorable Muppets and more energy devoted to showing social skills. Your little one will be entertained and will also learn about sharing, manners and how to keep trying (even when you're 30).

Teletubbies

Targeted Ages: 1 to 4

PBS

You may not be able to stomach Teletubbies but little ones do (over and over). The Tubbies are cute little things who play in a field of flowers. The sun has a face a child would draw. The TV sets in the Tubbies' stomachs display segments of the show where real children play and explore. Often the Tubbies will yell "Again!" after a segment ends and indeed, it plays once more. Shows such as this are often criticized for trying parental patience. Undoubtedly though, most children react in a very positive and delightful way to television shows such as this (as part of a carefully balanced diet of varied activities).

Wimzie's House

PBS

Meet the wonderful world of Wimzie! She's spunky and perky and her show is award-winning. Wimzie and friends gather at her house for child care where social and family issues are faced. Learn about sharing, trust and diversity and don't forget fun and song. This is the number one show in Canada and look out, U.S.—Wimzie's here to stay!

Zoboomafoo with the Kratt Brothers

PBS

Those wacky and wild Kratt brothers are now on a PBS pre-school show called "Zoboomafoo." It just premiered and we have high hopes for it. Martin and Chris Kratt and all of their animal friends meet at Animal Junction and it looks like your child should meet there, too.

Blue's Clues on Nickelodeon and The New Adventures of Winnie the Pooh on ABC and the Disney Channel are both good shows, but earmarked for children beginning at age three. Wait a bit. The same goes for those Rugrats.

Mom and Dad TV

We thought we'd mention the new trend of parenting television beginning to crop up. On FX, the newest programming includes a parent hour brought to you by the experts at *American Baby* and *Healthy Kids* magazines. What should you do when baby wakes you really early on the weekends? Try tuning in on Saturday and Sunday mornings (check your local listings) to "The American Baby Show" and "The Healthy Kids Show"; 60 minutes of parenting power.

The Family Video Library

VCRs let you create a library of appropriate material. For starters, you might want to pick up a copy of *Leonard Maltin's Movie & Video Guide* (Signet, $7.99) or *Jeffrey Lyon's 101 Great Movies for Kids* (Fireside, $11.00). Along with those guides and our suggestions, you will build a library of videos that will enter-

A "Smart Start" is Babyscapes™ Dancing Balls, moving to the rhythm and beat of classical music, holding baby's attention.

tain, use mild language, avoid excessive violence and be tolerable for you to sit through (often over and over again).

Designer's Choice

Baby & You

Price: $19.95
(888) 8-BABYNU

Baby & You gives you and your baby a wonderful workout, together. Mom can get back into shape and share quality time with her little one (baby is worn in a front carrier throughout the routine). Instructor Kathy Stevens divides the workout into five segments. Do them all at once or separately. Imagine getting a cardiovascular workout or toning those muscles while feeling really close to your infant! Go ahead and work up a sweat—together.

Baby Einstein

Price: $14.95
I Think I Can Productions
(800) 793-1454
Ages: Birth to 1 year

Did you talk to your tummy while you were pregnant? If so, this video is for you. Baby Einstein is all about exposing your baby to many languages before she can even speak. Conceptually, the video is based on recent research which suggests that the sounds of languages can help make new connections in the infant brain's auditory cortex. Whether it will or not, the English, Russian, Hebrew and French soundtrack is fascinating. The nursery rhymes, alphabets and counting are accompanied by bold and colorful objects moving on screen. Some sort of connections will be made. It's pretty intriguing stuff.

Best Baby Buy

Baby's Smart Start™

Price: $14.95
Babyscapes™
(888) 441-KIDS
Ages: 3 months and up

We all want our babies to have a "smart start," and this is just the video to help parents stimulate baby all through that very important first year. Baby's Smart Start™ was so intoxicating we sat watching mesmerized until our daughter said "what are you watching?." Six carefully selected classical musical arrangements accompany computer-generated red, black and white recognizable shapes. These dance and move to the rhythm and beat and hold baby's attention (and ours, too). There's even an informative guide about stimulation and the Smart Start™ but we say put that video on and sway to the music along with baby. It's an instant classic (as is their second video, Celebration of Color)!

Barney's Great Adventure

Price: $23.00
PolyGram Video
(800) 367-7765
Ages: 2 to 6 years

We think Barney gets a bad rap; he's happy and upbeat and bursts into song. This may not be your baby's foray into great music, but what Barney does do well is engage your child. The combination of the purple dinosaur and his friends is honest and appealing in this great adventure. The scenery is great, too. Just keep in mind your little one will love and adore Barney and thankfully she will grow out of it! Until that time, this is a good musical choice to pick up just before your baby turns two.

Cool Classic

The Best of Kermit on Sesame Street

Price: $12.98
Sony Wonder
(800) 221-8180

We had to include Kermit! You can buy this for your toddler's upcoming second birthday. Kermit is winning Frog of the Year at a gala event and you and your little one are invited to view some of the best of Kermit's 30 years on Sesame Street. "It's Not That Easy Being Green" we all know and adore. Kermit is a wonder—a Sony Wonder.

Cool Classic

Elmopalooza!

Price: $13.00
Sony Wonder
(800) 221-8180
Ages: 2 to 8 years

Elmo is just an adorable excuse to make this musical tribute to Sesame Street. It's an hour long extravaganza, or Elmopalooza if you will, and the celebrities will brighten it up for moms and dads, too. Your child will sing along, again and again.

Designer's Choice

Exercise with Daddy and Me

Price: $14.95

Available through: (888) 741-BABY

Another great fitness video for your library, this one shows dads how to bond with their baby through movement, music, massage and exercise. It's instructional, and full of good information about the importance of dad in baby's life. It's a perky award winner, a 1998 Parent's Choice Honor.

Here Come the Teletubbies: Dance with the Teletubbies

Price: $15.00 each

Ages: 1 to 4 years

Warner Home Video

Okay, you may have had enough of Laa-Laa, but your baby can't get enough. Two new video releases will allow your child to see the Teletubbies over and over. "Again" they'll cry. In "Here Come the Teletubbies," the creatures try to deal with a theft of "tubby custard" and a toaster gone haywire. We like the second tape better—junior can copy the simple moves and dance to the upbeat (yet generic) music. We always find ourselves saying we can barely live through Barney and Teletubbies but these videos do provide some reassuring and familiar explorations about respect and learning.

Hey, That's My Hay!

Price: $13.00

Ages: 2 to 8 years

Farmer Small Productions

(800) 968-2261

Created by a Massachusetts woman trying to save her family farm, little viewers will learn just how hard it is to make hay from start to finish. It's quite adorable with a cranky old cow, lovely pastoral scenes and carefully chosen banjo, harp and fiddle music to accompany it.

Maurice Sendak's Little Bear: Parties and Picnics

Price: $9.95

Paramount Home Video

Ages: 2 to 6 years

What your little one adores about Little Bear on TV, she can now watch over and over again on video. There's cheerful, bright animals, little endearing plots (with happy endings) and pretty good animation at work here. There are four tales where Little Bear and his gang learn to cooperate and help one another despite being so different from each other. Nice lessons for baby to learn.

Best Baby Buy

Miracle of Mozart™

Price: $14.95

Babyscapes™

(888) 441-KIDS

Ages: 3 months and up

Babyscapes™ present their third video, the Miracle of Mozart™. Teaching numbers and shapes with computer generated graphics, accompanied by Mozart, of course, this video will have your child stimulated and learning. Not to mention your child will be listening, and what can be better than that? We really enjoyed all of the Babyscapes™ videos and they certainly do give babies "smart starts."

Cool Classic

Peter Pan

Price: $19.99

Walt Disney Home Video

Some Disney movies, like Bambi, are better for older children. Peter Pan flies for any age! Peter is the boy who won't grow up who helps the Darling children fly off to Neverland. The adventure begins; an Indian princess needs rescuing, the Lost Boys need to be saved and along the way, Captain Hook needs to be taught a lesson or two. The animation is terrific, the story full of fantasy and flight and the music is memorable!

Cool Classic

Sesame Street Sleepytime Songs & Stories

Price: $8.99

Sony Wonder

Your toddler will enjoy seeing how everyone on Sesame Street goes to bed—each character has a little routine (Big Bird has to fluff his nest and Ernie dances himself to sleep). Enjoyable songs and stories will inspire you and your little sleepyhead to find her own way of going to bed.

Designer's Choice

So Smart! A Learning Video for Babies

Price: $14.95
Ages: 3 months to 3 years
Available through: The Right Start Catalog
(800) 548-8531

There are a few of these get a head-start educational forays. But So Smart! is smartly designed; the animation is engaging, and the simple shapes encourage baby's visual tracking, recognition and memory. Music is of course classical including Bach, Beethoven and more. Chosen among *Parenting* magazine's "Best Videos of the Year."

Swim, Play & Learn

Price: $28.00
Ages: 6 months to 14 years
The Training Camp
(800) 284-5883

This video is for mom and dad, and it begins with some basic water safety. You'll learn how to help your child feel comfortable in the water and then how to introduce swimming skills. Techniques like floating, kicking and arm strokes are well illustrated. You'll see them via underwater and above-water photography. There are even tips on swimming fun with songs and activities.

Which Way Weather?

Ages: 2 years and up
Bo Peep Productions/Big Kids Productions
(800) 477-7811

What do you wear in windy weather? What do you pile on in the cold and snow? This fun video will inform children on what to wear, and the proper gear as well as what to do in all sorts of weather. So, splash in some puddles and search the skies for rainbows—you'll see how and what to do for outside fun. Nature can be exciting and fun and we like getting so inspired by this video that we turn it off and run outside to play, splash and fly a kite!

On-Line Video Purchase Power

We know you can probably get to your neighborhood video store, but these web sites offer many hard-to-find titles and also provide extras like reviews, advice and parental message boards. You may not come out ahead cost wise; with the shipping, it ends up about the same as in stores, but you may end up making wiser purchases for your growing child and her video library.

Try these web sites:

- Brainplay.com: Search over 5,000 children's videos by different parameters; age, category or title. You can also check the reviews for even more information.
- Kidflix.com: Wow! Over 25,000 kids' videos and an advice and message board for parents. Get on-line and discuss new releases.
- VideoServe.com: This is a multipurpose site with over 5,000 children's videos, this way you can look for your toddler and for yourself.

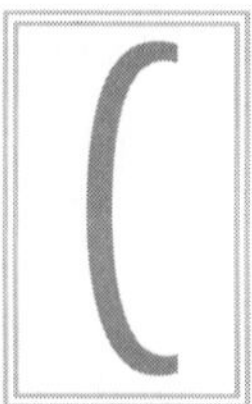

omputers and Software: The best bargains for you and your growing baby.

Introduction

Wondrous animation, education, adventure, entertainment and humor await you and your baby; they are as close as your family computer. Most parents really want their children to be technologically aware but at what age do you start them off? You may also wonder if the computer really is a tool which will really boost skills in reading and math, for example, or if it's just a glorified television set.

Like other pieces of technological wonder, it is neither. Just because we give our child some interactive software doesn't mean she'll be an early reader or turn into a math whiz. But the computer can be a great tool in helping your child develop a love of language and numbers—just as books can. In addition, well developed educational software will encourage your child to try things and will reward persistence.

Widespread computer usage is still significantly less than a generation old. Most parents had no exposure to a personal computer as a child and very many have had limited interaction as an adult. It is only in the past two years that a personal computer has been a viable purchase for the home. The market for computers and peripherals (as the computer industry likes to term add-ons such as printers, scanners, modems, speakers and such) is daunting and ever changing as manufacturers keep pace with technology. We don't think the purchase of a personal computer should revolve around the needs of an infant; it is a sizable investment, one that really ought to reflect the needs of an entire family. Certainly however, the equation for computer selection can include the availability of software for young children. Incredibly, it's likely that in 10 years, should the pace of development keep its current momentum, your infant will be using software only dreamt of a decade ago, and on a computer that would be the envy of early Apollo missions. As with many things in this book, we marvel at how things change in a generation. Undoubtedly, your parents, your baby's grandparents, are full of stories of how things were when you were a baby! Given this outlook, what are some of the good current software titles that might help your child? Should she be starting right away? Most education experts seem to think books and constructive toys, like blocks, are the way to go and that computers are best for older children. Certainly, there is some credence to this philosophy. However, new software is being introduced constantly, and we know that there's plenty of potential for meaningful interaction between you, your baby and a computer. There's certainly no harm in spending some quality computer time together. You may just be setting a very good computing habit.

Before you start, take a little time to consider safety issues when computing. As with all electrical appliances, protect cables and outlets from inquisitive youngsters (inexpensive cable organizers are readily available at most hardware stores and computer vendors, and you ought to be using outlet covers throughout your home). If you don't know already, liquids, spills and baby are synonymous; to reduce the risk of shock, or of damage to your computer system in the likely event of a spill, plan on having a separate surface on which to place bottles or cups for your hungry computer pal. It's a good idea to keep that surface below the computer. You might also consider a "no food or drink" rule while computing; that's actually the most sensible rule of all, for both you and baby. If you must reach for sustenance, then take time to get up, stretch and move away from your computer. Anyone who has worked at a computer knows how quickly time flies sometimes—stretching muscles and giving eyes a rest are important for both you and junior. Make sure, too, that you have a comfortable chair that provides good support for you and the baby on your knee. We always found our daughter sat on our knee, one hand sharing the mouse with us, and one hand free to bang on the keyboard. Oh yes, you might want to get one of those transparent keyboard covers too! Now that you've baby-proofed your computer and are comfortable with baby's inevitable use of the keyboard as a surface to slap, bang and pound on, you should set some time to explore technology together.

If you decide not to expose junior to a computer yet, don't worry. For children computing is almost intuitive, they pick it up very quickly whether now or later. If you decide to encourage the use of computers with your infant, go ahead and check out some of the software we like. Good toddler-friendly software will have levels of difficulty built-in which you can increase as your child's manual dexterity increases. These programs help children understand cause and effect, as pressing icons moves the cursor along, which initiates action.

Don't forget to use the computer as an opportunity for enjoyable quality time with your child—just as if you were reading a book, or singing together. Communicate and talk through everything you do together, place your hand over your child's to move the mouse, touch the screen together. It can be a delightful experience—don't even worry about being ambitious. It hasn't taken you long to learn how to surf the web, so just imagine what your baby will be doing a few years from now.

What computing moms and dads should do:

- Begin by baby-proofing your computer.
- Purchase a kid-friendly mouse, ergonomically designed to be easy to grasp and click.
- Increase your child's involvement through your involvement—sing-along, clap and dance.
- Talk to your child about what will happen when you click on a character, for example. This helps your child learn how to make choices and assumptions.
- Institute a time limit, it's a good habit.

Make some art with Elmo and your baby—Courtesy of Creative Wonders.

- If you are buying a new computer, assess your budget. Find out not only the cost of the computer, but the software and peripherals that you plan to use with it.

We have suggested some software titles authored specifically for this age group (birth to two years). But with a little creativity on the part of mom or dad, you can tailor "grown-up" software to entertain and captivate your baby, too. An illustration or painting program (such as Corel Draw®, Photoshop®, Freehand or Illustrator®) can be used to draw shapes of different colors, or other simple forms. We used a presentation program (such as Microsoft® Power Point or Acrobat™) to link together a series of simple icons created in a painting program; clicking the mouse advanced this sequence and our daughter had a home-made set of computer flash-cards. She loved it! Some word processing software supports voice technology and can read what you type (Simple Text which comes with Macintosh systems is one such program). Features such as these allow you to improvise your computer to become baby-friendly, too. If some of that is beyond you, at the very least, we insist that baby's photo is your start up screen!

Software for Children, and Mom and Dad

ActiMates Interactive Barney

Price: $110.00 for Barney—$65.00 for PC Pack; Runs on Windows 95
Manufacturer: Microsoft Corporation
Ages: 2 to 6 years

We couldn't believe that Barney is already celebrating 10 years of television fun and song. This year the purple dinosaur gets interactive! The ActiMates Barney is really three toys in one—the animated plush Barney can be hugged and cuddled, or it can work with the specially designed videos and/or software. Speaking for himself, Barney can say over 2,000 words and can sing any one of 17 songs. He can count, play peek-a-boo and even more. When Barney interacts with the PC Pack, his vocabulary explodes (up to 14,000 words). Prop him up by your computer and he'll offer guidance and encouraging words to your child. Play some games and learn about shapes, colors and counting. This is a product for your child's upcoming second birthday and although quite an investment, it's worth it. It's fun and engaging, and if you're still not sure about Barney, remember your child is!

Crayola Make a Masterpiece

Price: $19.99

Manufacturer: IBM Software

Ages: 2 to 12 years

Yes, that's a wide age span but the level of use, technique and creativity develop with age. Your toddler will just be able to begin to use this (just before her second birthday) but it's an incredible animated art tool! Artistic endeavors are great for developing creative instinct and the educational component is especially nice. You may even enjoy learning all about famous artists. You'll keep this around for quite awhile—Crayola does many things well, and this program is one of them. Other programs in the series include: Crayola's Magic Princess, Magic Wardrobe and Paint 'n Play Pony—try them all.

Dr. Seuss Preschool

Price: $20.00—Win95 and PowerMac CD-ROM

Manufacturer: Brøderbund

Ages: 2 to 4 years

This program features one of our favorite characters come to life on CD-Rom, Horton the elephant. He helps adorable Elma Sue search for her mom in this lesson-teaching title filled with classic Seuss charm.

JumpStart Baby

Price: $19.99 Windows/Mac CD

Manufacturer: Knowledge Adventure

Ages: 9 months to 2 years

JumpStart on some computing fun! Your baby will marvel at the music and fun and won't even know he's sharpening his developmental skills at the same time. Sing-along with your baby and Teddy (and his furry friends) while you both explore the eight learning activities.

JumpStart Toddlers

Price: $19.99 Windows/Mac CD

Manufacturer: Knowledge Adventure

Ages: 1 to 3 years

More JumpStart fun—curious toddlers will learn their alphabet, numbers and even some delightful nursery rhymes.

My Very First Farm

Price: $19.99 Macintosh

Manufacturer: Knowledge Adventure

Ages: 1 1/2 to 3 years

It's just like Fisher Price to come up with such a cute day on the farm. Explore and delight in feeding the animals and growing crops! This program will help baby develop listening skills and learn how to follow directions. If you like this one, and we think you will, you might want to select from another title in the Fisher Price software repertoire, "My Very First Playhouse."

Play With the Teletubbies

Price: $29.99

Manufacturer: Knowledge Adventure

Ages: 1 to 4 years

Go on, your kids love the Teletubbies. It's lighthearted fun and games, and like the show, your child will want to play it "again."

Reader Rabbit's Toddler

Price: $30.00—Windows and Macintosh

Manufacturer: The Learning Company

(800) 716-8506

Ages: 18 months to 3 years

We really like all the Reader Rabbit programs. This is a fun adventure into basic learning skills especially geared for little ones, emphasizing skills such as counting, sorting and working with colors and shapes. Reader Rabbit and Mat the Mouse introduce keyboard skill and before long your little computer tot will be moving the magic wand cursor around to pop bubbles and send bees off to pollinate musical flowers. The new upgrade has an alphabet activity and new features (print things out, personalize graphics and some game playing without clicking). You'll like it, too.

Ready for Math with Pooh

Price: $27.99

Manufacturer: Disney Interactive

Ages: 2 to 6 years

A personal favorite, Winnie the Pooh, gets your toddler ready for math; making it a mathematical adventure—sparkling activities all set in a magical garden. Your little one can learn at her own pace. Don't buy it too early; wait until just before she's two, so she can really grow into it.

Sesame Street Toddlers Deluxe

Price: $34.95—Windows 95 & 3.1 and Macintosh
Manufacturer: The Learning Company
(800) 716-8506
Ages: 2 to 6 years

Who would be better than our friends from Sesame Street to introduce your toddler to computer discovery and adventure, not to mention early learning concepts? Sesame Street Toddlers Deluxe is a three CD-ROM set, with each CD covering an important learning area. Sit with your child as she discovers over 30 activities which will really engage both of you. Elmo helps her through instructions on the first disk filled with creative activities. Pre-reading skills are encouraged on the second, introducing letters, rhyming, shapes and phonics. Intertwined are classic video bits of Sesame Street—the songs and familiar action reinforce the learning done on the computer. Your toddler will be counting along on Disk 3, as she learns to identify numbers and other early math basics. As if that isn't enough, the very best part might be calling her favorite Sesame Street muppet on the special interactive phone! It's fun and it's good learning.

Come compute with Elmo and Big Bird.

Computer Systems–The Hardware

Having your baby isn't necessarily justification for purchasing a family computer; baby won't be really active on it for awhile. New parents might, though. Web access offers incredible amounts of baby information, sources and shopping. Today's computers can help you balance your checkbook, run some terrific software and even edit those home-made videos.

Whether this is your first computer purchase or you've decided to upgrade to a family friendly choice, the hardest part will be deciding which computer system is best to buy. The argument over Macintosh versus PC-Compatible is as large as breast-feeding versus bottle-feeding. And you'll decide in much the same way: what you're comfortable with, what you have experienced, and simply, what you like best. We came up with several options for the best family computer. Remember that the highest rated might not match how you use a computer—your work style, your gaming sense or your graphic instincts.

First, take a peek at the criteria we like to look for:

- User-Friendliness—You take your computer home and you open the box. You now have to get this purchase up and running. How long will that take and how easy is it to sort out? Are the attachment cables color-coded? Is there a pre-installation guide to installing software etc.?
- Power—faster computers mean you have less down-time where you sit waiting while the computer is "thinking." In budgetary terms, more speed usually equates to higher cost. However, the faster your computer, the longer it will be compatible with the growing technology in software and the internet.
- Technical Support—Things sometimes go wrong. How good is the service when you call for tech support? How long do you have to wait on the telephone for a human voice who is willing to assist you? How good are the manuals—are they easy to understand and follow? One-year warranties are fairly standard and many companies offer toll-free support (thank goodness, with how long you sometimes have to wait), and some offer web pages, e-mail responses and on-site service. Particularly if you feel computer illiterate, you might consider buying your computer from a local store. You might pay a premium, but you'll be able to find a friendly face when you get into trouble with your PC!

- Price—You knew we'd get around to your pocketbook sooner or later. With computers you pretty much get what you pay for. Many family styled computers are now in the $1000.00 range, and we think that's great. Look also at what the extras will cost you—extra memory, peripherals, etc.
- Software Bundles—Virtually all PC-compatibles seem to come with *Microsoft Works*, which combines spreadsheet and communications programs and word processing. Look for those which also include accounting, games, encyclopedias, etc. iMacs are now also complete with bundles—check the latest computer catalog for specifics. Bundles seem to change as new products appear.

Remember to check if that great-looking price you were quoted includes a monitor—often it doesn't. A 16- or 17-inch monitor is pretty fabulous for a family computer.

Our favorite and hands-down winner, in our (Macintosh) minds is the iMac. It even became this year's top selling computer (PC or Mac) and it's a marvel of invention. We give it all of our favorite awards: Best Baby Buy (the price is remarkable), Designer's Choice (what could be more ergonomic and better looking) and Cool Classic (it's just destined to be a classic—it has the lines and the technology).

iMac

Power: 266Mhz; 6 gigabytes
User-friendly: excellent, an over-achiever
Bundled Software: generous
Tech Support: 24-hour phone support; web site; 90 day on-site service
Price: $1199 *with* monitor

Its about time! Steve Jobs has not only revived our interest in Macintosh, he's come up with a super family-friendly computer and he's gotten the price right, too. The newest iMacs might be as hard to find as those Volkswagen Bugs. Pick your color—blueberry, grape, tangerine, lime, or strawberry, but remember you can take this computer seriously. It's fast, very fast. It's complete—it comes wit a 24x CD-ROM drive, and a 56k modem which will make you ooh and aah. For our die-hard Mac aficionados, you soon won't be alone on the bandwagon. And if you're a gaming person at heart, the iMac's got a high-end RAGE video card. They're nearly irresistible and incredibly easy to set-up. Take it out of its box and plug it in. Don't even fret you won't know which plug—it's got only one. Baby probably isn't picky about some of the nuances of the iMac, but consider this when you purchase: This will be a very good computer for your family, and an investment that your baby will appreciate up to the ages of five or six. By then, the whole family will be ready for something new—and for sure, there'll be something even more wonderful on the market by then!

Compaq Presario 4504

Power: 200 Mhz; 16MB
User-friendly: average
Bundled Software: average
Tech Support: 24-hour phone support; web site
Price: $999 without monitor

Average power with upgradeable memory (which we suggest), but the Compaq Presario 4504 has that great sticker price! Not for graphics specialists (a bit slow and a bit less color) but it will easily handle a family load of reference, accounting and entertainment. It's a good buy and a very reliable company with many happy customers in the personal and business markets. As with the iMac, we really see this computer as a good-value buy for the whole family, and something that a young child will appreciate, especially in early elementary school years.

Apple Power Mac G3/450

Power: 450 Mhz; 64MB
User-friendly: excellent
Bundled Software: generous
Tech Support: 24-hour phone support; web site; 90 day on-site service
Price: $2,859

Quick to set up so you'll be off and running. What we like best about Macs is clearly visible in the G3/450 - its incredibly user-friendly and the operating system is also a cinch to learn. Pick yourself out a nice monitor and you'll be in computing heaven. For the extra cost you get a fast, efficient and easy to use computer. This is a more serious computer with more potential for expansion - ideal for use by a family and home office. It is an excellent computer, if you will be performing hardware-intensive explorations, give it a closer look.

Sony VAIO PCV-150

Power: 233 Mhz w/MMX; 32MB
User-friendly: excellent
Bundled Software: generous
Tech Support: 24-hour phone support; web site; 1 year on-site service
Price: $2399 without monitor

A bit more serious, this Sony computer is a fully-loaded multimedia experience. It comes with a full video-editing package and you'll find it easy to play those incredible fast games. There's even a built-in tuner so you can watch TV. We aren't so sure about the colors—purple and gray—but it is a no nonsense, technologically advanced buy. Its gaming and multimedia capabilities will appeal to children, but baby won't notice the difference when using most of the software we have reviewed. If you are planning to do some video editing to produce slik edits of your baby videos, then a more powerful computer such as this, along with the right software, can be a good purchase. Again, it is an excellent computer, but there's nothing that comes with this package that makes it a better buy for baby than the iMac or Presario.

And Others Others worth looking at are the Dell Dimension XPS M233s (a bit more of a business buy), the Packard Bell L197 (compact and affordable), and the Hewlett-Packard Pavilion #8140 (an upper bracket item but with a Pentium II and loads of attachments like AirMedia for live news). For baby and parent interaction, we can't hesitate to recommend those two computers in the lower price bracket (the iMac and Presario). Check around, too, for competitive pricing. The bottom line on computers is always in flux.

ooks: The best books for you to read to baby.

Instituting a Reading Routine for Your Infant, Toddler and Growing Child

This year my daughter and I celebrated Family Literacy Day (November 1) and Children's Book Week (November 16–27) by reading together. Actually, we still cuddle up with books on a regular basis (even though she reads on her own and does so incessantly). We thought that the best gift we could give our infant was to help her develop a love of reading and to come to know the joy books provide. Research shows that as little as 15 to 20 minutes a day can really make a difference to your baby. All the books in the world won't mean as much as the time you spend looking at and reading them together. For infants and toddlers, reading will help them learn how to listen and increase attention span. They'll also be able to recognize and identify things from real-life.

Reading aloud to your baby helps stimulate early childhood brain development. Yet research has shown only 50% of infants and toddlers are routinely read to. What is really incredible is that children ages 9 to 14 are only spending one percent of their time reading. So how do they spend their time? No surprise really, they're watching television, almost 20% of their time, according to the Carnegie Council on Adolescent Development. What can you do now so your child doesn't grow up doing everything but reading? Buy books; classics, entertaining, beautiful and fun ones. Most importantly, read them aloud and read them often. Try to instill a love of reading so that once your child learns to read on her own, she'll continue to read. Remember that spending just a few minutes a day reading to your baby will make a dramatic difference in her development. You will provide a foundation for learning, not to mention the fun and adventure which awaits.

With all of the lovely, fun and adorable books around, how do you know which you should buy? Just what should be in your baby's library? What's a Caldecott or a Newbery Book Winner? (Authors win Newbery

Awards; illustrators win Caldecott Medals). Which books did you adore when you were small—Curious George or Cat in the Hat? Fussy, irritable babies might calm down when looking through a nursery rhyme or a lullaby book. Bedtime stories can help set the tone for relaxing and calming down. A story-time in the afternoon might give you and your toddler a chance to take a midday break. So pick up some of your favorites and look through some of ours.

Reading Tips For Infants

Perhaps you are a natural storyteller, then again maybe you aren't. Here are some tips that will help you determine what's right, what's encouraging and when baby is ready.

- Make the routine pleasurable. Make it more of a tradition. Celebrate the story time you spend together. If at first your baby only wants to grab the book or chew on it, that's okay. Eventually by reading every day, your baby will understand.
- Choose books with rhythmic repetitive prose. It's not only more fun to read, but your baby will respond more.
- If baby wants the same story over and over, re-read it.
- Vary your tone to keep baby's interest.
- Offer Dad, Grandma, and Grandpa opportunities to read to junior as well. If they don't think of it themselves, include a book with baby's bag of tricks.

Baby's First Board-Books

At baby's first birthday, board-books are ideal—they're tough and delightful. Our daughter wore out two *Pat the Bunny's*, so we're delighted that classics like that are now available as board-books. Some board-books are adaptations and feature repetitive and rhythmic prose as well as bold, bright graphics delighting all readers. Here are some that convey simple, useful everyday concepts such as manners, animal names and bedtime routines. Read them to your child and be sure to reinforce the ideas all day long.

Baby Animals: Zoom Zoom

Author: Kimika Warabe
Price: $3.95
Publisher: Chronicle
Ages: 6 months to 2 years

An accordion-style mini-board-book unfolds to display eight pictures on one side and one long picture on the other. The simple, watercolor illustrations are just perfect for your little one. It's a cheerful and bright book and you can add the words.

Baby's First Library: The Runaway Bunny, Big Red Barn, Goodnight Moon

Author: Margaret Wise Brown
Price: $21.95
Publisher: HarperCollins Juvenile Books
Ages: Baby to Preschool

A mini-library of fun and delight—this trio of Margaret Wise Brown classics will keep you engaged over and over again. *The Runaway Bunny,* illustrated by Clement Hurd, speaks about a parent's love, care and protection. *Goodnight Moon* will help your child learn how to say goodnight as a bedtime ritual which will become comfortable. It also helps your child name familiar objects in a room which will somehow bear resemblance to baby's room. Say goodnight to everything together and bedtime might be a bit smoother. *The Big Red Barn,* with illustrations by Felicia Bond, is an exploration into farm life. Children love animals and animal sounds and in the end, the barnyard animals are fast asleep. If you're lucky, your baby will be, too.

Barnum's Animals

Author: Joanne Barkan
Price: $8.99
Publisher: Little Simon
Ages: Baby to Preschool

Animal cracker fun in this package of four books in one. Pick up this set, which helps with the alphabet, opposites, counting and shapes.

Dr. Seuss's Bright and Early Board-Books

Price: $4.99
Publisher: Random House
Ages: Baby to Preschool

Where would any book list be without Dr. Seuss? It would be incomplete. Seuss is the master of the phrase and of making it so much fun to recite, remember and read, that children forget any difficulty. *ABC—An Amazing Alphabet* is classic Seuss—smart, sassy and a great addition to any child's board-book library.

Hopper

Author: Marcus Pfister
Price: $6.95
Publisher: North-South Books
Ages: Baby to Preschool

Here's our adorable little hare learning how to survive in the arctic. Hopper is both sweet and sensitive, a small bunny being shown the right path by "Mama." Marcus Pfister provides some memorable images of Hopper and his world. The story is a modern classic. *Hopper* is also available in full picture book size (also issued in many languages). Pick up the others in the *Hopper* series, including *Hopper Hunts for Spring.*

I Spy Little Book (I Spy Books)

Author: Jean Marzollo, Walter Wick (Photographer)
Price: $6.99
Ages: Baby-Preschool
Publisher: Cartwheel Books

Do you have to get through dining out or a long car trip? I Spy books can help with their version for little sleuths. It's the usual I Spy formula: the left-hand pages have some rhyming couplets along with some pictures of the objects named, and on the right-hand side is a more complicated picture which contains all the objects on the left. Your job, should you choose to accept it, is to pick them all out. The fun is doing it together. The images are simple and clear, the colors bold and graphic.

Little Cloud

Author: Eric Carle
Price: $9.99 approx.
Publisher: Philomel

Eric Carle is a master of collage, and Little Cloud is another beauty. Little Cloud drifts across the sky—joins together with other clouds, and then they make rain!

Little Polar Bear

Author: Hans de Beer
Price: $6.95
Publisher: North-South Books
Ages: Baby to Preschool

Lars is the little polar bear who gets swept away from home and lands in the tropics. His exciting adventure is just the first in the Little Polar Series; we love them all. *Ahoy There, Little Polar Bear* is also available as a board-book and your baby will love the thoughtful and tender illustrations and the endearing story.

Pat the Bunny and Friends

Author: Edith Kunhardt (Contributor), Dorothy Kunhardt
Price: $17.95
Publisher: Golden Touch and Feel Board-Books
Ages: Baby to Preschool

Pat the Bunny was a big part of my daughter's childhood and it seems a big part of many children's. One of the first interactive books of its kind, Dorothy Kunhardt's story for babies and toddlers was first published in 1940, and has now sold over six million copies. It's hard not to like patting the bunny's soft fur, playing peek-a-boo, looking in the mirror and doing it over and over again. If it's as big a hit as we think it will be, next read the two sequels (*Pat the Cat* and *Pat the Puppy*) written by Edith Kunhardt, the daughter of the author of the original classic. Here are the basics, which are tried-and-true: tough cardboard pages, eight activities and simple line drawings. This is a boxed set that will occupy and fascinate your baby for quite awhile.

Raffi's Songs to Read®

Price: $6.99
Publisher: Crown Publishing Inc.
Ages: Baby to Preschool

Ten years later, we can still recite the Raffi songs. Here are two cute little books, *Five Little Ducks* and *Down By the Bay*, which encourage putting the words to the songs. Making that connection is important, we think—more important than whether or not you can stand to listen to the songs one more time! Raffi has easy to remember lyrics and these corresponding books encourage speech and reading aloud.

Spot Block Books

Author: Eric Hill
Price: $5.00 each
Publisher: G.P. Putnam's Sons
Ages: 1 year and up

Everyone loves Spot! He's the star of this series of extra-chunky books which fit easily into your baby's hand. Together you can identify familiar objects and things when you choose from Spot's *Favorite Words, Numbers, Colors* or *Baby Animals.*

Crib Books and Soft Books

Cool Classic

Nursery Novel™

Price: $12.00
Manufacturer: Wimmer-Ferguson
(800) 541-1345
Ages: Birth to 18 months

The Nursery Novel™ is an adorable, stimulating first book which can be tied to baby's crib or changing table. Every child will love discovering those famous black and white graphics and contrasting colors. The fun mirror is an added bit of enjoyment for baby. She'll adore this and won't even know the Nursery Novel™ helps her engage her visual skills.

Best Baby Buy

Soft Stories

Price: $20.00 approx.
Manufacturer: Wimmer-Ferguson
(800) 541-1345

Your baby's crib will soon have a great view and a story to tell. Soft Stories attaches with Velcro so you can even take it along on trips. Each foam-filled design can be placed to create a storyboard, in the country, city or thrown into the back pocket. Baby will enjoy finding the two squeakers and the mirror. Soft Stories is literary fun but also encourages visual activity, eye/hand coordination and helps baby recognize herself as well.

Reading Tips for Toddlers

Have you ever heard a one-year-old repeat over and over a word she has recently mastered? They love demonstrating their recent knowledge of objects, animals and people. They poke, push, discover and sort everything around them. At about 1 1/2 years, language really explodes so books with prose, music and repetitive words and sounds are especially good.

- If you are reading from a longer story, just point out objects or re-word the text. Keep it simple, short and familiar.
- Include some books which illustrate objects a baby will recognize and be able to verbalize.
- Cuddle up together. Encourage concentration; be interested and enthused.
- Take books with you; pack some favorites in your diaper bag.
- Try to recite some favorite passages during the day to reinforce your readings.
- Remember to make reading a celebration of time spent together.

Activity Board-Books

We came across a few board-books that help with learning yet also provide some eye-hand coordination with their simple activities like touching, flipping up, and fitting shapes. These are great for a toddler, although they get rough play—they're made of pretty durable board stock. A real favorite just might get so much use you'll need more than one copy before baby's second birthday.

The Cheerios Play Book

Price: $4.99

Publisher: Little Simon

Bring baby's favorite food, Cheerios, and use them to complete all of the pictures in this great little book! Baby will practice her grasp, developing eye-hand coordination, as she fits those Cheerios into their spaces. The graphics are cute and eye-catching. The only problem is when baby turns those pages the Cheerios will fly. But should you get baby to eat them and count them before turning the pages . . .

Fit-a-Shape! (Series–Wheels, Tools and More)

Price: $5.95

Publisher: Running Press Book Publishers

Your young reader will learn to fit the little plastic-edged shapes into their slots in this clever book series which helps eye-hand coordination as well learning to recognize common objects and words. It's a lovely and smart little series.

Touch and Feel (Series–Farm, Home, Clothes and Wild Animals)

Price: $6.95 each

Publisher: DK Publishing, Inc.

We all loved these books, they're simple yet complex enough to both entertain and challenge your toddler. DK Publishing has come up with some great books for children. This particular series allows touching and feeling, which really helps your child put reading and recognizing together. In *Touch and Feel Farm* you can stroke fur (we like that it feels really good, not a cheap feeling fur) and in *Touch and Feel Home* you can even see in the mirror. You and your child can compare and contrast familiar objects and animals. These are good, attractive, well-designed activity board-books—touch and feel for yourself!

Pop Up and Lift the Flap Books

Pop up books are great fun, but they never seem to last. They're a bit fragile, so you may want to wait until your toddler is a bit older or use only those you won't mind replacing eventually. There are many versions often based on baby's favorite stories and books. Here are just a few of the ones we really like:

Little Polar Bear Pop-Up

Author: Hans de Beer

Price: $15.95

This is a three-dimensional, interactive version of the classic tale about Lars, the little polar bear we've all come to know and love.

Oh, Dear!

Author: Rod Campbell

Campbell Books, London

Price: $12.95 approx.

Oh, Dear is the repeated phrase when Buster sets off to search for eggs for Grandma. It's a simple lift-the-flap book with cute graphics. You'll really enjoy saying "Oh Dear" with such emphasis that it becomes very funny. You and your little bookworm will want to read it over and over. Oh dear.

Twinkle, Twinkle Little Star—A Lullaby Book with Lights and Music

Illustrated by: Jannat Messenger
Price: $10.95
Aladdin Books

Twinkle, little book—how you become baby's favorite! You pull down the tab, and the music and lights start. The classic words with lovely illustrations and a peaceful blue sky border make this a book baby will want to look, listen and see every night before bed.

Picture Books–Big and Small

There are some must-have picture books: a sprinkling of Dr. Seuss, some elegant Eric Carle and of course, Mother Goose. You could go absolutely crazy buying picture books and if your budget allows, you should. Don't forget your local library, too. Many libraries have created great kids' spaces and on that day when you've got to get out of the house, it might just do the trick. You can sift through the shelves and shelves of picture books and test some out.

To help you decide what you've just got to have in baby's library, we've highlighted just some of our all-time picture book favorites:

Brown Bear, Brown Bear, What Do You See?

Author: Bill Martin, Jr., Eric Carle (Illustrator)
Price: $15.95
Publisher: Henry Holt & Company, Inc.
Ages: Preschool

I can almost remember the entire text and with a bit of prompting I probably could. The gentle rhymes of Bill Martin, Jr. and the gorgeous collages of Carle are quite the combination. *Brown Bear, Brown Bear, What Do You See?* Eric was such a favorite in my house that it never left my daughter's bedside table. You meet a delightful new animal with every turn of the pages and each one is associated with a different color. The repetition and rhythm of the phrases encourage beginning readers (and make for good listeners as well). Carle is a master at tissue-paper collages: a plump purple cat, a soft yellow duck and a handsome blue horse and more prance across the pages. Of course, you'll both have to add the animal sounds yourselves!

Chicka Chicka ABC

Author: John Archambault
Illustrator: Lois Ehlert and Bill Martin Jr.
List Price: $4.95
Publisher: Little Simon
Reading level: Baby to Preschool

This is a board-book version of one of our favorite alphabet books. It's so much fun to read, all the letters of the alphabet racing one another up the trunk of that famous coconut tree. When baby gets older, pick up the award-winning picture book version, *Chicka Chicka Boom Boom*—you'll both love it.

Hush, Little Baby

Illustrator: Shari Halpern
Price: $15.95
Publisher: North-South Books
Ages: Baby to Preschool

Here's the famous lullaby brought to life through Shari Halpern's fresh, invigorating collages. It's a beautiful book with familiar and soothing lyrics. Sing it, read it and enjoy it. Halpern is at her best illustrating this classic song!

My Very First Mother Goose

Author: Iona Archibald Opie (Editor)
Illustrator: Rosemary Wells
List Price: $21.99
Reading level: Baby to Preschool

Mother Goose is a classic treasure which we should not forget to include in our libraries. Opie and Wells have collaborated on an enchanting version of Mother Goose rhymes so that we can put these endearing poems into our child's repertoire.

The Peter Rabbit Nursery Book and Toy

Author: Beatrix Potter (Illustrator)
List Price: $17.99
Publisher: Frederick Warne & Co.

This is one of those times you just might as well break down and buy the gift set. *The Peter Rabbit Nursery Book* and Toy gives your little one the famous plush bunny and a great book. This nine-inch Peter version has a squeezable (and washable) body and an adorable carrot to munch on. The miniature hard-cover Nursery Rhyme Book is just full of poems guaranteed to entertain you and your baby as they have been doing for generations of little readers. Cuddle up in bed, all three of you (Peter is really soft and huggable) and read some of Beatrix Potter's best poetic works.

The Rainbow Fish

Author: Marcus Pfister
List Price: $18.95 hardcover
Publisher: North-South Books

A simple, elegant story about a beautiful but vain Rainbow Fish who along the way learns some lessons about sharing. The glittery holographic foil stamping makes a shimmering imprint on readers. (This is also available as a board-book and as a big book edition).

The Rainbow Fish will shimmer in any child's library.

The Very Hungry Caterpillar Book with Plush Caterpillar

Author: Eric Carle
List Price: $15.95
Publisher: Philomel Books
Reading level: Baby to Preschool

The set features a sweet, fuzzy, eight-inch very hungry caterpillar with colorful fringe and felt antennae to play with, while Mom and Dad read the classic tale. This is a new way to introduce the bestseller (over 12 million copies sold) to your child. This is a miniature edition, but it's still a nice size for little hands to flip through. Baby will enjoy the metamorphosis and the counting, and how the hungry caterpillar eats his way through the pages.

There were a few books we had more than one version of—*The Very Hungry Caterpillar* was one of those. We had one in the diaper bag and a full-sized picture book to poke through at home when we were hungry for a good tale.

Golden Books

Doesn't everyone remember Golden Books and *The Poky Little Puppy?* Golden Books first rolled out their 25-cent 42-page hardcovers back in 1942. Many years and stockholders later, the company became golden again. In 1997 it became Golden Books Family Entertainment with a five-year license agreement with Disney Book Publishing. Currently, the Golden Book legacy seems uncertain; whatever happens in its future, Golden Books has tremendous history and appeal. The books are concise, perfectly scaled versions for children. If Golden Books ceases to exist, there are a lot of us who'll be searching antique stores (and online auctions like eBay) for old copies with their golden stories and glowing illustrations. After all, every child deserves a copy of *The Poky Little Puppy.*

On-line Book Buys

With a Borders or a Barnes and Noble popping up around every corner, why should you search the web for books? We found that almost every publishing company has a web site, and even many authors and illustrators are now online. We also found that there are some good sites which encourage reading, not purchasing. And then once we were loaded up with all the information we could find, we could be shopping at Amazon.com, Barnes & Noble or Chosen for Children. There's a wealth of literary information out there and it is pretty easy to search for on-line.

- American Library Association—ala.org/booklist

  This is the on-line version of the American Library Association's (ALA) annual book review which includes over 2,500 titles for children. With articles and interviews to support it, you'll find plenty of useful information.
- Amazon.com—www.amazon.com

  A powerful site with amazing search power. Enter in your child's age and great gift info pops up, or look for Caldecott winners. You'll find it all here, and at a pretty darn good price.
- Children's Book Council—www.cbcbooks.org

  This site offers special sections for parents, teachers, librarians, publishers, authors, and more. The parent's section guides you through choosing great books for your child. There are also bibliographies, news, and interviews.
- Children's Literature Web—www.ucalgary.ca/~dkbrown

  A great literary place to start—information about books, about reading to your child, links to helpful sites, resources, bulletin boards, booksellers and lots more.
- Chosen For Children—www.chosenforchildren.com

  Search and buy classic children's picture books on-line. We like searching by unusual topics: Bedtime, or Folktale and Myth. Shipping is free, it's chosen for children and when you spend $50, two books are donated to a local shelter for kids in need. We certainly like that.

reserving Memories.

Introduction

You have so many memories now of baby; her birth, coming home, her first birthday, etc. How do you preserve them? What should you keep and how much should you keep? How do you archive and organize your prints, negatives, baby's first T-shirt? Where do you go to bronze baby's shoe?

We have located some products that will help you preserve your memories and do it with care, not to mention style. Here are those we like—some are just plain fun, and others use the same materials your local museum might to preserve memorabilia for prosperity. Our daughter loves looking through photo albums of her first few years and looking at old videos. She snickers at the cute little outfits we dressed her in, and wonders over the newspapers we saved from the day of her birth. Nostalgia is a wonderful human trait, and a little care and attention now will be the source of much joy for years to come.

Baby Books and Memorabilia Albums/Kits

Usually baby memory books cover the first year or two of baby's life. Many are themed to your nursery or favorite character. Filling out information such as baby's date of birth, weight, and first outing are just some of the details these books help you preserve. Add some fabulous baby photos, and you have a wonderful memory of the first years. What's nice about a baby book is that it gives you a format, organizing you to collect certain data, images and thoughts; if you don't have much faith in your own creativity (or even if you do), in amongst the mayhem of baby's first year, this is a great way to document those special moments and events.

Baby's Time Capsule

Price: $17.15
Available through: Baby Catalog of America
(800) 752-9736

This is a timeless keepsake and fun to compile. Do it with friends and family, filling the capsule with all sorts of memorabilia and family mementos from the year baby was born. Seal it up and store it to be opened some day in the future. Your baby will enjoy the opportunity to look back at her first year.

Cool Classic

Classic Pooh Baby Album

Price: $10.88
Available through: Baby Catalog of America
(800) 752-9736

Classic Pooh will help keep baby's 3" x 5" or 4" x 6" photos tidy and arranged (vertically), flip up and see the one beneath. If you like Pooh and like this album, you may also want to order the Winnie the Pooh Baby Book, too.

ClearHold Mounting Corners

Manufacturer: Light Impressions
(800) 828-6216

If you are going to use any other type of photo album which has paper pages, try the ClearHold Mounting Corners. They will hold those images tight. These are especially nice in those beautiful handmade photo albums with colored pages. We prefer the longevity of using mounting corners in albums, rather than getting a book with so-called "magnetic" pages which are inclined to deteriorate and possibly damage precious photos and paper over time. It takes a little longer to put together an album using photo corners, but your patience is rewarded in the long term. We always took extra time to lay out pages and plan our albums in advance, rather than just starting in one corner of a page and working across. The ClearHold corners are easy to apply, and as with all Light Impressions products, are good quality and worth the money.

Decorative Scrapbook Page Kit

Price: Varies
Manufacturer: Frances Meyer Inc.

Another great helper is this kit from Frances Meyer—choose from 12" x 12" or 8 1/2" x 11" formats. Each kit has a theme and includes suggestions, paper, stickers, shapes and tips on the best ways to "scrapbook." This is a nice flexible product. The suggestions are great for those of you who feel "creatively challenged." Just add some of those cute baby pictures and a little time.

Heirloom Fabric Box Kit

Price: $40.00 for quilt size/$35.00 for garment size
Manufacturer: Light Impressions
(800) 828-6216

How do you store baby's first "blankie," the one crocheted by Grandma? Fabric items such as blankets, quilts, and clothing like the layette hand-made for your little one, will yellow or deteriorate from exposure to acids, moths, or moisture. Don't shove them into a wooden chest or the back of your closet. Protect these treasures with a Fabric Box Kit which offers archival protection and is also roomy and substantial. The acid-free, nonbuffered wrapping tissue will support the fabrics and the polyethylene bag will help guard against insects and moisture. It ships flat and is easy to assemble, although you might find it hard to put these tiny treasures away. At least you will know they will be protected. If you have a wedding dress that's still hanging in the closet, Light Impressions has a great box for that, too!

Designer's Choice

Keith Haring Baby Book

Price: $12.95
Available through: The Pop Shop
(800) K-HARING

Everyone seems to know and identify with the baby image Keith Haring painted graffiti-style. It's very uplifting and almost spiritual and perfect for the baby book where you'll compile memories and more. The simple, vibrant iconographic images seem inherently appropriate for a baby book. This is part of a well designed collection of products designed by the Keith Haring estate.

Memorabilia Album Kit

Price: $50.00
Manufacturer: Light Impressions
(800) 828-6216

You have boxes filled with impressions of baby's footprint, pictures of baby's birth and kind letters from family and friends sent to welcome home junior. What now? This Memorabilia Album Kit will inspire you to dig through; helping you to organize and preserve. The kit comes with a TrueGuard Album with a Slipcase to keep it fresh. A variety of inserts such as TopLoaders (insert those letters right into these protective sleeves), Off-White Acid Free Paper Inserts and ClearHold Corners (for securing those great shots of the delivery!). The album and slipcase are both made of acid-free materials covered in a durable, attractive buckram cloth. With roomy dimensions, you can hold approximately 50 pages of treasures. This is a marvelous product for long term storage. Light Impressions is a well respected firm that provides museum-quality products through an extensive catalog. Indeed, their archival products are found in many museums where preservation is crucial.

Cool Classic

My First Year: A Beatrix Potter Baby Book

Author: Beatrix Potter
List Price: $10.00
Publisher: Viking Press

Baby's first year is filled with milestones you'll want to record, and here you can do it in Beatrix Potter style. Fill in and attach mementos like prenatal scans, photographs, baby's hospital bracelet, and more. We really like the addition of a pocket in the back to store some additional keepsakes. It's a wonderful, delightful way to register all of baby's first year alongside the charming, timeless art and stories of Beatrix Potter. This is a charming book and a beautiful compliment to a traditional nursery.

Our Baby's First Seven Years Memory Book for Our Adopted Child

Price: $26.60
Available through: Baby Catalog of America
(800) 752-9736

This is specifically and thoughtfully designed to record details of your adopted child's life with her new family. Preserve the memories of your first meeting and bringing her home. Includes pages for the first seven birthdays, and even has advice and information to foster baby's development. Portrait pages are also included in this three-ring binder memory book.

Paper Pizazz™

Price: $6.50–7.50 each book
Manufacturer: Hot Off the Press
(503) 266-9102

You can turn all of baby's precious snaps into the most wonderful memory albums. Special papers are packaged together in a book—select the one you like best. They range in topic from Baby and Pooh Bear to some lovely Metallic Papers. The sheets are acid-free and examples are included to help you put it all together. If a baby book seems too limiting for you, here's an opportunity to be a little more creative within the format of a nicely designed book. This is simple, straightforward and good value.

PhotoArchive Box

Price: $40.00 Double Box Size
Manufacturer: Light Impressions
(800) 828-6216

What happens when Grandma calls and wants those reprints to show to everyone she knows? Can you find them? A great tool for keeping prints and negatives accessible and organized are these PhotoArchive Boxes. You can label and cross-reference your images, making them all easy to find. All the components are of archival quality. A Double Box will hold up to 900 photographs and will provide the base box, envelopes for the prints, clear, polyethylene sleeves for your negatives, number tabs to help you link photos to negs, and even an index for the box lid.

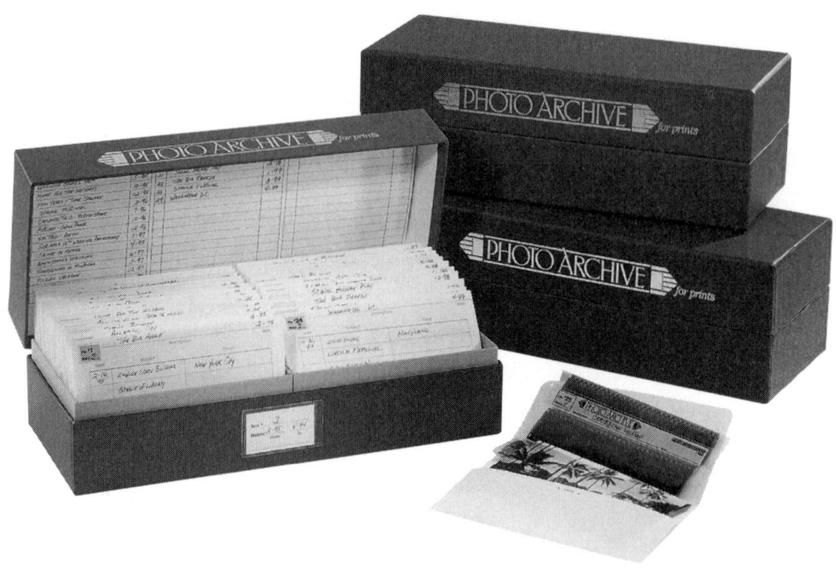

Photo Archive Boxes

Frames

Frames are everywhere—you can order them on-line, by catalog or pick them up at your favorite store. There's so much variety and so much choice. Pick frames that make that snapshot of baby shine—don't pick frames that detract from the images. Here are just a few classics:

All-Metal Portrait Stand with Bronze Baby Shoes

Price: $54.95

Contact: American Bronzing Company

(800) 423-5678

Order this memento on-line or toll free: either way, the American Bronzing Company's been transforming baby shoes for over 60 years. This is a frame and bronzed shoe combination. You get to use an 8" x 10" of baby, and bronze two shoes (as long as they're under 5 1/2" in length). They send you a pre-addressed mailing bag and you can ship those little shoes off. Six to eight weeks later, you have a marvelous, metal portrait stand and tiny bronzed shoes. Also nice is being able to choose the finish: antique or bright bronze.

Petit Prince Frames

Prices: $35 (4"x6"), $41 (5"x7")

Available through the: Rue de France Catalog

(800) 777-0998

Frame up your little royal one with these enchanting frames! The motifs are drawn from the famous tale, *Le Petit Prince.* So go ahead and make a memory of your little prince or princess!

Present a picture of your little prince. Courtesy of Rue de France.

Recording and Measuring Growth

We didn't always find products we thought were useful for preserving memories. Casper Enterprises, Inc. makes a Measure-Up portable height recorder. For $16.95 it seemed an unlikely combination of technology and memory. It's a rather clumsy piece of equipment that didn't really appeal to us—it is rather awkward as an heirloom. There's something more delightful about lining junior up against it and marking off the growth. Most of us have wonderful memories of a printed wall chart, or even of Mom or Dad making pencil marks on a wall or notches in a door frame. Rather than adding graffiti to the walls at home, here are some of the store-bought growth charts we like:

Beatrix Potter Growth Chart

Price: $7.88
Available through: Baby Catalog of America
(800) 752-9736

As soon as baby hits 26" you can begin to record her height on a lovely, full-color Peter Rabbit growth chart. It's 9" wide and made of thick card stock which will hold up well. It comes with a wooden border on top complete with a tassel hanger.

Our Baby's First Seven Years Photo Growth Chart

Price: $7.88
Available through: Baby Catalog of America
(800) 752-9736

Baby's own pictures will help illustrate her growth on this custom growth chart. Themed with baby fun, this chart is made of durable card stock with a wooden border and tassel hanger. It also coordinates with the *Our Baby's First Seven Years Mini Photo Album* and *Baby Book.*

Self-Stick Growth Charts

Price: $12.99
Available through: JCPenney Stores and Catalog
(800) 222-6161

A washable, self-stick vinyl chart in Winnie the Pooh, Mickey Mouse and Big Bird to measure junior's growth. Lots of choice here in the catalog, along with a great price and self-stick convenience, makes this something you don't want to forget. Choose Winnie the Pooh (#R825-5366A), Mickey Mouse and Company (#R825-2553A), Big Bird (#R825-2579A), and even that purple dinosaur, Barney with Baby Bop (#R825-5374A). JCPenney, if you haven't already discovered, is a remarkably reliable source of sensible, necessary, value driven products for baby. The range of products they stock is remarkable, even down to these four growth charts! If in doubt, JCPenney more often than not will have what you are looking for.

Transfer-Mations™ Height Charts

Available through: Camp Kazoo, Ltd.
(888) 60MURAL

Pick from 14 designs to help you keep track of your growing child! Use the iron-on transfer and then paint-by-number, what could be easier! There's a rocket, a cactus, a flower, a crown and royal staff and many, many more to choose from.

Professional Photography

Even though your camera seems always to be in tow, there may be an occasion where you'll want to use a professional photographer to capture baby on film. Many department and chain stores have portrait studios where there are seasonal and topical backdrops to choose from. Look in your local yellow pages for other professional studios in your community, and talk to other parents and friends to see who they would recommend.

Getting the Most from Your Photographic Sitting

You've found a photographer or a studio and you want to be prepared. Schedule your appointment at a time when baby or toddler is most likely to be well-rested and happy. Is it after nap-time for example? Then be sure to arrive just on time (or just a tad early). Long waits might make your child apprehensive as will fussing about clothes and hair. Try to keep casual and relaxed. The photographer should be able to help calming and making baby at ease. Toddlers can be told what to expect—try to make the photo shoot fun, and be enthusiastic. If going to a portrait studio, remember to think ahead about how many prints you think you want and what kind of background you're interested in. We've found most photographers and studios to be incredibly helpful with the child (and a bit overwhelming when it comes time to ordering those package deals). Order what you need; you can always re-order.

Professional Photographers of America (888-97 STORY ext. 333)

If you want a picture to tell a great baby story, contact the Professional Photographers of America (PPA). Contacting "the World's Great Storytellers," as they call themselves, will give you access to their database, and their representative will put you in touch with a certified PPA photographer near you.

Many large stores have portrait studios. Some of these are:

- JCPenney
- KMart
- Sears

Photo Imaging

Price: $140.00 for an 8" x 10"
Contact: Liquid Image
(212) 334-4443

Little Angel

Liquid Image is a high-tech company with a sense of humor, ready to take your child's image and blend it (or the entire clan) into one of 75,000 outrageous backgrounds. Pick from baby being a Raphael angel or on the cover of a comic book. Not inexpensive but definitely different; this portrait is for when you really want to try to express something unusual. If you can't get to their New York studio, a surcharge will allow you to send in a snapshot. Just be sure you love the way baby looks in the photo and they'll turn it into a Liquid Image like no other.

Castings

Bronzed shoes have been a tradition for generations. Chances are, somewhere, your parents bronzed your first shoes. Perhaps not as popular as it once was, the tradition still continues. Now you can even obtain a casting of your baby's hand or foot to treasure forever!

Cool Classic

Certificate for Bronzing One Pair of Baby Shoes

Price: $29.95
Contact: American Bronzing Company
(800) 423-5678

The traditional baby keepsake—preserving that first shoe in rich, antique bronze. You can order on-line or by the toll free number. Then you'll receive a certificate which you send with the shoes or sneakers (we're often asked if they're okay to bronze) to the American Bronzing Company. Then you'll receive that hefty bronzed memento which will last a lifetime.

The Bronze Photo courtesy of American Bronzing Company.

Hand & Foot Casting Kit

Price: $32.95
Available through: One Step Ahead Catalog
(800) 274-8440
Ages: Birth to 12 months

You can buy them separately, but why not get them both at once? Order a Hand & Foot Casting Kit; it's easy to use in its two-step kit. Everything you need comes with, and it's all nontoxic, nonallergenic and baby-safe. We couldn't get our daughter to do this on her own, so Dad and her held hands and did it together—it made a delightful sculpture that she painted when she was a little older; it's a real treasure.

Designer's Choice

Porcelainized Baby Shoes

Price: $49.95
Contact: American Bronzing Company
(800) 423-5678

We thought this was a pleasant change from the traditional bronzing. Porcelainizing gives those little baby shoes the look of fine china. You can even trim them in baby pink or blue, or even gold. To add a delicate touch, hand lettering of baby's name and birthdate is included.

Porcelain Baby Shoes—a delicate change from traditional bronze. Courtesy of American Bronzing Company.

Tiny Imprints Keepsake Kit

Price: $7.99
Available through: Baby Catalog of America
(800) 752-9736

This is a complete kit for creating a plaster representation of little baby's hand (it won't stay little long). You prepare the nontoxic plaster mixture yourself with ease, and then pour into the decorated tin; then press baby's hand into the plaster. You can add baby's name and date of birth (write it in using a toothpick) When it dries you can put it on a small easel (not included) for all admiring eyes. Pick a pink, blue or mint tin, and create that tiny handprint memory.

Going Places With Baby

oing Places: Essential equipment and tips to help you get around while you and baby are on the go—from little errands to international air travel.

Introduction

Traveling with your baby for the first time is invariably more complex than it might have been before. Even the simplest and shortest of journeys will now require more planning and require parents to bring along baby's favorite things, not to mention necessities such as food and diaper supplies. Whether traveling by car, foot, or cycling, it is imperative to select gear that fits your needs, budget and lifestyle.

Planning for a bigger trip is exponentially more complex. Have you gotten a passport? Which travel companies and destinations best cater to families with infants and toddlers? Does a car rental agency go the extra mile to make kids happy? You may not even know the questions to ask when faced with the first big trip with baby in tow.

Here are some suggestions for trips big and small, questions to be sure to ask and our best of everything for your baby who is on-the-go.

Safety Before You Go

If you are about to go on vacation it might be wise to jot down some medical facts, and pack them first.

Just grab some note cards and indicate your baby's:

- pediatrician's phone number and beeper number
- weight

- any chronic conditions or allergies
- any prescription drugs (or over the counter) being taken as well as the dosage
- identification numbers, such as social security and health insurance policy number

Hotel Safety Savvy—Childproofing Your Hotel Room

Safety is always a priority even when staying at a hotel. Supervision is the best precaution, but there are also a few things to check:

- Call to see if the hotel cribs meet current Consumer Product Safety Commission standards. If manufactured after 1976, slats should be no more than 2 3/8" apart. If they aren't, or the hotel isn't sure, why not pack a portable crib?
- Create a travel bag of safety equipment such as outlet covers, night-light, toilet-lid latch and even a bathtub spout cover.
- Place a piece of furniture so that it blocks the windows.
- Check that all windows and doors lock securely.
- Tie up any long electrical or drapery cords, keeping them out of baby's reach.
- Put toiletries out of reach.
- Check the water temperature.

Shopping Safety Savvy

Going shopping? It may be a journey you take for granted, not a fancy vacation, but some preparation is still important. Grab that shopping cart but be sure to buckle your baby in! We find that although most shopping carts now have seat belts attached, they may be dirty, broken or worn—all of which discourage their use. So what can you do to protect baby from an unrestrained fall? Buy one of these belts or harnesses, listed below, and take it with you to your favorite stores.

The Baby Comfort Strap

Price: $10.00
Manufacturer: The Baby Comfort Company
(877) 774-2229
Ages: 6 months to 2 years

This strap is simple and sturdy with a two-inch thick pad that hugs baby's chest. The one-piece construction makes it extremely easy to use while keeping your little one from being able to wiggle out of it.

Baby Best Buy

Baby-Hold-Me-Safe

Price: $20.00
Manufacturer: Carrousel Concepts from One Step Ahead Catalog
(800) 274-8440
Ages: 5 months to 4 years

Aside from its great name, we really like that the Baby-Hold-Me-Safe does just that! Unfolding into a fully padded seat, this fastens directly to the back of the shopping cart's seat and around the front bar. It even comes with a mini-duffel, so carrying it around with you is convenient and tidy. Getting it up and holding took about a minute and it also fits snugly, keeping baby secure. An added plus is that the coverage of the front bar is also nice if your baby is teething.

Ride 'N Stride

Price: $12.00
Manufacturer: Leachco
(800) 525-1050
Ages: 6 months and up

This walking harness converts into a shopping cart strap. The adjustable straps, Velcro fasteners and quick-release buckles make it a success. It is quite strong and especially difficult for that adventurous toddler to get out of.

Going Out—Using and Purchasing Carriers, Slings and Backpacks

The first time we went to use our Snugli, it was exasperating trying to get it secure and feeling right. It was like learning how to diaper baby. After the first time, we couldn't understand how it had seemed such an immense task. If you have a friend who can show you how, ask them to help you. Once you get the hang of getting that carrier feeling right, you'll enjoy the hands-free way you can move around with baby.

Which do you choose though—front or back carrier, backpack or frame carrier? You may need more than one carrier depending on how active your life is. We managed with one Snugli and our stroller. If you hike or take on long excursions, you'll probably want a backpack. A baby carrier is a hands-free alternative to a stroller. There are basically two types—one is a pouch-like carrier out of fabric that you can wear in the front or back, and the second is a framed carrier worn only on the back. Pouch-style carriers are great for young infants needing head support (around six or seven months). Use frame style carriers only when baby is sitting up by herself. It's often difficult to get around with a stroller—wait until you try to board a crowded bus, for example. That's when a carrier is terrific. You will also feel much more secure with baby attached to you when moving through crowds. Best of all, babies love them, they feel so close to mom or dad and the rhythm is very soothing.

There always seems to be a downside and there is. Parents often complain about the aches and pains which seem to accompany carriers. As baby grows and gets heavier, the carrier and baby will become quite a heavy load. If it really is uncomfortable at some point, curtail the use and pull out your stroller. All in all, carriers can be very useful and many are now designed to help with a heavier load of an older child or a child with differing abilities. Go look at the options, try them on if possible, and most definitely, ask your friends.

Here are some of the carriers we liked for their features, cost and availability:

Designer's Choice

Baby Bjorn Infant Carrier

Price: $74.95
Manufacturer: Regal Lager®
Models manufactured 1999 only

Safety Note: Baby Gjorn carriers had an earlier recall on models dated 1991-1998. (Please be sure to purchase only the newest models, manufactured in 1999) and if in question, contact the U.S. Consumer Product Safety Commission. Regal & Lager have redesigned the new models to address this issue.

Baby Bjorn wasn't around when we were looking for comfort and quality in a carrier. It certainly is now. An award winner, the Baby Bjorn Infant Carrier grows with your baby. There's no fidgeting with hard to adjust back straps, either. All adjustments are made from the front. Newborns can face toward you and use the head support. As she grows, your child can face you or face out. The Infant Carrier fits babies up to 33 pounds We've only seen it in classic navy, but by catalog you can find it in denim, black gingham, lime, orange and khaki.

Home and Roam Carrier

Price: $79.99

Manufacturer: Baby Trend

The Home and Roam is a versatile carrier. It converts from a framed backpack to a soft carrier just by zipping and clicking. The sturdy aluminum frame for the backpack also folds for travel. You can adjust the seat height for your growing child and there's an extra large head support. It's machine washable and comes in some nice multi-jewel colors.

Cool Classic

Original Babysling

Price: $29.99

Manufacturer: Nojo

(800) 854-8760

The original Babysling was developed by Dr. William Sears as an environment for carrying your baby that was secure, yet intimate. Strong, soft fabric can carry a baby up to 30 pounds, and for your sake, is comfortably padded at all pressure points. We like the versatility, too. You can carry your baby in many different positions: cradle hold, kangaroo carry, snuggle hip, or hip straddle. The Babysling is also discrete enough for nursing in public. Thankfully and thoughtfully, there's an illustrated instruction book. If you buy it through the One Step Ahead Catalog (800 274-8440) for $34.95, it comes with a video demonstrating how to use it.

Snugli Double Take Soft Baby Carrier

Price: $20.00

Manufacturer: Gerry

(800) 525-2472

This Snugli allows you to put baby face in or face out, whichever she prefers. Our niece always wanted to face out so we appreciate this option in carriers. There's chest padding so baby is nicely cushioned when she's facing in. Other features include fully padded leg openings and head and neck support. There's that removable bib we like and a strap to hold a toy. For ages 0 to 12 months.

Best Baby Buy

Snugli Front & Back Pack Soft Baby Carrier

Price: $45.00

Manufacturer: Gerry

We used to affectionately call it the "Ugli Snugli" but we really loved the way baby fell asleep every time she was in it. And it wasn't really ugly, made of blue denim it was quite trendy. This version of the Snugli offers three carrying positions, facing in, facing out, and as a backpack. The backrest flips front to back to change position and the padded belt strap carries one-third of baby's weight so maybe your shoulders won't ache quite as much. There's a fully padded head pillow and adjustable seat height, too. Something we appreciate is the drool bib. For ages 0 to 20 months.

Stallion Deluxe

Price: $189.99

Manufacturer: Tough Traveler®

(800) 468-6844

Here's the ultimate backpack for walking or hiking with your baby (if you are between 5'4 and 6'6). There's an adjustable shoulder harness and control straps. Water resistant with storage pocket and upright bottle holders right under the seat, this Stallion has many features we like. Of course, I am only five feet tall so I'm out of luck, but for those in this height range, it's a good buy. The sturdy frame makes it stable and easy to load and easy to put on and off, too. The Stallion can be used for kids up to 60 pounds and it's made to last—even through a few kids. The safety harness really holds baby in (there are some extra accessories by Tough Traveler® you'll like too—a rain and sun hood, insulated bottle holder, mesh netting, and an adorable insulated kid's backpack! For shorter-backed adults, Tough Traveler® suggests trying the Filly™ model).

Trailblazer Frame Carrier

Price: $109.99

Here's the one for my build—the Trailblazer works for parents 5' to 6'2" and is designed for infants from 6 months to 45 pounds. I doubt I could carry more than that anyway. The Trailblazer has five hip support positions which help ensure a proper fit and balance the load. There's a contoured waistband for extra comfort and foam back support. With a three-point harness, baby is secure and you can carry toys in those loops provided. The loading stand with retractable kickstand allows you to keep the Trailblazer stable while you load it up.

Trekker Carrier

Price: $89.95
Available through: One Step Ahead Catalog
(800) 274-8440

Mom-invented, this carrier is really comfortable and easy to wear. It's versatile with front and rear-facing positions and nursing is especially easy with it. The Trekker goes on and off easily and quickly and it supports baby's neck.

Strollers and Accessories

How do you choose a stroller when there are so many variables and so many to select from? Begin with the most important factor to you—weight, size, or portability. We looked at carriage-style strollers for infants, lightweight strollers super for running errands and shopping, car seats that even convert to strollers, jogging strollers and special feature strollers. We like all of these listed because they are durable, come with safety restraints, have front swivel wheels, and rear brakes.

Other sources to take a look at are The Baby Catalog of America, with an enormous range of strollers available (800) 752-9736. Your local Toys "R" Us, JCPenney and Sears all maintain a good selection of strollers.

Stroller Safety Savvy

After the notorious walker, statistics indicate the next most dangerous culprit is the stroller. Babies slide out, climb out, and fall out. Small parts are choking hazards. Seat belts break and brakes fail. Here are some stroller safety do's and don'ts:

- Don't hang shopping bags from the handle of the stroller. It unbalances the stroller and it may fall backwards. We know it's tempting. Buy yourself a backpack or a stroller with a basket underneath.
- Don't leave baby unattended. Your baby could get her head caught in the leg openings between the front edge of the seat and the handrest bar.
- Don't rely on the brakes. Don't leave baby unattended while perched on an inclined surface.

- Really follow those weight limits. Don't overload a stroller.
- Always use the restraining belt.
- Don't use or carry the stroller with your child in it up stairs, escalators or steps. You could all fall or baby could fall out.
- Stop using the stroller when your child weighs more than 35 pounds—yes, that's a lot of weight for safe use of a stroller. Check the manufacturer's guidelines.
- If using a multiple stroller, follow the manufacturer's guidelines for taking your children out. You wouldn't want the stroller to tip.
- Check for the JPMA (Juvenile Products Manufacturers Association) certification, which now requires strollers to have a locking device (preventing accidental folding). Other standards must be met including those for brakes. For a list of certified strollers, call (609) 231-8500.

Buy the safest stroller you can afford, and use your safety savvy. Never leave your baby unattended when in a stroller.

We also found a few innovative, helpful products for stroller use and travel:

Stroller Extension Handles

Price: $14.95
Available through: One Step Ahead Catalog
(800) 274-8440

This is such a good idea we wished we had thought of it—extension handles for those strollers which have been giving all of us back pain. Many of us stroll along bent over, and these handles easily attach with locking knobs to fit all umbrella strollers. For added comfort, the grips are foam, and the handles extend from 3" to 6." After using a stroller for a couple of days, if it seems uncomfortable, then go out and buy this elegant and simple product. It's a back-saver.

Stroller Tote

Price: $39.95
Available through: One Step Ahead Catalog
(800) 274-8440

Here it is—a tote for that (standard) stroller which really helps for travel adventures. It's made of tough Denier Nylon and features a carry handle and an adjustable shoulder strap.

Carriage Strollers

We know we love them for their comfort. Our Peg Perego gave our baby such a smooth ride, but it was heavy. We picked it despite that, because it later converted to a sitting up stroller as well. You want to look at the weight, the folding mechanism, the alternate positions (does it recline?) and whether it comes with a handle that reverses (so baby can choose whether to look at you, or in the direction of travel). Here are our favorites:

Kolcraft K-2001

Price: $109.00
Manufacturer: Kolcraft
(800) 453-7673

This is bit on the weighty side, coming in at 21 1/2 pounds, but reclines in two positions plus fully reclining. It has a foot-release mechanism for folding, and a reversible handle. Some nice extra features we like are the large storage basket, three-tiered canopy and double front and rear wheels.

Full-size Stroller #7528

Price: $110.00
Manufacturer: Graco
(800) 345-4109

Weighing in at 25 1/4 pounds, this stroller is hefty. We really like the extra-thick seat pad and how it locks in the fold position. Go ahead and go shopping, as this is another stroller with a large storage basket. The baby head support is removable, another nice feature. As for basics, this stroller has them: it reclines, has a foot-release mechanism and a reversible handle.

Amalfi

Price: $220.00
Manufacturer: Peg Perego
(800) 728-2108

Peg Perego is a personal favorite—the Amalfi is 17 pounds and has all the basics: reclines fully and with two positions, has a foot-release mechanism and a reversible handle. We already mentioned that Peg Perego carriage strollers offer your baby a smooth ride; the Amalfi's shock-absorbing suspension system is a definite plus. Other nice features are the double front and rear swivel wheels, and an oversized hood.

Lightweight Strollers

We enjoyed a carriage stroller—it was great for our urban, walk-everywhere lifestyles. When we took a trip though, the lightweight stroller was the only way to go. We could have managed with just one stroller, but having two afforded us the flexibility to tailor our vehicle to the situation and conditions (lightweight was the way to go in summer, more often than not).

Calais Royale

Price: $199
Manufacturer: Aprica
(310) 639-6387

The Calais Royale is only 14 pounds, which is a delight. It has a reversible handle, a one-handed folding mechanism and it reclines in three positions. After the basics, Calais Royale offers some nice features we really like: one-touch reclining, double front and rear swivel wheels and it stands and locks in the folded position. The only down-side is the cost.

Eclipse

Price: $54.00
Manufacturer: Kolcraft
(800) 453-7673

The Eclipse is a pretty good buy; low price and low weight (15 pounds). It has all the basics like a two-handed folding mechanism, and it fully reclines with two reclining positions. It doesn't have a reversible handle but the plusses include a large storage basket and locking in the fold position.

Kidsport

Price: $89
Manufacturer: Combi
(800) 99-COMBI

On the weighty side, the Kidsport is still a reasonably priced buy. It has all the fundamentals we like, such as a two-handed folding mechanism. It only reclines in one position and fully, but it does stand and lock in the folded position. We also like the large storage basket and the canopy window offering your baby some peeks outside even in inclement weather.

Stroller and Safety Seat Combinations

Century was the first to do it, combining an infant child safety seat with a stroller. The stroller also converts from an infant one to a toddler stroller. This was big news to parents, as the price was less than the price of just a stroller. Other companies followed suit, and now there are several on the market. Here are a few we really like:

Adventure 4-in-1 System with 5-Point Harness

Price: $199.99

Manufacturer: Century®

Here's a smart fit from the folks who started it all. The Adventure includes a SmartFit Plus car seat with a stay-in-the-car base that can be used as an infant carrier, a stroller for use with the carrier and an all-purpose stroller for when baby gets older. The seat connects to the stroller frame and you can use it as either rear or front facing without removing baby. When your child outgrows that infant carrier, use the Adventure stroller as an all-purpose one. The infant car seat carrier has a four-position handle which makes it so convenient to carry. It also adapts to shopping carts. The stroller features an oversized basket, an extra large storage pouch and oversized wheels for all sorts of terrain. The pad and canopy are removable and washable. Here's the best bit—there's a five-point harness in both the carrier/car seat and in the stroller. It's an adventure and a smart fit.

Secura Infant Car Seat and Travel System

Price: $160.00

Manufacturer: Kolcraft

(800) 453-7673

This is an infant car seat for babies up to 20 pounds that comes with a contoured handle for carrying. With a tilt and squeeze you can place the seat right onto its base for car trips or directly onto the stroller for walks. Once baby outgrows the infant seat, you can make good use of the stroller.

Sit 'N Stroll, 5-in-1 Car Seat and Stroller

Price: $199.99
Manufacturer: Safeline®

There are so many permutations we don't know where to begin. Use the Sit 'N Stroll as a rear-facing car seat for infants (5 to 25 pounds), then use it as a forward facing car seat for toddlers (up to 45 pounds). Unfold those wheels and pull up the handle and there's an all-purpose stroller. It's certified for use on an airplane and you can use the booster seat at mealtime. There's a five-point harness plus a two-point harness tie. It even includes a removable seat cover for washing and a shade for the sun.

Kar Seat Karriage "Snap 'N Go Lite"

Price: $39.99
Manufacturer: Baby Trend®

Already have an infant car seat? Pick up this lightweight stroller frame that is ever so easy to travel with. Just snap in your infant car seat—almost all of them work—Century, Evenflo, Kolcraft and Cosco. Just snap and go. It also fits into most airline overhead compartments.

Jogging Strollers

Stay healthy—buy one of these jogging strollers and get on the path to fitness and fun. Active parents really swear by them, whether they're running, hiking or just plain walking. Look for features like wheel sizes geared for different terrain, lifetime warranties and accessories like canopies, baskets and water bottles. Even though these jogging strollers now offer smoother rides, you might want to check with your pediatrician to see what age you can start using yours (about one year). Then pull on your Lycra gear, pop baby in, and off you go. There is no reason why you should give up your jogging time, just because you have a baby! Here is another product that affords you the opportunity to do something for yourself, and bring your cool new companion along also.

Baby Jogger II®

Price: $310.00
Manufacturer: Baby Jogger Company
(800) 241-1848

An excellent all-around jogging stroller, the Baby Jogger II has quick-release wheels and a lightweight, padded aluminum frame, so it's easy to push or carry. It comes with a handbrake with a parking button and holds up to 75 pounds. Choose from three wheel sizes: 12" all-terrain, great for walkers; 16" all-purpose, great for jogging moms and those who want to stroll, and the 20" for serious runners. The large wheel size is also a plus in snow and sand. All of this, and you can select from great colors like jade, cranberry, raspberry, batik and more.

Kool Stride Runner

Price: $269.95
Manufacturer: Kool Stop
(503) 636-4673

The Kool Stride Runner is loaded with features and comfort. Your baby is secured into a five-point safety harness. The zip back seat lets your little one recline or sit up, and a removable canopy with see-through windows protects in sun, rain and heat. Best of all, it assembles without tools. Recommended age is 6 months and up to 85 pounds, so get you and baby on that jogging path.

Special Needs Jogger

Baby Jogger
(800) 241-1848

A version of the Baby Jogger II, this one is designed so challenged kids can enjoy being outdoors with mom or dad. This stroller works well at the beach or in snow; and can be used for hiking. It's easy to take along and isn't heavy. Pick from two wheel sizes, 16" or 20." The washable seat has been made wider and can accommodate up to 150 pounds. A lifetime warranty and even modifications are available.

For anyone with twins and triplets, Baby Jogger makes jogging strollers capable of handling the entourage—(800) 241-1848.

Jogging Stroller Blanket–Cozy Rosie

Price: $45.00 - 50.00
Manufacturer: Sew Beautiful
(914) 666-9792

Want to keep baby warm when the temperature drops and you still want to jog? Order a Cozy Rosie, made in the U.S. out of durable Polarfleece®. The blanket bag attaches right to the stroller frame with Velcro fasteners and colorful ribbons, and best of all, the Cozy Rosie will fit all types of jogging strollers. It won't come untucked or drag on the ground, and it keeps the back of a child's legs warm, too. Machine washable and available in navy, red or leopard, it's a great cozy addition to your stroller.

Stroller Toys and Accessories

One of the most important considerations about your stroller, is what you can put on it to keep baby entertained and enthused. Sometimes being outside isn't enough, or parents need baby to keep involved and concentrating on something other than mom and dad. Here are a few helpful stroller toys and accessories:

Designer's Choice

Busy Bugs Activity Bar

Price: $20.00
Manufacturer: Hoopla by André™
(800) 541-1345

Little busy bugs you and your baby will like! These creatures attach to the stroller (or crib) for hours of fun. Bees, butterflies, flowers and even frogs stick to the purple worm who transports them. Squeakers and rattles make delightful noise when baby finds them. This little busy bug parade will keep baby having traveling fun.

Drive-N-Melodies Toy

Price: $24.99
Manufacturer: Combi®

Baby's first dashboard, a musical one, will keep her occupied while in her stroller. There's spinning animals, electronic melodies and a squeaky horn. It secures easily to the stroller's front bar with two straps. Fits all strollers.

Stroll'R Hold'R®

Price: $7.99
Manufacturer: Kel-Gar, Inc.

This is a unique stroller accessory we were always thankful was invented. It's a carry-all container which features a drink holder for sodas or bottles. It clamps to most tubular handles on strollers and removes easily. Made of durable plastic.

Best Baby Buy

$ Whoozit ©1994 André Sala

Price: $20.00

Manufacturer: Hoopla by André

(800) 541-1345

Ages: Birth to 24 months

Fanciful and cheerful, this multi-sensory toy is a winner, an award winner to be exact. This imaginative creature will captivate your child through a variety of different activities. Fun noises, a cheerful mouth that can bend, a hidden mirror and hide-and-seek legs will keep your baby or toddler busy. Whoozit© can travel anywhere baby goes; on the crib, the stroller or on the high chair. For infants, the black and white target is stimulating while the bright and wacky colors and patterns will delight toddlers. There's also a Baby Whoozit© size!

Car Seats and Accessories

Using child safety seats has saved many lives and prevented injuries, but car-related accidents are still the leading cause of death among children in the U.S. Just like adult safety belts, child seats must be used—buckling up will help keep baby safe, even if she doesn't like it.

The millennium will bring some new baby regulations into place. All new cars and car seats will need to have a uniform attachment system by the year 2000. Straps on either side of the car seat will buckle into anchor points and a tether strap will attach the top of the seat to a bracket near the rear of the car. The tether strap reduces the forward motion of the seat that often occurs in a crash. You will be able to install the anchor point behind the spot behind where you will situate the car seat.

Read your owner's manual carefully and always use your car seat, even when baby is upset. Resist taking her out of the seat to calm her (even when you aren't the driver); just don't get into that bad habit. It just isn't safe.

For car seats which also convert or snap into strollers, please refer to our section "Stroller and Safety Seat Combinations" found in "Essential Equipment—Strollers." You might want to call for a free copy of "The What to Expect™ Guide to Car Seat Safety," a public service booklet from those award-winning authors of the popular "What to Expect" parenting series. Call (800) 955-4500 for yours.

Journeying By Car Young babies are pretty good travelers—they get sleepy. As for keeping on schedule on a road trip, if a trip would have taken two hours, it might take four now that you have baby in tow. What you can do to keep her from getting fussy is have one parent sit in the back to entertain her, if possible. Take along some of baby's favorite music and books to look at. Bring a blanket and extra clothes. Don't forget baby's favorite traveling toys and a must-have is a sun shield to prevent glare and heat. Is baby potty training? If the answer is you think so, don't forget to bring that along, too. If you scale down your trip and your expectations, and you're prepared—your car travels with baby might just be fun!

Car Seat Safety Savvy

Just buying a car seat isn't enough; many parents are making mistakes installing and using them. These mistakes could be deadly. Here are some do's and don'ts:

- Back seat, back seat, back seat! Air bags and car seats don't mix. You will get used to baby being in the back when you remind yourself it's safest for her. And put her in the middle of the back seat, if your seat belts allow it.
- Do not install a car seat too loosely—it should be fastened securely against the back of the seat. To secure an infant seat (rear-facing), lean into the back of the seat (use your arm) while fastening the seat belt. For a forward-facing car seat, push down into the seat (try using your knee). If the seat moves an inch or so when it's fastened, then it's too loose. Try it again. Follow the manufacturer's installation directions carefully.
- Don't use a forward-facing car seat too soon. For baby's safety, keep using that infant seat until she's one year old and weighs at least 20 pounds. If your baby weighs that much sooner than a year, use a convertible seat (holding up to 30 pounds) and use it in the rear-facing position.
- Don't stop using your booster seat too early. A booster seat should be used until your child can sit against the seat back with knees bent at the seat's edge. The lap belt should fit snugly across the top of her thighs and the shoulder belt should fit without slack. Often, children are itching to get out of their boosters; be sure you don't give in too soon.
- Use the harness correctly. Make sure that the car seat harness straps are threaded through the proper slots. For rear-facing seats, thread the

straps at or below infant's shoulders. When the seat is forward-facing, thread through the top slots (on most seats), but check the manual. Harness straps must fit snugly, even when junior doesn't like it. You don't want them to pinch, but they must be close-fitting. Try the finger test: if you can slide more than one finger between the strap and your baby, the harness isn't being used correctly.

- Don't put the retainer clips in the wrong place. Car seats which have that little retainer clip (which holds the straps together) need to have it located at the child's armpit in order for it to do its job—which is keeping those important straps from slipping off.
- Register that car seat immediately. That way, you'll be notified of recalls if necessary.

Canada requires child safety seats to meet slightly different standards and because of these differences, not all car seats sold in the U.S. are available there. For information on Canadian issues of child car seat safety, contact the Transport Canada's Road Safety Office at (613 998-1978) or find it on the web at www.tc.gc.cal. You can also check recalls by calling the British Columbia Automobile Association (800-663-4636).

As you know, many child safety seats are recalled when a flaw or defect appears that could cause injury (seats are among the most commonly recalled products). If you aren't sure whether your child safety seat has been recalled or if you want to check a hand-me-down (we don't really recommend hand-me-downs with all the constant changes and recalls), contact the Auto Safety division of the U.S. Department of Transportation (DOT) at (800-424-9393). You can also report any problems you have had at the same number. The National Highway Safety Traffic Safety Administration who services that hotline also has a web site at www.nhtsa.dot.gov. The number for Safety Belt/Safe USA is (800) 745-SAFE.

Purchasing and Using Safety Car Seats

Which safety seat is right and at what time? If you buy a convertible seat can you skip buying an infant seat? Yes and no; most experts seem to think that an infant seat is designed more efficiently to accommodate a smaller body and because of the semi-reclining position of the seat, the baby has better head and neck support. Not to mention the duality of an infant car seat; most of us like to use them as carriers when detached from the base. This is an added benefit when your baby has fallen asleep in the car. With a convertible seat, you'd probably end up waking her when you unbuckle her. To add even more versatility to an infant car seat, you can now purchase a stroller frame which the seat snaps into. It's a sensible mix of design and budget.

Infant Seats

The infant seat is well-designed to help protect your baby's head, neck and back. They are intended for rear-facing use. Very small babies (or preemies) may need to lie flat, so check with your doctor. To provide extra support for a smaller infant, roll a diaper or a receiving blanket along the sides of her body, neck or head.

These infant seats are comfortable, safe and well-designed.

Smart Fit Infant Seat

Price: $60.00
Manufacturer: Century
(888-5CARSEAT)
Weight limitations: 0 to 20 pounds
Harness system: 3 pt.
Removable carrier seat: yes

The Smart Fit is fairly light, weighing 7.6 pounds, but has everything we like in a car seat: it's machine washable, made with plush fabric, has raised belt slots for easy installation, a level indicator showing correct installation, and a curved ergonomic carrying handle. It also adapts to shopping carts. The sculptured "All Ways" handle makes for easy carrying.

Travel-About with Smart Handle

Price: $69.99
Manufacturer: Kolcraft
(800) 453-7673
Weight limitations: 0 to 20 lbs.
Harness system: 3 pt.
Removable carrier seat: yes

We wanted to know what was so smart about the "smart handle," and we found out. The foam handle pivots for easier carrying, which is most pleasant especially with its eight-pound weight. It would have also been smart to make it machine washable, but we do appreciate that it also comes with a level indicator showing correct installation.

Turnabout Infant Car Seat #760

Price: $55.00
Manufacturer: Cosco
(800) 544-1108
Weight limitations: 0 to 22 lbs.
Harness system: 3 pt.
Removable carrier seat: yes

The Turnabout Infant Car Seat by Cosco has a carrying handle that rotates 360 degrees for extra comfort; labeled seat belt paths; a level indicator which shows correct installation; and a push-button harness adjustment. It weighs eight pounds and has a machine-washable seat.

Convertible Car Seats

Convertible seats do exactly that—they convert from a rear-facing infant seat (again, when your little one is a year old and at least 20 pounds) to a forward-facing seat (use until 40 pounds). When you do switch to the forward position, be sure to install it correctly—upright—and readjust the harness straps to the top slots. Review the manufacturer's directions and check that the seat isn't installed too loosely.

You'll hear a lot about five points, as in harnesses. What does it mean and do you need it?

Convertible safety seats have one of three types of harnesses:

- five-point—with straps at the shoulders, hips and crotch
- overhead shield—this tray-like piece swings down around the child
- padded T-shaped shield—attached to the shoulder straps that buckle into the seat at the crotch

The five-point is the least easy type of belt to put on your child, especially a fidgety one. The shield of course, is the simplest—it just slips over the child's head in one motion and snaps into place easily. The five-point is the most adjustable for personal size; remember the best fit means safety.

We thought we'd mention seeing an Eddie Bauer convertible car seat recently. It was priced higher than most and although the car seat might be appealing for its masculine, auto-styling, we couldn't find much information on its safety merits. We'll have to wait and see some reports on its safety record.

Guardian Folder Car Seat

Price: $110.00

Manufacturer: Early Development

(704) 643-8409

Weight limitations: rear: 0 to 20 lbs.—forward: 20 to 40 lbs.

Harness system: 5 pt.

Recline Positions: 3

Machine Washable: yes

This is a pretty good choice if you travel a lot—the Guardian folds easily. It also comes with an automatic seat belt adjustment and extra thick padding for added comfort.

Safe Embrace Car Seat

Price: $135.00

Manufacturer: Fisher-Price

(800) 432-5437

Weight limitations: rear: 0 to 22 lbs.—forward: 22 to 40 lbs.

Harness system: 5 pt.

Recline Positions: none

Machine Washable: yes

The Safe Embrace may not recline but it does a lot of other things very well. It has color-coded seat belt paths we really like. Best of all—should you need help installing it, you can contact Goodyear Tire & Rubber Company (Call 888-439-7786 for locations where you can get free assistance).

Smart Move

Price: $169.99

Manufacturer: Century

(888) 5CARSEAT

Weight limitations: rear: 0 to 30 lbs.—forward: 20 to 40 lbs.

Harness system: 5 pt. or overhead shield

Recline Positions: 2

Machine Washable: yes

The Smart Move by Century *is* a smart move. It is the only rear-facing infant seat for babies up to 30 pounds Even smarter—on impact the seat rotates to a protective upright position and the optional tether strap secures the seat to the car frame. It was designed for superior infant fit and will accommodate a growing toddler. There's a two-position infant head support. We like that there's a tether strap attachment kit for extra-secure installation, one of the most important things around. The Smart Move can also recline when facing forward. The five-point harness has a one-piece harness tie. Machine washable, removable cover for cleaning and the head area lined with EPS (used in bicycle helmets) are two really nice features.

1000 STE Classic

Price: $49.99
Manufacturer: Century
(888) 5CARSEAT
Weight limitations: rear: 0 to 20 lbs.—forward: 22 to 40 lbs.
Harness system: 5 pt.
Recline Positions: 2
Machine Washable: yes

This car seat meets all the basics and at half the price. The two position buckle will accommodate growing children and their heavy winter clothes. The shoulder harness also has adjustments designed to grow with your child. For a real budget buy, pick one up at Midas wholesale ($42). When baby grows out of it, return it and get a rebate for $42 of Midas services. What a deal!

Toddler/Youth and Booster Seats

Breverra Contour Booster Car Seat

Price: $74.99
Manufacturer: Century
(888) 5CARSEAT
Weight limitations: 30–60 lbs.
Harness system: 5 pt. shielded
Washable: yes

This is a high-backed (for extra headrest support) booster with a shielded 5-point harness, and a 3-position comfort clip which adjusts for a variety of children's heights.

NextStep

Manufacturer: Century
(888) 5CARSEAT
Weight limitations: forward: to 65 lbs.

Harness system: 5 pt.
Recline Positions: yes
Machine Washable: yes

Century has designed the "Next Step" in car seats; this has been developed for use after an infant seat all the way to 65 pounds That's a big leap. NextStep is a deep, forward-facing seat which transitions your little one (from an infant seat) all the way to adult seat belts. Century has made it as easy to use as possible, and it's loaded with the features we want: a 5-point harness and the seat buckle and shoulder positions adjust. The harness can even be removed, so you can use the car's restraint system. Reclined or upright, your toddler or "big kid" will be comfortable.

Car Seat Toys

Need something to interest your child so traveling in the car is more enjoyable (for you as well)? We found several toys and products that we think will help.

Car Seat Gallery™

Price: $12.00
Manufacturer: Wimmer-Ferguson
(800) 541-1345
Ages: Birth to 12 months

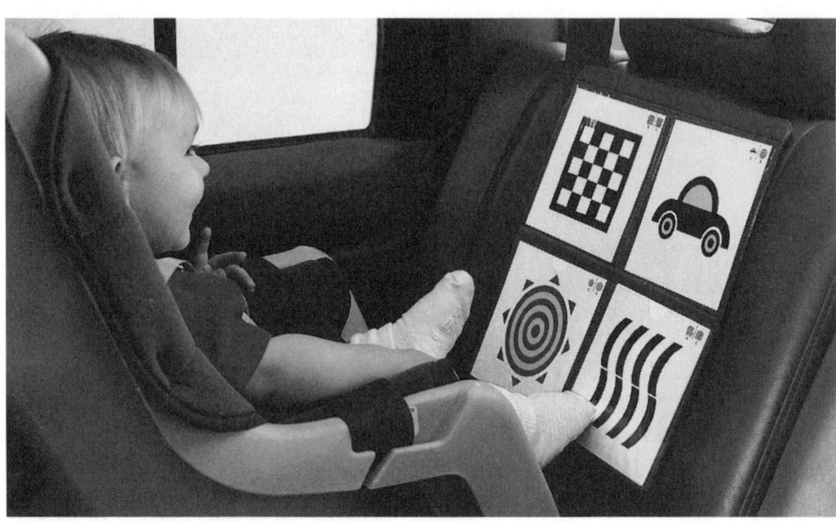

A little interactive art gallery for traveling babies

Every car needs its own little art gallery. Here's an easily installed toy (for both front and rear facing infants) which features ten double-sided cards, thoughtfully displayed in plastic pockets. The cards are graphic and stimulating, ten in black and white and ten in vivid colors. Change them and interchange them, making the gallery different all the time.

Car Mobile™

Price: $8.00
Manufacturer: Wimmer-Ferguson
(800) 541-1345

For a very small investment, you might receive lots of stress-free travel time. The Car Mobile™ is a great way to engage baby and keep her interested while in the car. Favorite toys will hang just above the car seat, in view but securely fastened to the locking rings. The Car Mobile™ also encourages early visual activity like focusing, scanning and tracking. While baby's doing that, you can track your progress on the road.

For a mobile baby

Bicycles, Bike Helmets and Bicycling Safety

Not riding your bicycle as much as you used to? Attach a trailer to it, and hit the road.

Biking Safety Savvy

Just when is it safe to put a helmet on your child and take her for a bike ride? Where can you find a proper, extremely small helmet? Is it safe for any infant less than 12 months to be in a bike seat, trailer or any other bicycle type carrier? Make sure you ask your pediatrician's advice on this—we think you should. The answer we found is no, children under age one should not be riding along. This explains why you won't find a child helmet on the market sized for infants. Many states have made it illegal to ride without a helmet, and some have even passed laws against biking with children under one year of age (even with a helmet).

We know avid bike riders will be looking forward to having baby aboard, whether on the bike or in a trailer. Why not wait until baby is older? The risk is so great. Remember to ask your doctor before you take baby on the road in any way.

When baby is older (one year at least) trailers are perhaps the safest way to take a baby along. They are lower to the ground and in the event of a crash, your baby will fall a shorter distance. Try out the trailer yourself, ride in it. How does it feel? Riding in a trailer can be a rough ride—checking it for yourself might just show you how rough it can be. Then take your baby and the bike seat along to your doctor for advice. Let her see what type of protection it will offer. Check out the Bicycle Helmet Safety Institute's web pages regarding safety (using wedges and pillows and more to help secure your child in a trailer). Questions to ask the trailer manufacturer include:

- If the trailer hits a bump too fast with one wheel will it turn over?
- Is the trailer constructed to protect the child in a rollover (a fairly common occurrence)?
- Is there protection for your child's bottom if you hit a rock passing between the two wheels?

ASTM is working on trailer standards, but they aren't finalized and so consumers and new parents should be extremely cautious.

What about child carriers—child seats mounted in either the front or back of your bike? Are they safe? Front mounted ones allow the parent to look at their toddler while riding, and unfortunately, you could fall on your child in a crash. Although children balance better in front-mounted carriers, these also obstruct views while riding.

What is it about the one year mark? Baby's neck can tolerate the weight of a helmet, but only while awake. Unfortunately, babies often fall asleep when in a bike seat. Ask your doctor about this, and you'll be waiting until baby is awake. Again, show your doctor both the helmet and your toddler at a visit and get an opinion. Each child's development and readiness for tolerating a helmet and a ride is different.

Would you believe that reports indicate over a third of biking injuries happen when the bicycle falls over when standing still? The scenario is, the baby gets positioned and the bike is leaning against something and the parent turns to put on their helmet or do something, and in an instant, the bike can crash to the ground. ASTM labels on child carriers also state that stability of bikes change when a child carrier is attached. Be sure the carrier you purchase meets the ASTM standards, also requiring a shield to prevent your child from getting fingers or toes into the rear spokes. Check out the Ottawa's Citizens for Safe Cycling web site which presents several problems with child carriers and concludes about the safety hazards they present.

There is always a risk in cycling, and certainly parents will do their best to be cautious and concerned. Yet, there isn't any training available for using trailers or child bike carriers, and so parents gear up and ride off with baby. Read all you can about biking safely with your child, check out the following web sites and always check with your doctor. Don't set a bad example, either. Wear your helmet—it makes asking baby to wear hers a lot easier.

Child Bike Seat

Price: $99.95
Manufacturer: Kettler®
Available through: Right Start Catalog
(800) 548-8531

Here's a bike seat system for your baby (12 months and up). The mounting bracket attaches to your bike's mainframe seat post and stays there. Then you can add or take off the baby seat in just seconds. The baby seat is actually cantilevered up and away from the rear wheel so baby will ride more comfortably. The sturdy seat has a removable, washable pad and there are adjustable body straps that provide the five-point harness fit we think is essential. The child foot pads also adjust to accommodate baby's growth, and the large splash guard on the rear wheel keeps baby dry. Use up to 50 pounds.

Cool Cap Bike Helmet

Price: $14.95
Available through: Right Start Catalog
(800) 548-8531

Here's a bike helmet for those little riders (one year and up). There are three vents and extra Velcro padding to keep your toddler protected and comfortable. Passes ANSI and Snell tests. Accommodates ages one through four years and one size fits all. It even comes in pink (or white).

Front Row Bike Seat

Price: $70.00
Manufacturer: Leisure Sports Accessories

Everything we used to hear about how you shouldn't ride your bike with someone on the handlebars has changed with the development of the new Front Row bike seat. Approved by the ASTM, this new seat, designed by Leisure Sports Accessories, attaches to the handlebars of your bike and will keep your child's hands and feet away from the spokes. (The shoulder harness, lap belt and adjustable leg supports help make this a well designed product for children eight months to four years or up to 40 pounds. At $70, this innovative seat is a good buy. Purchase it at bike and sporting goods shops but please remember that just because a seat or product is usable at an age under 12 months, we don't recommend it—ask your pediatrician.

Hitch 'N Go Bicycle Trailer

Price: $199.95
Manufacturer: Fisher-Price
Available through: One Step Ahead Catalog
(800) 274-8440

Tow your kids along in the Hitch 'N Go designed for safety and riding comfort. It attaches easily and securely to your bike—no tools are even required. The nylon shell is water-resistant and allows air to circulate and the body is made of reinforced steel and high-impact plastic. The front windshield can roll up, but an inner mesh screen stays in place keeping pebbles and bugs away. Seats two children and includes an adjustable five-point harness and safety flag. Holds up to 100 pounds.

If you happened to have purchased the Baby Jogger II, there's also a Bike Trailer Conversion Kit for it.

Going to Class

Now that you and baby are mobile, are you putting her in school? Classes for babies are growing in popularity and in variety, engaging your child in everything from music to water play, computers to physical fitness. What does your baby really gain by all this early education and social experience? Should you go for swimming or playgroups? Do you feel pressured to enroll your baby in classes?

Although we aren't sure of the true educational value (nor are authorities on the subject) or its lasting significance, we think babies love activity and yours might really enjoy splashing, running, bouncing and jumping around in a classroom setting. You might also enjoy the chance to get out; many classes provide Mom and Tot activity so you'll get to meet other new parents. You can compare notes and discover what other babies are doing and what they're like.

Check out classes before enrolling. This is for your baby—observe the instructor. Do they seem to understand cognitive, emotional and physical development theories? In other words, do they look like they know what they are doing? Are they having fun with the kids? What types of classes are there?

Music Classes

Although we think they're fairly new, music classes for babies under two seem to be tied to those studies which link music exposure to the development of spatial reasoning skills. Check out the classical music we listed under "Musical Notes." It follows those same studies. What will you and your baby do in a music class? You'll probably be holding her as you sing and dance around the room. Toddlers will be able to begin experimenting with musical cause and effect—bashing and shaking instruments. You should also work on rocking songs, lullabies and hello/good-bye songs which you can find ways to incorporate into life at home.

Contact:

- Kindermusik International (800-628-5687)
- Musikgarten (800-216-6864)
- Music Together (800-728-2692)

Swimming and Water Fun

Babies aren't really ready to swim, but they can learn to love the water and not to be afraid of it. Babies can learn to put their faces in the water and blow bubbles—both good starting points. Water games are also good, and having fun is a big part of it. We recommend your local YMCA, but if you're going to try your local fitness center, be sure they follow the YMCA national guidelines which prohibit baby's head from being submerged. Don't forget those rubber pants over diapers, or pick up some special swim pants.

- Call the YMCA of the USA (800-872-YMCA) www.ymca.net

Movement Classes

Gym for babies? Indeed, there's plenty of moving going on in these classes for your budding gymnast. Gymboree Play Programs offer 45-minute classes which have circle time (singing and talking), free play (exploring the equipment), and parachute time (babies get a moving ride on top of the parachute, billowy and colorful, which parents gently pull along). If you go to any other similar fitness program, look for an emphasis on discovering and becoming acquainted with gym equipment for kids—including mats, balls, foam wedges, etc.

- Gymboree Play Programs (800-520-PLAY)

Other Classes and Activities

Looking to fill some afternoons? Try story hours for babies. Pick up schedules at your local bookstore and library. You can come and go when you choose, and you'll get a changing group of participants. It's informal and easy.

Going Places By Air

Traveling by air with your baby is quite an adventure. You cannot control those long, airport delays, missed connecting flights or being bumped, but you can organize yourself and your baby to make traveling by air as simple and enjoyable as possible. You may consider it a selfish notion, but when travelling with an infant, your needs are quite exceptional relative to some of the other passengers. Take advantage of this. Make sure everyone involved, from making your reservation to checking in, knows that you are travelling with a young child. Airlines do tend to recognize your needs, and will cater to you and your baby's requirements to the best of their ability.

- Use a sling or backpack (if baby is old enough) for moving through a crowded and noisy airport. This will help baby feel safe and reassured.
- Try and keep baby a little bit hungry—breast-feeding or giving a bottle on takeoff and landing distracts junior during this novel experience (it sure is novel for her). More importantly, the sucking and sipping helps the ears adjust to the cabin pressure changes. If your baby is asleep on takeoff that's fine but upon landing wake her up. The Eustachian tubes of her ears don't equalize pressure as well when she's asleep (and this phenomenon is a bit worse when landing).
- Ask your pediatrician about using a nasal spray (saline) to ease the dryness in nasal passages.
- Be like *Felix the Cat* and bring a baby-bag full of essentials. A layover might have you desperately seeking diapers. It will only take one delay to realize how important it is to bring lots of baby's (small) favorite toys and books to amuse your new flyer. Yes, it is yet another thing to carry—but no one ever promised that you would be travelling light with a baby.

Carry-on rules have gotten stricter. If baby is flying with you but you're paying one fare, you are only entitled to your number of bags, no extras. Here are some carry-on rules.

- A laptop will now count as a bag.
- Some airlines will count your purse as a bag.
- Carry-on bags should measure less than 22" x 14" x 9"—a hanging garment bag can measure slightly larger.
- Car seats can be brought on in addition to your two bags, but double check when you make your reservation.

- Strollers are usually checked at the gate. This is actually a plus, because most airlines then have it waiting in the jetway when you deplane, so you can use it in the airport terminal.

With the increasing numbers of families flying each year, airlines are responding by offering special menus, programs, airport play areas, and other distractions and amenities. Some airlines are more kid-friendly than others. As a rule of thumb, the larger scheduled carriers are likely better equipped to meet your needs. Chartered flights tend to be more unpredictable anyway—while travelling with a baby in tow is hardly an unusual circumstance, charter airlines tend to provide less service, and may not be able to respond to your requests.

What are some of the perks and who is offering them?

- American Airlines (800) 433-7300

  The first major national airlines to halve the child's fare for those under age two was American. We think that's incentive in and of itself to fly with them. If you call ahead, you might be able to get a peanut butter and jelly sandwich, a hot dog or a hamburger instead of the usual. The staff is pretty helpful to families.
- Continental Airlines (800) 523-3273

  Continental is trying to keep the family happy by creating some indoor playgrounds at major air terminals and some children's meals with great finger foods.
- Delta Airlines (800) 221-1212

  Delta Airlines has their great Fantastic Flyer program ($35/year) that offers some discounted fares, inflight freebies and a quarterly kids' magazine. If you're flying a lot, it'll be worth it with its flight and hotel discounts.
- Northwest Airlines (800) 225-2525

  You can order special meals ahead—hamburgers and hotdogs. They have airplane trading cards, too.
- Southwest Airlines (800) I-FLYSWA

  Southwest Airlines, which is now the fourth-largest domestic carrier, will allow pre-boarding and will also take your stroller from you at the gateway. It will be ready for you and your baby when you get off the plane (it's a small detail, but one that's greatly appreciated in an airport whose baggage carousels are seemingly miles from the gate).

- United Airlines (800) 241-6522

  United offers McDonald's Friendly Skies meals even if there aren't any french fries. Call ahead to make arrangements. There's even some age appropriate meals for younger children. Kids can get an activity kit on international flights.

Going abroad? Try Virgin Atlantic, surprisingly tot-conscious. Free toy-filled backpacks are distributed to children coming aboard. British Airlines also offers cartoons and filled fanny packs. Air France has a special children's menu; toys and drawing supplies are available (order meal in advance).

What happened to just getting a wing pin for your lapel? Airlines want to keep children happy. With a day's notice almost all of them will dish out a special kid meal. They tend to cater more to the toddler than the infant, though, so you should still be prepared to cater to baby's idiosyncracies! What you should look for in an airline is a combination of service, value and whether or not they're kid-friendly. Although a baby under two can travel for free if sitting on her parent's lap, there comes a time when your baby doesn't want to sit still. To make your flight more comfortable and enjoyable (for you), reserve a separate seat. Airlines will often cut the fare for your toddler anywhere from 50% to 90%, depending on availability. You can chance it and try to book off-peak flights in the hopes of finding an empty seat. Some airlines will also lend or rent you a car seat or bassinet. What isn't so kid-friendly is that it isn't a bargain to fly with your family. The demand for air travel keeps the carriers from offering their previous "family fare" discounts so while the airlines try to better accommodate our growing needs, it's rare to find a "deal" that is sympathetic to a young family—especially one that is cost conscious (and who isn't?).

Some final thoughts:

- Pre-board whenever possible.
- During peak seasons, skip e-mail tickets, stick to a hard copy set with pre-assigned seats.
- Allow plenty of time. Even if flying is routine for you, it isn't for baby.

Airports with Kid-friendly Spaces

A final word on airports: there was a time when the last place you'd consider for a day out was the airline terminal. That's changing as travelling by air is such a commonplace occurrence. Also helping families survive the traumas of air travel are the airports themselves. Many have gone ahead and provided kid-friendly zones, areas where you can almost forget that three-hour delay or missed flight. Some of these are so much fun, you might want to visit the airport as a destination itself (not to mention that some airports have great shopping too!). The best of the best of these are:

- Cleveland—On a recent flight to Cleveland, we observed modest (but well appreciated) areas with straightforward play equipment. Conveniently located in the gate area, it's a simple gesture, but one that children (and parents) seem very grateful for.
- Houston Intercontinental—Scattered through the busiest terminals at Houston International Airport, five play areas and nurseries complete with cribs, rocking chairs and changing tables will keep you comfortable and entertained.

Kids on the Fly is imagination in flight—Photography, Doug Snower.

- Logan International Airport—The Boston Children's Museum and Store has some space in Logan where families can relax and play. The store is better than the playspace but when you're tired and looking for diversions, this will work.
- O'Hare International Airport—Kids on the Fly is imagination in flight. Located just outside of Terminal Two in Chicago's O'Hare Airport, this playspace is a collaboration between the Chicago Children's Museum and the Department of Aviation. Your delay might not be long enough to enjoy it fully; be sure your toddler crawls through the shipping crates to spin, feel and discover what's inside of each. You can check on your flight with the on-site information kiosk.
- Pittsburgh International Airport—Be a sport at Pittsburgh International's Kidsport with its planes and ramps to ride, fly and take-off. Couches offer a comfortable opportunity to nurse or grab a quick nap.

These kid friendly zones are popping up all of the time—watch out for them on your next trip.

Interactive Museums—Children's Museums and Science Museums

A great destination for a baby (and mom, dad or caregiver) is an interactive museum. There are more and more of them every time we check.

Learning can certainly be fun for baby, and you, too. Many museums now have areas dedicated to early learners; children under the age of five. Filled with opportunities to discover, investigate and role-play, these are perfect places to frequent. Look around at your local or nearby museum to see if they have a separate zone for toddlers. If not, check to see if they offer some programming for your toddler where he can have the run of the place (without larger children around). You will find that many museums (and not just the children's museums) cater to your needs.

Our museum picks do it all. They are inventive, secure, exciting and interactive. Here are some favorites—large and small, urban and suburban:

The Boston Children's Museum

Dedicated Programming

Take advantage of the wonderful weekly programming using music and movement at the Boston Children's Museum for babies and tots (6 months to 2 1/2 years). The Boston Children's Museum was a pioneer of such programs and they certainly do it well.

The Chicago Children's Museum

Dedicated Spaces/Zones: Playmaze and Treehouse Trails

More than half of the children visiting The Chicago Children's Museum are under five years of age, which probably accounts for the museum's two dedicated early learner exhibits. Pump some gas, bake some cheesecakes, or even drive the city bus in PlayMaze, a colorful, mini-metropolis. PlayMaze offers your child wonderful opportunities for role-play and discovery. And just next door is Treehouse Trails, where your tot can crawl into a tent, explore nature, and learn to trail and track.

Your baby will enjoy exploring the "Tot Lot" in Playmaze—Photography, Doug Snower.

kidscommons–Columbus, Indiana

Dedicated Space/Zone: Yes
(812) 378-3046

kidscommons is a uncommonly good little museum for kids, especially little ones. There's an assembly line and an incredible art-making area. Blow bubbles at the bubble table or just hang out in the tot-lot, expressly designed for non-walkers (and not a bad place for a parent to get down on all fours with junior, too).

Louisiana Children's Museum–New Orleans, Louisiana

Dedicated Space/Zone: First Adventures

Older kids will love the giant math and physics lab and the rock wall for climbing. Tourists will love an authentic French Quarter scene, but baby will love First Adventures with its playscape.

The Louisville Science Center–Louisville, Kentucky

Dedicated Space/Zone: KidZone
(502) 561-6100

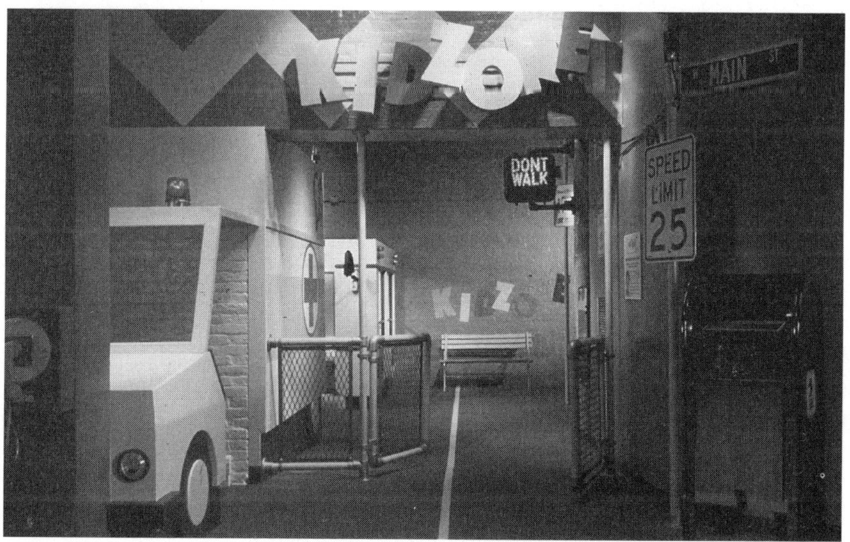

Kidzone is especially for little scientists—Photography, Doug Snower.

Begin a scientific journey in KidZone at The Louisville Science Center for children under six, with a secure and delightful tot lot. Recently renovated, the new KidZone allows your toddler an introduction to science and investigation. Splash at the water table (at toddler height), serve your passengers a meal in the multi-story plane and delight in the weather clouds. Especially wonderful are two quiet areas: the textural, soothing space ship for reading to your tot and the resource room which looks a lot like Grandma's house, comforting and complete with a rocker—nurse or read in an area of semi-privacy.

Fox Cities Children's Museum–Appleton, Wisconsin

Dedicated Space/Zone: Happy Baby Garden

Even the name is uplifting! Babies, older babies and toddlers all have distinct areas geared to different developmental needs. Babies who are crawling will love the underground tunnel and those exploratory toddlers will try out the celery-stalk slide, over and over again.

One last thought—these museum experiences provide wonderful social opportunities for you and baby; if you live close to a children's museum, you'll find yourself frequenting it on a regular basis not only for your child's experience, but because you'll find it a great place to interact with other parents too. Think about buying a museum membership. It's a great value, supports your community, and being able to drop in and out whenever you please is something you and baby will really appreciate. Most museums have great web sites and often give good travel directions. Some even include other tourist information which might be helpful.

Hotels and Rental Car Agencies

When we looked at hotels for family friendliness, we weren't really surprised that the ones doing it the best were the best hotels. It really comes down to customer service—will you be able to get cots and cribs, extra blankets and highchairs? The Marriott and Hyatt chains seem willing to fill such needs as does the Embassy Suites. Hilton, Doubletree, Westin, Wyndham, Hampton, and Sheraton also accommodate family requests. If you can afford the Four Seasons, they really treat kids especially well (as you would expect for those rates).

What really helps you get what you need is to call ahead. Often you have to keep reminding the hotel. Upon check-in, ask again if that crib has been set up. Often rooms with microwaves or refrigerators are handy for traveling with infants—that way, you can heat and store food and essentials.

To get you where you're going you need a car that's safe, clean and reliable. Avis wins a lot of praise for their pricing, quotes that stand firm. Enterprise will pick you up upon request, which could be very useful with a family. Hertz is huge, so the variety and availability always seem good. Remember to think about what you need ahead of time. Many car rental agencies will now book mini-vans but they usually require notice. Always check that a car seat is available if you don't have your own. In our own experience, we prefered using our own; the rental companies we saw were either out of car seats, or had rather well used models. We felt more at ease with supplying our own seat.

APPENDICES

Toll-Free Numbers for the Parent/Consumer

Here are some of the toll-free consumer relations numbers you may find necessary as you purchase products, toys and equipment for your baby. Call for replacement parts for toys or with questions. Check our internet guide as well; although we found customer service on the web to be useful, it usually takes a day or so. The web does offer many other convenient resources and listings.

Tips for Dealing with Consumer Relations Departments

- Call during nonpeak hours if possible.
- Have the product, instructions and warranty in front of you. You may need to provide the model, serial number, or code.
- Know where and when the product was purchased.
- Be prepared for waiting—you'll be put on hold. If you have a speaker feature on your telephone, it's a good time to use it.
- Ask for the addresses of on-line resources which may be able to help you solve your problem more conveniently.

After the Stork
800-441-4775

Ameda Egnell
800-323-8750

American Bronzing Company
800-345-8112

Audio-Therapy Innovations, Inc.
800-678-7748

Avent America Inc.
800-542-8368

Babessentials™
888-613-6383

Babyscapes™
888-441-KIDS

Baby Songs™
800-745-1145

Baby Trend®
(800) 328-7363

Baby Catalog of America
A Division of the Baby Club of America, Inc.
800-PLAYPEN (800-752-9736)

Baby Jogger Co.
800-241-1848

Biobottoms
800-766-1254

The Bumpa Bed™ Co.
800-241-1848

Camp Kazoo, Ltd.
888-60MURAL

Carrousel Concepts from One Step Ahead Catalog
800-274-8440

Century
800-837-4044 888-5CARSEAT

Chinaberry Books
800-776-2242

Colorado Kids Clothing Company
800-500-4182

Company Store
800-285-3696

Cosco Inc.
800-544-1108

Diaper Genie
800-843-6430

Discovery Toys
(800) 426-4777 U.S.
(800) 267-0477 Canada

Dr. Possum's World
800-827-4086

Dutalier Inc.
800-363-9817

Edutainment Catalog
800-338-3844

Evenflo Bottles/Nursing Items
800-356-BABY
Information available in French, English or Spanish

Evenflo Juvenile Furniture
800-233-5921

Exposures (Frames, Photo Albums)
800-222-4947

First Years
800-225-0382

Fisher-Price Inc.
800-432-KIDS

Fitigues
800-235-9005

Genius Babies
888-388-1003

Gerber Baby Products
800-4-GERBER

Gerry Baby Products
800-525-2472

Gifts for Grandkids
800-333-1707

Graco Children's Products, Inc.
800-345-4109

Hand in Hand
800-872-9745

Hanna Anderson
800-222-0544

Healthtex
800-554-6737

Hoobobbers
800-533-1505

Hoopla by André
(800) 541-1345

JCPenney
800-222-6161

Kid Classics - Learning Curve ™
(800) 704-8697

Kolcraft Juvenile Furniture
800-453-7673

L.L. Bean Kids
800-341-4341

Lamaze Infant System
800-704-8697

Land of Nod
800-933-9904

Land's End Kids
800-356-4444

The Learning Company
800-716-8506

Learning Seed Catalog
800-634-4941

Lego Systems, Inc.
(800) 453-4652

Light Impressions
800-828-6216

Lilly's Kids (Lillian Vernon)
800-285-5555

Little Forest Toiletries - Dr. Possum's World
800-827-4086

Little Tikes
800-321-0183

Manhattan Toy - Manhattan Baby™
800-541-1345

Mattel
800-524-TOYS

Mead-Johnson (Enfamil)
800-BABY-123

Medela, Inc.
800-TELL-YOU

Mondial Industries Limited (Diaper Genie)
800-843-6430

Morigeau Furniture USA
800-326-2121

Munchkin, Inc.
800-344-2229

Natural Baby Company
800-388-2229

Omron
800-634-4350

One Step Ahead
800-274-8440

Panasonic
800-211-7262

Pappa Geppetto's Toys
(800) 541-1345

Patagonia Kids
800-638-6464

Peg Perego U.S.A., Inc.
800-798-4796

Perfectly Safe
800-837-KIDS

Playskool
800-PLAYSKL 800-752-9755

Perfectly Safe
800-999-3030

Playtex Products, Inc.
800-222-0453

Pottery Barn
800-922-5507

Radio Flyer Inc.
800-621-7613

Ragazzi Furniture
888-324-7886

Right Start Catalog
800 LITTLE-1 800-548-8531

Room & Board®
800-486-6554

Ross Laboratories (Isomil, Similac)
800-515-7677

Rue de France
800-777-0998

Safety 1st, Inc.
800-723-3065

Safety Zone
800-999-3030

Soko (Decorative Hardware)
888-828-7656

Step2
800-347-8372

Susan Sargent Designs Inc.
800-245-4767

Tyco Preschool/Sesame Street Products
800-488-8697

Tough Traveler
800-GO-TOUGH
800-468-6844

Walt Disney Records
888-WDR-SING

Wimmer-Ferguson Child Products, Inc.
800-747-2454

Internet Baby Shopping and Information Guide

You are exhausted. You just finished the two A.M. feeding and can't get back to sleep—all you can think about are all the things your baby needs. Don't worry about getting a baby-sitter or calling after hours—just get on-line. The internet is open 24 hours a day and it lets you browse, search, and comparison shop. Cybershopping can save you time, energy and even money. Transactions have become as safe as those in stores. (Look for secure servers or encryption software to prevent sensitive information like your credit card number from being used.) So park your mouse by your favorite web site and buy exactly what you and your baby need.

Safeguarding credit information:

To be sure the site you are shopping on has a secure connection, look for the key symbol (icon) in the lower left-hand corner of the Netscape Navigator browser or a gold padlock icon in the lower right-hand corner of the Internet Explorer browser. These icons represent a service which encrypts your credit card number so it's almost impossible for those unauthorized to have access to it. Many websites will let you know that they are secure but if you're still uneasy shop and preview. You can always call in your order.

Now you know how to see if your surfing is secure, here's a guide to the best baby (and mom and dad) sites on the web:

BABY PARAPHERNALIA

BABY-GO-TO-SLEEP
www.babygotosleep.com
Check out the unusual Baby-Go-To-Sleep Tapes created by Audio-Therapy Innovations. They've been helping infants (and adults) fall to sleep and even sleep through the night. These recordings include an actual human heartbeat as the rhythm of traditional lullabies. Really!

BABYSCAPES™, INC.
www.babyscapes.com
Babycapes™ is an educational products company, maker of those great stimulating, learning videos with dancing geometric shapes set to classical music. Check out the informative on-line presentation and the three great videos all reasonably priced.

BABY CATALOG OF AMERICA
www.babycatalog.com
Order on-line all of the name brand and hard to find baby products you liked in the catalog. There's toys, childproofing items, furniture and all sorts of baby gear. You can often save as much as 50% off retail prices. There's even a membership club so should you be needing several larger ticket items, the $25 membership fee will be offset by your savings (an extra 10% off everything).

GENIUS BABIES
www.geniusbabies.com
When grandparents, aunts and uncles want to know what to give your newborn, give them this web site address. Genius Babies puts together great gift packages from the best award-winning developmental toys, CD's and more. There are two age groups to order for: newborn to 12 months and 12 months

through 36 months. Choose from packages such as the classic baby, the busy baby, and the deluxe baby gift set. Isn't it nice to find a developmental video, CD, book and a toy all geared for your baby's age and level of learning all in one easy to order package? Order some for your friends as well.

HOOHOBBERS
www.hoohobbers.com
Check out some the products well recognized for their quality (and design). With over 100 patents awarded and even voted into the permanent collection of modern art and design at MOMA in New York, you can pick out some wonderful things for your baby! We found these products well designed, ergonomic (easy for baby to grasp and use), attractive and fun. Don't miss the soft toy box, starter silverware and baby rocker and even more.

iBaby.com
www.iBaby.com
Rack up some big kid sized savings at iBaby.com! It's easy and convenient and filled with all the top baby products you want and need. There's even a Baby Gift Registry making giving and getting even simpler than ever before. In just a few cases, the variety is limited but there's still plenty to choose from and the descriptions are complete and full of information.

KIDSTUFF.COM
www.kidstuff.com
This is a great web site which supports a great catalog filled with baby stuff we like: baby slings, baby joggers, bath and baby products, wooden and educational toys and products, music, videos and more.

LAND'S END
www.landsend.com
Land's End is a great source for everything from crib sheets to diaper bags. You'll love checking it all out on-line.

SUSAN SARGENT DESIGNS INC.
www.susansargent.com
Check out this Designer's Choice site for Susan Sargent's rugs and bedding. You'll find her children's collections—ABC and Circus—elegant and lively, colorful and whimsical. While you're there, you may even want to indulge in some new bedding for yourself. There's a multitude of hand-painted, handmade and fine quality items, all of which you can indulge in to decorate the nursery, the toddler's room or even, your own.

BEDS, CRIBS & BEDDING

BELLINI
www.bellini.com
Check out the Avanti line—stylish and full of wonderful collections for the nursery.

THE COMPANY STORE®
www.thecompanystore.com
There's plenty to shop for at The Company Store. Start with some great bedding for your infant and toddler. The Company Kids™ Collection is colorful and bold, and easy to care for.

LEXINGTON FURNITURE INDUSTRIES
www.lexington.com
Home to Betsy Cameron's Storybook Collection of beds, armoires and more. Many first beds to choose from.

RUE DE FRANCE
www.ruedefrance.com
Rue de France carries some of the loveliest bedding, draperies and accessories. You may forget what you originally searched for as you get lost in the lace and details.

BABY CLOTHING (MOM & DAD, TOO)

Point your mouse at these:

FOR A SPECIAL BABY
http://foraspecialbaby.itool.com
For a Special Baby makes special clothing for special babies (those really tiny ones). Exceptional parents have two needs that this company meets: tiny, precious clothing in a variety of styles and easy dressing, wearing and fit.

JCPENNEY FOR BABY CATALOG
www.jcpenney.com/shopping
Find all your clothing basics for newborns, infants and toddlers and more and at good prices.

LANDS' END KIDS' CATALOG

www.landsend.com

Lands' End is a great catalog and now you can shop on-line for their clothing and outerwear for infants and children.

L.L.BEAN KIDS' CATALOG

www.llbean.com

Another great source of clothing and outerwear for kids.

LITTLE ME

www.littleme

Little Me's whimsical designs are backed up by 80-year history of manufacturing babywear. What an incredible teaming of whimsy, aesthetics and well-made merchandise! Little Me babywear is so cute you often forget how well made and how comfortable it is. Paying special attention to how quickly baby grows, the Little Me garments feature wider bodies with extra room for growth and slightly longer shirts and tops in two-piece sets help keep backs and tummies covered. This sweet site also provides a section on parental expectations in clothing (what features should you look for) and another section on garment care (how do you get those tough stains out?). A pretty and informative site, not to mention being able to check out a great collection of babywear!

ENTERTAINMENT, FILM, MUSIC & VIDEO

How do you find out reviews of videos for your growing child? Many of these web sites offer extras like reviews, advice and even parental message boards. The Disney site has so much information on it, you'll probably run out of ideas to search for. None of these sites are real purchasing bargains but they will help you make decisions on family viewing and entertainment, even travel.

BABY SONGS

www.babysongs.com

Find out about all of the award-winning Baby Songs videos and audios. Go behind the scenes, too and you'll be ordering these great tapes and videos for your baby.

BEST BUY

www.bestbuy.com

We can't imagine that there isn't a Best Buy close to you, but for convenience you can find all of baby's musical favorites on-line.

BRAINPLAY.COM
www.brainplay.com
Search over 5,000 children's videos by different parameters; age, category or title. You can also check the reviews for even more information.

DISNEY.COM
www.disney.com
The Disney magic comes alive at Disney.com. Search for family vacation destinations and weekend getaways. Browse for gifts for any occasion and buy it conveniently on the web. You can send some character greetings and even take a few minutes to try out some interactive games on-line.

KIDFLIX.COM
www.kidflix.com
Wow! Over 25,000 kids' videos and an advice and message board for parents. Get on-line and discuss new releases.

REEL.COM
www.reel.com
It's hard enough to get out of the house and perhaps, if you do make it to the video store you have about five seconds to decide. Much easier for new moms and dads is surfing reel.com with over 85,000 movies for sale and even rentals ($4.50 plus shipping for a seven-day period). You can use a movie matching search to get suggestions or pick from the American Film Institute's top 100 movies of all time.

VIDEOSERVE.COM
www.videoserve.com
This is a multi-purpose site with over 5,000 children's videos, this way you can look for your toddler and for yourself.

FOOD, DINING & GROCERIES

Imagine not wasting time running to the grocery store and the drugstore. Now stop imagining and shop on-line! More and more markets and stores are offering a wide range of foods and products to moms and dads who have more errands to do than time. Convenience aside, you can also avoid impulse-purchases and tantrums over candy.

CARNATION BABY FORMULAS

www.carnationbaby.com

Want some information on formula? Here on-line Carnation will answer all of your questions and more.

KIDS HEALTH ORG

www.kidshealth.org

Created by a group of children's hospitals, this informative web site will help provide you with nutritional and health advice, info and tips. There are some great recipes, too.

KRAFT FOODS

www.kraftfoods.com

Once junior starts eating food, this Kraft Foods site is a good one to bookmark. Find all the Kraft favorites and more.

MUNCHKIN INC.

www.munchkininc.com

Check out the inexpensive well-designed silverware, temperature telling yellow ducky

NETGROCER

www.netgrocer.com

A nation-wide service, NetGrocer is tough to beat. It offers convenience, competitive pricing and a way to make grocery shopping a whole lot easier. Netgrocer also sells health and beauty products, computer software, baby supplies and even books. When they arrive in your neighborhood (cities being added all the time) be sure to check out the small delivery fees.

PEAPOD

www.peapod.com

A fast and convenient way to order groceries (although it isn't quite national yet). Create an on-line shopping list, even set up regular orders. There's a small delivery fee on top of what you would just about pay at a supermarket.

RECIPES ON-LINE

www.recipes.wenzel.net

An easy to search, browsable database filled with over 25,000 recipes. We really appreciated the simple ones.

WELL FED BABY®, INC.

www.wellfedbaby.com

Check out the Well Fed Baby® foods, they're 100% organic, vegetarian and Kosher. Soy milk and tofu are the foundation of many of the recipes and all foods fill the nutritional needs of growing infants.

PARENTING & WORKING PARENTS

AMERICAN BABY PARENTS SOUP

www.parentsoup.com/american baby

You turned to the magazine (American Baby) for advice and information while you were pregnant. Now you can go on-line to get support and advice every day, all day.

AT-HOME DAD

www.athomedad.com

This site offers at-home dads lots of resources and information including a newsletter.

FAMILY.COM

www.family.com

Owned by Disney (the parent company of Family Fun Magazine), this web site offers lots of family information. There's a section on travel and even on last minute (spur of the moment) trips. The family-friendly city guides help introduce you to 12 U.S. cities.

THE HOME-BASED WORKING MOM

www.hbwn.com

Read a monthly newsletter, follow some networking opportunities, and resources for starting your own home-based business.

PARENTS.COM

www.parents.com

Parenting information on everything from diapers to discipline, basic food groups to child rearing. You can sift through the parental advice, swap tips with other moms and dads and more. It's easy to use and you can customize your searches based on your child; her age, her interests. All this information without charge.

WORK AT HOME PARENTS' CAFE

www.workathomeparents.com

A site filled with message boards, chat rooms and an e-mail discussion list especially for parents working at home, check it out.

PRESERVING MEMORIES (ALBUMS, BRONZING, PHOTOGRAPHY)

AMERICAN BRONZING COMPANY
www.abcbronze.com

This is your on-line adventure into bronzing—make those memories last forever! American Bronzing has also come up with porcelainizing, a delicate finish option finished off with a hand-lettered name and birthdate.

FRANCES MEYER, INC.
www.francesmeyer.com

This is the scrapbook leader as Frances Meyer, Inc. says, but it's pretty true. You can find some great kits to start you off and then add some themed stickers (especially cute are the baby ones) and more to decorate, commemorate and compile all sorts of mementos and memorabilia.

LIGHT IMPRESSIONS
www.lightimpressionsdirect.com

We'll let you in on professional photographers' secrets—order some great archival albums, preservation kits and scrapbooks. They've got hints and techniques to help you along and a full line of products which are archival (helping you preserve all of baby's memories and more).

LIQUID IMAGES
www.liquidimages.com

Liquid Images can make an angel out of your little angel (a photographic one, that is). Any snapshot can be turned into the sweetest memory, check out on-line their photographic wizardry.

SAFETY

FIRST ALERT
www.firstalert.com

JPMA (Juvenile Products Manufacturers Association)
www.jpms.org

Check out product safety on-line at the JPMA—Don't feel overwhelmed by the sheer volume of recalls—there are many wonderful products being produced for baby. This web site has a lot of very useful safety tips and data as well. Add a bookmark to the page.

THE CHILDPROOFER

www.childproofer.com

The Childproofer has just about everything we've heard of and safety items we didn't know exist. You can order on-line or call 1-800-374-2525. After ordering latches, gates and more you can really childproof your home.

TOYS

All the big toy companies and some great small ones are now on-line to assist you.

eToys.com

www.eToys.com

eToys is the leading Internet toy retailer and a great way to purchase on-line. Thousands of toys are easy to browse and with competitive prices you'll find a lot to like about eToys. Pick brand names or specialty manufacturers and even have your purchase gift wrapped. This past holiday season proved to me at least that avoiding the crowds in the toy stores was as easy as shopping at eToys.

FAO SCHWARZ

www.faoschwarz.com

Discover the latest and greatest in toy trends from the most famous toy store of them all.

FISHER PRICE

www.fisherprice.com

Fisher Price has put together a thoughtful, helpful site. It's a shame it's a bit slow because you might quit before you find some very good tips. There's information on where you can purchase Fisher Price (of course), the newest products and toys (it's fun to feel privileged) and some terrific play tips (these are set up by age and are very well written). There are some "Color Me Fisher Price" pages for older children, a parent's handbook and even an on-line gift registry. If they were to get it up to speed, I'd like it even more.

HOLT EDUCATIONAL OUTLET

www.holtoutlet.com

Pick up some discounts (they vary from 10 to 50%) on educational toys, books, art materials, and even furniture. When your baby is old enough for

Playmobil this is a site you'll want to go to. It may not be the most intriguing site around, but where can you find some of these discounts?

LITTLE TIKES TOYS
www.littletikes.com
Home to some really great classic toys and lots more.

RADIO FLYER, INC.
www.redwagons.com
Many shapes and sizes of little red wagons are available, so be sure to check out the My First Wagon on-line. Radio Flyer is a classic.

RED ROCKET
www.redrocket.com
Red Rocket stocks a very thoughtful selection of educational and specialty toys plus books and software. There are some great descriptions and tips on safety and play. The purchase procedure needs a bit of work but its worth the effort to find such a pleasant selection.

STEP2
www.step2company.com
Step2 are the makers of some terrific, inexpensive baby toys and equipment. We love the Bigger Family, Penguin Sled and Scribble Center but there's an awful lot to like.

TRAVEL

Here's some traveling websites—so globe-trot on-line and check out the travel books, clothing and gear, not to mention the adventures themselves.

BENTLEY'S LUGGAGE & GIFTS
www.bentleys.com
Bentley's is one of the largest luggage and gift stores in the U.S.—their site often offers specials where savings are considerable. Check out their travel tips as well including a great chart of airline carry-on luggage policies. Then you just might need some new traveling bags.

CHRISTINE COLUMBUS
www.christinecolumbus.com

Clever name—this is also a lively and informative site packed full of clothing and gear, mostly aimed at woman travelers. The company will e-mail your gift list to your relatives and friends. If you've a birthday coming up and wouldn't mind having that new palm-size travel hair dryer, call up Christine.

EXPEDIA
www.expedia.com
Scan the best available flights, hotels and rental cars with this do-it-yourself travel agency.

PRICELINE.COM
www.priceline.com
Want to travel on your own terms and at your own prices? Try priceline.com and name your own prices—always read all the fine print but it can be the best way to get somewhere and stay somewhere.

RAND MCNALLY TRAVEL STORE
www.randmcnallystore.com
Not everyone has a Rand McNally nearby, so here's the spot to locate atlases, maps (software and paper), globes, books, puzzles and more. Rand McNally gift wraps and if you're feeling indecisive, go ahead and travel to the personal shopper link.

USA CITY LINK
www.usacitylink.com
Does the big city attract you and your little one? Check it out in advance for all the specifics you'll need to know.

Index

A

B

D

E

F

G

H

I

J

R

S

T

U

V

W

Y